D1241581

ALLIANCE
FOR
MURDER

ALLIANCE
FOR
MURDER

*The Nazi–Ukrainian Nationalist
Partnership in Genocide*

For the Committee:
B. F. SABRIN

SARPEDON
New York
In association with Shapolsky Publishers

Published in the United States by
SARPEDON
166 Fifth Avenue, New York, NY 10010

© 1991 by Sarpedon Publishers, a division of S. Smith, Inc.

Published in association with
Shapolsky Publishers
136 West 22nd Street, New York, NY 10011

ISBN: 0-9627613-0-3

Library of Congress catalog card number: 90-063301

MANUFACTURED IN THE UNITED STATES OF AMERICA

This book is dedicated, first, to the memory of a group of secular and religious Jews, residents of the town of Trembowla, who were among the first victims of the inhuman barbarism which beset the region.
On July 5, 1941, this group of 20–22 was rounded up randomly by local (and other) Ukrainian Nationalists, and driven to perform work in the military barracks, called 'koshary.'
After cleaning up the barracks, this group was brutally massacred by Ukrainian Nationalists. Only one young Jew managed to escape the bloodbath to tell the grisly story. According to this eyewitness, some Jews were forced to massacre each other with iron bars and shovels.
The cries of the victims could be heard miles away.

This book is dedicated also to small groups of Soviet soldiers (of different nationalities) who tried to join their units in retreat from the Nazi onslaught. They never made it. After being forced to lay down their arms, these defenseless lads were massacred by Ukrainian Nationalists on the spot, their dead bodies remaining for days on the streets.

Lastly, this book is dedicated to the memory of Moses Hütler (née Hitler), the brother of Jacob and Adolf Hütler, who was shot by the German Nazis in front of his house. His dead body was left hanging (head down) for three days because he dared to carry the same name as the Führer of the Third Reich.
The father of the brothers mentioned above (Isac M. Hütler) was murdered by the Nazis on the same day.

ACKNOWLEDGEMENTS

We would like to express our sincere thanks and gratitude to the Holocaust survivors who wrote down their personal stories, and to all those who made the publishing of this book possible.

For having commissioned the translation of the most important chapters of this work, from Hebrew into English, Mr. I. Goldfliess, a Holocaust survivor and a resident of Israel, deserves full recognition. The actual translator, Mr. M. Bobrovsky, an Israeli resident, is to be commended for doing an excellent job on the translation itself.

For some of the old pre-war pictures in this book, Samuel (Sol) Selzer from Trembowla deserves credit. He was not in Europe during World War II. He died in 1987 in New Jersey, while in his eighties. Almost all of his family perished during the Nazi occupation.

Our sincere thanks also to Mrs. H. Gans, wife of the late Josef Gans, for supplying the pictures of David Salomon Gans (Josef Gans' father), a Holocaust victim.

And to Mr. Adolf (David) Hütler, whom we have known for many years, our gratitude for his extraordinary patience in telling his story, and detailing the events of the Nazi occupation.

Our special thanks to Mrs. Halyna M.G. for her effort in obtaining the Documentary Archive material in the Ukr. SSR. Without this help and understanding *Alliance for Murder* would not have contained the documentary evidence. Recognition and sincere thanks go also to Mr. Volodia for his efforts in this direction.

And for the photo-documentary material, we wish to express sincere thanks to Mr. W.A. Lavrenyuk, Tarnopol State Museum, Ukr. SSR.

Mr. Sam Halpern, a Holocaust survivor, deserves recognition for bringing over from Israel the translated (into English) part of the *Trembowla Memorial Book* that he received from Mr. I. Goldfliess.

Our sincere thanks, too, to Mr. M. Heliczer, a Holocaust survivor, for the *Tarnopol Memorial Book*.

Mr. S. Brinstein, a survivor of World War II, deserves credit for his effort in the compilation of the many survivors' stories, translation work, and contribution in general.

Mr. I. Gartner, a survivor of World War II, is to be commended for his research on the Holocaust, and history of Ukrainian Nationalism.

The book committee hopes that the reader will find *Alliance for Murder: The Nazi–Ukrainian Nationalist Partnership in Genocide* interesting, useful, and educational, and that he will come to look upon it as a contribution to a more correct understanding of the tragic events of the Nazi era. There is no doubt that militarism, fascism, racism, and war were the main reasons for the Holocaust. But this is a subject for scientific historians.

Soviet archives contain a wealth of captured Nazi and Ukrainian Nationalist documentary material. Interested U.S. historians would do well to investigate these in their quest for the answers to the question of why and how the Nazi era occurred.

For the Committee: B. Sabrin

Committee Members: I. Gartner,
B. Sabrin,
A. Hütler,
S. Brinstein, and
I. Goldfliess

CONTENTS

In July 1919, the short-lived Ukrainian Nationalist regime which had formed a government in the wake of the Russian Civil War was forced out of Galizia and Western Ukraine and the territories were incorporated into the newly reconstituted nation of Poland. The following chronology of events are the concern of this book:

September 1, 1939. . . .Germany invades Poland from the West

September 17, 1939. . .The Soviet Union, in cooperation with Germany, invades Poland from the East, re-annexing Western Ukraine

July 22, 1941. . . . . . .Germany invades the Soviet Union

July 2, 1941. . . . . . . .German troops enter Tarnopol

In Trembowla, Tarnopol Region:

    October 5, 1942 . . .The First "Action"

    April 7, 1943 . . . . .The Second "Action"

    June 3-5, 1943 . . .The Third "Action"

November 6, 1943 . . .The Red Army reoccupies Kiev

March 22, 1944 . . . . .The Red Army reoccupies Trembowla

July 27, 1944. . . . . . .The Red Army reoccupies Lvov

May 11, 1945 . . . . . .The final surrender of German forces to the Allies

PREFACE

B. F. Sabrin

Alliance for Murder: The Nazi-Ukrainian Nationalist Partnership in Genocide contains, among its eyewitness accounts, selections from the *Tarnopol Memorial Book* and the *Trembowla Memorial Book,* both of which were published many years ago in Israel.

The tragic stories recounted here are the survivor's own, and nobody has a right to alter them. This rule has been faithfully observed throughout, with the exception that some stories have been rendered slightly abridged.

During my post-war visits to Tarnopol and Trembowla, Ukraine SSR, I had a chance to meet some elderly Gentile residents. I was astounded at how well they remembered the bloody events of the Nazi occupation. Also, I was given documentary evidence that described in detail the Holocaust tragedy in the area. Some of the material is included in this book.

Mr. Z. Turevich, a resident of the outskirts of Trembowla, was able to describe with amazing accuracy the different Nazi "Actions" committed against the Jewish residents. He mentioned the loaded train transports to the Extermination Camp Belzec* (located between the cities of Rawa Russka and Tomaszow Lubelski), the cold-blooded murders and subsequent mass burials of the Jews in the mountain village Plebanovka, another Trembowla outskirt. All this was done with the help of the Ukrainian Nationalist Police. Mr. Turevich also described the liquidation of the Jewish Ghetto in 1943. After the final "Action," the Nazis declared Trembowla *Judenfrei,* (free from Jews). This important event was published in the Nazi newspaper.

According to Adolf David Hütler, a survivor of the Holocaust,

---

*A detailed description of the human tragedy in this camp can be found in Rudolf Reder, *Belzec,* Cracow, 1946.

I

a 1944 Allied International Commission investigated the Nazi atrocities in the village Plebanovka, counting and photographing the excavated bodies from the mass graves. The findings of this investigation are preserved in the Soviet State Archives.

During my recent Tarnopol and Trembowla visits, I was given Documentary evidence that described in detail the Holocaust tragedy in the area. The material is included in this book.

Contributing Holocaust Survivors

Some of the Holocaust survivors in the U.S. agreed to contribute their stories. The others did not respond to my request for various reasons, be it their old age, or unwillingness to relive the bitter wartime experience they suffered during the Nazi era.

The following remarks about the contents of this book are not intended to offend any contributing Holocaust survivor. I do remember most of the survivors (and victims), and realize that some are no longer alive. In any event, all have my full respect for making their contribution to keep alive the memory of those who perished during the reign of the bloody fascist "New Order" in Nazi-occupied Ukraine.

Only a broader view of events can give us a clear, objective picture. This precisely explains the reason for the diversity of voices and opinions presented in this book. If a reader finds an event described differently by different authors, it is because this book stands behind the memories of the actual participants in the events, and not the generalizations later bestowed by observers who were farther removed. What is truly remarkable is the consistency of the accounts in imparting the horrors that are also documented facts.

The tragic events in Western Ukraine during the Nazi era are little known to the American and Canadian public. To blame the German Nazis for everything that happened there, and leave out the Nazi henchmen and collaborators of all shades, would be a distortion of historical truth. It would be a disservice to the memory of the victims of Nazism and Fascism.

A more complete picture of events in Nazi-occupied Ukraine (and the Baltic states) during World War II will be a job for future historians. Microfilmed archival documentary evidence is already available in the United States. Let's hope it will see daylight in the early 1990s. The time is long overdue.

Introduction:
The Nazi-Ukrainian Nationalist Partnership

B. F. Sabrin

The bloody collaboration between German Fascists and Ukrainian Nationalists in the Nazi-occupied territories during World War II was on an unbelievably wide scale. In every city, every town, and every village under Nazi rule in the Ukraine, Ukrainian Nationalist civil administrations, police, and committees coexisted side by side with the German Nazis. Theirs was not a collaboration at gunpoint, with one side bruised and suffering under the other's iron heel, but rather a partnership, in which the Ukrainian Nationalists saw in the Nazis the means to achieve their own ends.

As is now well known due to recent trials in the United States and Israel, many Ukrainian Nationalists served as guards in slave labor camps, extermination camps, and Jewish Ghettos. Tens of thousands of Ukrainian Nationalists also served as *Hiwis* (helpers) in the Nazi army, while others accepted arms and fought alongside the Nazis in numerous special action and anti-partisan battalions, as well as in the larger formation, SS Division Galicia.

In its short and murderous history, the Third Reich did not enjoy the advantage of more devoted hirelings and henchmen than it found within the Nationalist movement in the Ukraine.

History of Ukrainian Nationalism

In view of the fact that almost all survivor stories in this book mention the role in the Nazi Holocaust tragedy played by Ukrainian Nationalism, it is appropriate first to explain this movement's brief and inglorious history.

One of the most extremist Ukrainian Nationalist organizations which emerged after World War I was the "Ukrainian Military Organization" (UVO), headed by Yevhen Konovalets. It was created

3

in September 1920 and had its headquarters in Berlin, Germany.

The UVO had its branches in Western Ukraine, then under Polish rule, with the city of Lvov its territorial center. During the 1930's, the UVO was remodeled and changed to the "Organization of Ukrainian Nationalists" (OUN), headed by Yevhen Konovalets and A. Melnyk (Konovalets was assassinated in 1938).

The OUN "patriots" had started to evolve their own model of Fascism before Hitler came to power in Germany. In the "Resolution of the First Congress of the OUN" (held in 1929, in Vienna, Austria), we can read the following: "Only national dictatorship will be able to preserve the internal strength of the Ukrainian Nation."

Ukrainian Nationalist "patriots" served their Nazi masters long before the outbreak of World War II. In the 1930's (and earlier), OUN had close connections with the Nazi Abwehr (intelligence service) in Berlin. Many members of OUN were Nazi agents, involved in subversion, espionage, sabotage, terrorism, and outright murder. In 1934, the OUN assassinated Bronislav Pieracki, Poland's Interior Minister, in Warsaw. (The OUN-UPA also boasted about the murder of Soviet Marshal M. Vatutin and Polish General W. Swierczewski — after the war.) Espionage information provided by the OUN network in the Western Ukraine before World War II was utilized by the Third Reich to its best advantage when it invaded the Soviet Union.

In April 1941, the OUN held its second Congress in the city of Cracow, which by then was already under Nazi occupation. One of the Congresses' resolutions concerned Jews: ". . . In the USSR the Jews are the most faithful supporters of the ruling Bolshevik regime. . . . The OUN combats the Jews." Stepan Bandera, Yaroslav Stetsko, and other OUN members, took an active part in organizing this "Second Great Congress" of the "Revolutionary OUN."

Blinded by its pathological hatred of the Soviet rule of the Ukraine, and infected with the racist virus, the OUN considered the Third Reich as its natural ally, seeing in the Nazi *"Drang nach Osten"* (Eastward Drive) its only hope of achieving an independent Ukraine. On the bloody path of treason and collaboration with German Nazism, no crime was too small or too big for the OUN "freedom fighters," seizing what they viewed as their historical opportunity.

The Third Reich, among other sources, gave financial backing to the OUN, which split into two camps in 1940: OUN-B (Bandera) and OUN-M (Melnyk). They even killed each other in rivalry. On August 30, 1941, two leaders of the Melnyk branch of the OUN were shot in the back and killed. Their assassin was immediately killed by

Ukrainian and German police, thus excluding the possibility of learning his true motives. Considerable evidence exists, however, that the Bandera group had ordered the assassinations.

On June 30, 1941, OUN-B proclaimed "Ukrainian Statehood" in Lvov, with Yaroslav Stetsko declared the "Premier." Stetsko was the son of a priest and an ideologue of modern Ukrainian Nationalism, an ardent believer in both "God and Ukraine." In the Lvov Cathedral of St. George (July 1, 1941), Metropolitan Andrey Sheptystsky, the head of the Ukrainian Greek Catholic Church, gave his blessing: "We recognize Yaroslav Stetsko as the Prime Minister of the State Government of the Ukraine. May God bless your deeds."

In many ways, Ukrainian Nationalist murderers surpassed their Nazi partners in perpetrating atrocities (Pogroms) against innocent people. On Bandera's order, thousands of Western Ukrainians, suspected of affiliation with Soviet power, had been slaughtered. Both groups, OUN-B and OUN-M, readied the so-called *Pokhidni Hrupy* (expeditionary groups) trailing behind the Nazi invaders into the Ukraine.

Here is what Holocaust survivor Adolf David Hütler remembers:

"One day, before the Nazi army entered the town of Trembowla, Tarnopol Region (Western Ukraine), on July 4, 1941, Ukrainian Nationalists rounded up a group of around 20 Jews (secular and religious) and ordered them to go to the *"Koshary"* (military barracks), located outside the town. The reason for taking them there was probably the desire of the Ukrainian Nationalists to clean up the barracks before the Germans came in.

   With the exception of one, the rounded-up Jews never returned home. After they finished the job, they were brutally massacred on the spot. Their cries could be heard miles away. It was a real Pogrom. No Ukrainian Nationalist prisoners were shot by the NKVD (Soviet Security Police) in the town's prison. There was no excuse and no 'outburst of anger' by the local population at that time. So why were innocent people massacred? Simply because they were Jews. No excuse was needed. Ukrainian Nationalists ran amok. . . . "

In testimony before the Nuremberg tribunal, German Lieutenant Erwin Bingel describes how Ukrainian militiamen (OUN members) participated in an action at the Vinnitsa airport in Western Ukraine. The Jews of Vinnitsa had been assembled at the airport and then:

"One row of Jews was ordered to move forward and was then allocated to the different tables where they had to undress completely and hand over everything that they wore and carried...Then, having taken off all their clothes, they were made to stand in line in front of the ditches, irrespective of their sex. The commandos then marched in behind the line and began to perform the inhuman acts...With automatic pistols and 0.8 pistols these men mowed down the line...Even women carrying children a fortnight to three weeks old, sucking at their breasts, were not spared this horrible ordeal. Nor were mothers spared the terrible sight of their children being gripped by their little legs and put to death with one stroke of the pistol-butt or club, thereafter to be thrown on the heap of human bodies in the ditch, some of which were not quite dead."

In 1946 I had a chance to meet a group of Jews who had been partisan fighters during the war. During the course of our conversations, one of them described in vivid terms a revealing event: "We fought the Nazis from the forests. One day our order was to eliminate a German outpost. After the job was finished, we were surrounded by a large group of enemies who pursued us without a stop. The only road left to retreat was back to the forest. The bloody battle lasted a few hours, until we started to run out of ammunition...our losses were very heavy. The enemy had the advantage in manpower and ammunition. They continued to pursue us into the forest. Some of our comrades managed to evade them, running faster than the rest.

"When it started to get dark in the forest, some others crawled on top of tall, thick trees. The enemy did not like to stay in the dark forest. They left the area. When I came down from the tree, I started to look for my brother. I found him dead. What could I do? I took off his shoes, took a piece of his bread (partly soaked with blood), gave him a last kiss on the forehead, and left the area, joining the other comrades."

Who were the enemies fighting against the partisans? Were they German Nazis? I asked. "No," was his clear answer. "They were Ukrainian Nationalists." This individual later emigrated to Israel with a group of people.

Ukrainian Nationalists in Western Ukraine viewed the Nazi invasion of the Soviet Union as a liberation, and welcomed the creation of a "free" Ukraine within the Fascist "New Order" in Europe. To them, partnership with German Fascism was their only means of achieving Ukrainian statehood; what is also true, however, is the enormous degree to which they shared with the Nazis murderous intentions toward whoever stood in their way, including the innocent.

I have a personal recollection of a broadcast, dating back to the year 1941, which I have never found mentioned in any book, newspaper, or magazine. Despite this, I don't think that I was the only person who heard it.

The first day (June 22, 1941), or the first few days, after Nazi Germany attacked the Soviet Union, I invited myself into the house of my friend, Moynio Pfefferblüth (a famous football player), who resided in the town of Trembowla, Tarnopol Region. I had a reason for doing so: My friend had a powerful SW-AM radio, on which one could listen to the news about the war directly from Berlin in Nazi Germany.

During the visit I asked Moynio to tune in Berlin. It took a few turns of the radio knob, and then the deafening sound of marching music was blaring. The marching songs and cries of *"Sieg Heil"* continued for 15 minutes or so, and then a brief pause followed. Right thereafter, an announcement came: "Radio Berlin, here is Berlin. An important speech will follow soon."

We didn't have to wait long: ". . . *Howoryt Berlyn"* (in the Ukrainian language). "Here is Berlin. Dear fellow Ukrainians, the long-awaited hour of liberation of our Motherland from Moscow Bolshevism has arrived. The dream of Ukrainian Independence will soon be realized. With the help of the glorious invincible German Army, we will destroy Bolshevism and reestablish a free Ukrainian State." What followed was a vicious tirade of slander and hatred against the Soviet Union, an open call for subversion, sabotage, and terrorism in the rear of the Red Army.

The tirade continued: "Greet the victorious German Army as liberators of the Ukraine, friends of the Ukrainian people. Help to destroy the hated enemy — Moscow, Russia. Hasten the day of our final liberation."

Despite the fast pace of the speech, I was able to understand its content (in Ukrainian) very well. The entire speech lasted around 25 to 30 minutes. The speaker's radio time was limited. He concluded his radio appeal with the following call to the Ukrainian people: *"Smert Zydam, Smert Kommunistam, Smert Kommissaram."* Translated into plain English, it reads: "Death to Jews, Death to Communists, Death to Commissars." Exactly in that sequence.

The open call to kill was made *before* the Holocaust started. It came directly from Berlin, Germany, and was made by an important member of the Organization of Ukrainian Nationalists, which had its headquarters in Berlin. OUN was, therefore, fully responsible, along with the Nazis, for the open call to kill.*

Death Battalions Before the Invasion of Russia

It is estimated that around 25,000 young Ukrainian Nationalists escaped from Western Ukraine (under Soviet rule) to the Nazi-occupied part of Poland after September 1939. It was from those Ukrainians that the Nazis trained and formed the two notorious death battalions — "Nachtigal" and "Roland."

Both Ukrainian volunteer battalions participated, along with German "Brandenburg" commando units, in the Pogroms of the early stages of the Nazi invasion of the Soviet Union. The "Nachtigal" and "Roland" death battalions committed bloody atrocities in Lvov, Tarnopol, and other cities and towns in Western Ukraine, in which thousands of Jews were massacred.

The two murder battalions were disbanded in 1942, and their men were merged into the volunteer SS-102 Punitive Battalion, which became known for its orgies and bestiality in its career behind the actual fighting front.

On July 15, 1943, the local newspaper, *Kremenetsky Visnik (Kremenets Herald),* in the Tarnopol region wrote with jubiliation: "We, Ukrainian Nationalists, are fighting the Jewish clique. Forthcoming generations will be glad that the Jews were exterminated."

During the middle of 1943, Banderite Armed Bands, known as the UPA (Ukrainian Insurgent Army), were formed. Their main activity was terrorism, violence, sabotage and suppression of Soviet partisan activity in the rear areas.

Side by side with the German Wehrmacht, helping to "build a better Europe," was the Ukrainian Volunteer Division of the Waffen-SS *"Galizien"* (14th SS Division), which numbered 12,000 to 15,000 men. This division was decimated by the Red Army during the battle of Brody (July 1944) and, just before the collapse of the Third Reich in April 1945, its beaten remnants were transformed into a new unit, called the Ukrainian National Army (UNA).

---

*The name of the Ukrainian Nationalist speaker was mentioned, but I fail to remember it. Since my archival research of recent years I have managed to narrow the suspects, however, and there is a strong indication that it was one of the following OUN leading members: V. Kubiyovych, S. Lenkavsky (OUN Propaganda Department), M. Lebed, or Y. Stetsko.

The opinion exists that, in comparison with the Eastern Ukraine, the "Galicia District" (Western Ukraine) was somewhat more fortunate in terms of people's suffering, because it was incorporated into Poland under Nazi administration in what the Germans called the "General Government."

In *Ukraine: A Concise Encyclopedia,* by Voldymyr Kubijovych,* a Ukrainian Nationalist collaborator, we read: ". . . in the middle of 1943, Galicia (Western Ukraine) was the only relatively peaceful island in the great expanse of Eastern Europe conquered by the Germans, and the only place where conditions were close to normal."

How "close to normal" and "peaceful" the Galicia district was during the bloody Nazi occupation in 1943 has been well known for some time, and will be elucidated in the chapters of this book. By 1943, the bloody, anti-Jewish Programs were almost over, and the mass pits, containing the murdered victims of multinational Fascism, had already begun to be covered with green grass.

Partners Despite Disappointment

Despite the OUN's initial disappointment with the broken German promise of an independent Ukraine (Lvov, June 30, 1941), Ukrainian Nationalists swallowed the bitter pill. The Soviet Union was proving to be more than a match for Germany on the field of battle and the Nazis' attention had necessarily to focus on defeating the Red Army, with post-war arrangments to be settled later.

It was not until after their defeat at Stalingrad, in early 1943, that the Germans formed the Ukrainian-manned *Galizien* SS Division, with the head of the Ukrainian Central Committee, V. Kubiyovych, exhorting his countrymen to "destroy the Bolshevik monster." As their fortunes waned on the battlefield, in fact, the ties that bound the Nazis with the Ukrainian Nationalist movement actually grew stronger. The Ukrainians reasoned, "Now, the Germans will need us more than ever." It became in both sides' interest not to let their crimes and abuses of power come to light. And both sides feared equally the retribution of the Red Army.

The OUN leadership, however, was not blind to the turn of events, and, like a chameleon, began to change its colors to adapt to a changed environment should the need arise.

In August 1943, the third OUN-B Congress (the Bandera faction)

---

*Kubijovych died in 1986, in Paris, France.

modified the organization's platform. Nazi henchmen, agents and collaborators, spies and terrorists, turned overnight into "freedom-loving patriots," fighting for "human rights and democracy." In one "Political Resolution" of the modified platform, it is stated in black and white: "We are for the full right of national minorities to cultivate their own national culture . . ." in a "free, independent Ukraine." The hope to achieve this aim (with the help of Nazi Germany) was still alive.

During 1941–44, Ukrainian Nationalists helped the German Nazis to exterminate Jews in the millions, and later they offered (the dead Jews) the full right to "cultivate their National culture" in a Nazi-liberated Ukraine. In July 1944, the Ukrainian Nationalist "Supreme Liberation Council" went even further in its verbal generosity to "Guarantee citizenship rights to all national minorities in the Ukraine." In the resurrected Ukrainian state they were prepared to "guarantee genuine rule of law" and "equality of all citizens before the law."

During the Nazi occupation of the Ukraine, millions of Jews, Russians, Poles, Ukrainians, and others found "equality" in the Nazi extermination camps and slave-labor camps, as well as in the open pits of unnamed forests. The Ukrainian Nationalist collaborators never received the chance to govern independently or put into practice their "ideals." What remains today is the evidence of their partnership in destruction.

For the Record

After a brief struggle, the Nazi Army marched into Tarnopol, Ukrainian SSR, on July 2, 1941. On Saturday, July 5, 1941, they arrived in Trembowla, Tarnopol region. Some Jews and non-Jews were killed the same day. The Ukrainian Nationalists (OUN) came out from the underground even before the Nazis entered, killing retreating Soviet soldiers, Jews and Polish citizens.

The first Nazi "Action"—the first mass round-up of Trembowla Jews—took place on October 5, 1942. Hundreds of people were loaded onto cattle cars and transported by train to the Extermination Camp Belzec.*

*Belzec lies on the line: Lublin, Zamość, Tomashow, Rawa-Russka, Lvov. It is located 15 km. from Rawa-Russka in Poland, near the border of the Ukr.SSR. The construction of the camp started in the early part of 1942. The Jewish slave-labor brigade that built the camp was exterminated directly upon the camp's completion; subsequent death transports began to arrive in March 1942. Outside

The second "Action" took place on April 7, 1943. The Jewish people were forced to walk in their underwear (3–5 miles) to the village of Plebanovka, where they were gunned down with machine guns. The disabled, the young, the sick, and the old, all unable to walk, were loaded onto horse-wagons (provided by local Gentiles on order) and delivered to the execution place.

The third "Action" took place on June 3–5, 1943. The round-up method was similar to that of the second "Action." Most of the Trembowla Jews (and nearby smaller localities) found their end in the mass graves, high up in the village of Plebanovka. Some other graves were found later behind the military barracks near the forest.

The Trembowla Jewish Ghetto was created in 1942, and liquidated in 1943. It was located in the old part of the town, starting from the military barracks (called *Keplovka*), and stretching all the way to the Jewish Synagogues and the old bathhouse. The victims were squeezed into a long, narrow strip of the town. From the smaller towns and the surrounding villages, the Jews were driven to the Trembowla Ghetto. Most of them perished in Plebanovka and other places. Some were betrayed by local scoundrels. There were cases where some Gentiles agreed to hide Jews at the beginning of the occupation, and then later murdered them, or handed them over to the Nazis, thus inheriting the Jews' possessions. Some Jews committed suicide, not being able to take it any longer. Others gave themselves up to the German or Ukrainian police.

The town of Trembowla was liberated by the Soviet Army on March 22, 1944. At the time of the liberation, only a handful of Jews (around two dozen) had managed to survive. From a small, vibrant Jewish community (approximately 1,500–2,000), only a tiny remnant remained alive. It is estimated that around 10 percent of the total escaped in time to the Soviet Union, before the Nazis arrived.

Were there any Jews collaborating with German Nazis in Trembowla? Sadly, there were some isolated cases.

Adolph David Hütler, a Holocaust survivor, relates the story of a former student classmate of his named Rudolf, who went hunting with some German Nazis to find hiding Jews.

the gas chamber was a machine, with a motor running on gasoline. Through a pipe, the exhaust was pumped inside the chamber. It took around 20 minutes until the victims suffocated. A detailed description of the human tragedy in Extermination Camp Belzec can be found in the booklet: "Belzec," by Rudolf Reder, Krakow, 1946. It is unfortunate that this small (65 pp.) booklet in Polish language has never been translated and published in English. — *I. Gartner*

Passing his own house, he pointed his finger to the camouflaged hideout where his entire family was sheltered. After the frightened group of unlucky people were forced to come out, the parents were astounded to see their own son standing together with the Nazi executioners outside. They took a sharp look into his eyes, not believing what they saw. The Nazi officer noticed it, sensing something. "Who are these people?" he asked the Jewish student.

"They are my parents, my family," he replied.

"If you could do this. . .you'll join them," said the Nazi officer, concluding the brief conversation. The Jewish group was led away to the nearby Nazi S.D. (Security Service). The entire family, including the student, perished.

In Trembowla, only a handful of Jews collaborated briefly with the Nazis, thinking that they'd save their own lives. In the end, they wound up in the pits, together with all the other Jewish victims of the time. From the very beginning of World War II to its very end, the Ukrainian Nationalists were a voluntary partner in crime with German Fascism.

Without the close collaboration of the OUN, especially in the occupied parts of the Ukraine, the Nazi killing machine could not have succeeded in annihilating so many victims. The Ukrainian Nationalist police were established in cities, towns and villages in the Ukraine from the beginning of the Nazi occupation. The Ukrainian Nationalist police were the last to leave the Nazi-occupied Ukrainian territories.

German Plans for the Ukraine

Had the Soviet Union lost the war against Nazi Germany, the Ukraine would have become an enslaved colony. After the Jews and the Gypsies, the Slav people were next in line to be enslaved and eliminated.

The Nazi "General Plan East" outlined the gradual extermination of tens of millions of Slavic people.

The first version of the "General Plan Ost" was prepared by SS leaders before the invasion of the USSR. It provided the guideline for colonization of the conquered lands to the east of Germany. This plan envisaged the "eviction" (read: extermination) of 31 million people in Poland and the western part of the Soviet Union within 30 years.

After the invasion, the Nazi leaders considered the first version of the plan to be inadequate. An Imperial Ministry for affairs of the occupied eastern regions, headed by Alfred Rosenberg, was set up in Germany. The Nazi ministry found it necessary to "evict" 45–50 million people, because "it is not so much a matter of defeating the state with its center in Moscow, as of destroying the Russians (the sub-human Slavs) as a nation."

It is known that SS leaders, and their "specialists," worked hard on every detail of the "General Plan Ost" right till the end of 1943. Their final conclusion was that in this future colony of the "Great German World Reich" (stretching as far as the Urals) there should be 80 percent "Germanization." Therefore, a minimum of 120–140 million Slavic people were to be physically destroyed.

In one of his speeches in 1936, the Nazi Führer, Adolf Hitler, said: "If we had the corn-chamber of the Ukraine, what a paradise the German Reich would be." The Nazi drive for *Lebensraun* (living space) in the East, never included the Ukrainian Nationalist (OUN-UPA) grand illusions of an independent Ukraine.

Did Ukrainian Nationalist ideologues and "patriots" understand the naked truth outlined clearly in Hitler's *Mein Kampf* in the 1920s? Just as they had collaborated to enact a tragic fate upon the Jews of the Ukraine, so too would they have fallen victim to an equally murderous fate, had their fondest dreams been realized.

Part One

THE

SCENE OF

COLLABORATION

> *"There is now a sociopolitical system which is developing the world over: in one country it manifests itself as Fascism, in another as Hitlerism, and we name it here as Nationalism."*
>
> Ukrainian Nationalist newspaper — *Nash Klich*
> June 3, 1938

1

On the Eve of
World War II

Dr. Zvi Parnes

In 1938, the Polish government worked out a law according to which all those residing for long periods of time in foreign countries, or whose ties to the country were weak, would lose Polish citizenship. The law was directed primarily against Jews residing temporarily in other countries.

The Nazi government found this to be a good excuse to get rid of Polish Jews residing in Germany. Despite the existing friendship treaty with Poland, the relations between the two countries took a turn for the worse.

During the same year, 1938, the Nazi regime expelled tens of thousands of Jews, and drove them to the Polish Frontier at Zbonszyn, where a large refugee camp was established, supported and supervised by the "Joint." When the camp was closed down, a number of these refugees were sent to Tarnopol. The public-spirited Jewish leaders of Tarnopol showed great compassion and did everything to help their unfortunate brethren, who had arrived in complete destitution. A special committee was created, of which the leading members were Dr. Parnes, Dr. Nusbaum, Dr. Horowitz, Dr. Seret, and Mr. Exelbirt. The job wasn't an easy one. There was a problem with the supply of food, clothing, and housing. Most refugees had neither shelter nor personal documents to prove their Polish citizenship.

The swelling of the population figure caused a price increase of many food products, rent, and other necessities. The Gentile people, many of whom were infected in those years with anti-Semitism, showed their discontent with the "invasion of the uninvited guests." Even a certain segment of the local Jewish population started to lose patience, especially as German Jews were revealed to consider their Polish brethren as "culturally backward." The tension grew even more when a story came out about a refugee who, wanting to cross the

Soviet Border, was caught by the Polish Border police for alleged espionage. Anti-Jewish elements used this episode to accuse Jewish leaders of helping the Communists. However, this familiar trick did not work.

Such was the situation when World War II started. Not long after, a new wave of Jewish refugees started to arrive from the western part of Poland — Bielsko-Biala, Katowice, Krakow — escaping eastward from the Nazi onslaught.

The outbreak of World War II found Polish Jewry in a state of extreme anxiety. Tarnopol was again flooded with refugees, and the Jewish community once again rushed to their rescue. Many refugees were provided with living quarters. A special folks-kitchen was created, supplying a warm meal for a small donation. In a few days, the Tarnopol population almost doubled. The refugee flow continued from everywhere. High Polish Government Officials, former Ministers, and Foreign Diplomats passed through Tarnopol, toward the Rumanian Border. The tension grew constantly. The defeats of the Polish Army on the front left no doubt as to the end of the Polish Government. The fear about the future was on everybody's mind.

On September 17, 1939, the first Soviet tanks entered Tarnopol. The town was spared from any destruction and war action. But who knew what the New Order would bring.

At the beginning of Soviet rule, various forms of social help, such as soup kitchens and handicraft cooperatives were quickly organized. But this was the "Swan Song" of Tarnopol Jewry.

After a few days of chaos, a cooling-down came. A special Jewish refugee delegation went to the City Commander, Major Zhukov, to bring up the refugee problem. Major Zhukov declared that there was no place for such activity under Soviet law, and he further added that it was the Soviet Government and not some other agency that would provide jobs for its citizens. But he allowed the committee to continue its work until a civilian authority was established in the city. He also assured the Refugee Committee that food rationing would include the folks-kitchen.

It was important to find work for the refugees. A start was made with organizing the shoemakers. It was a step in the right direction. City cobblers and other trades were next. After a short time, the small cobbler cooperative developed into a factory, which employed hundreds of people. The cooperative enjoyed the help also of the "Joint." After a comparatively short time, the cooperatives prospered and developed successfully. During a visit to Tarnopol, the head of the Ukrainian Cooperatives was not able to conceal his amazement.

With the creation of the cooperatives and the employment of the refugees, the role of the Elected Committee came to an end. The Jewish community leadership successfully fulfilled its mission, solving the difficult problem and overcoming many obstacles on the way.

The Soviet rule brought about a complete disappearance of all existing Jewish institutions and, with it, the liquidation of sources of livelihood for many others. The community was compelled to change its way of living, and at the same time, it was overwhelmed by new decrees.

The most cruel was the "Passportization" ordinance. Many Jews received passports which included Paragraph 17, prohibiting the right to live in large cities. By these means, masses of Jews were compelled to leave their homes and work. The real nightmare, however, was the exiling of Jews to Russia. Mass deportations took place in June 1940, when hundreds of refugees from western Poland who had escaped from the Nazis were deported to the eastern and northern USSR.

By the time the Soviet Army re-entered Tarnopol, in 1944, only 139 Jews remained alive. These had saved themselves by means of "Aryan" passports or by hiding with Gentiles. About 200 Jews had managed to escape to the Soviet Union before the Nazi onslaught. This pitiful number was all that remained from a community of 18,000 Jews who were living in Tarnopol when the Germans occupied the town.

2

The Dark Clouds

Abraham Ochs

THE CONTINUED GROWING TENSION in Europe after the Nazi seizure
of power and raging anti-Semitism in Poland did not bode well for
the future. The Polish Jews found themselves in a precarious situation,
almost without a way out. They started to lose the ground under their
feet, not seeing any ray of hope on the horizon. The news about the
Nazi invasion was perceived as a hard blow, and in their hearts the
Jews came to believe that bitter years lay ahead.

During the summer months of 1939, illusions prevailed in Poland
that war would be avoided. The peaceful Nazi takeover of the Saar
Region, and the Munich Treaty, strengthened those illusions. Nobody
believed that Hitler would dare provoke the Western Powers (England,
France) who had a defense treaty with Poland. Even less tenable was
the belief that Poland's fate would be decided in a matter of days.
After the deadly Nazi blows, the empty Polish illusions of being
"strong, united and ready" (*silni, zwarci, gotowi*) were shattered and
the pride of Poland crumbled into dust. The backbone of the Polish
Army broke. If this is the fate of a "great country," the Jews thought,
what can we expect? Not having even enough time to shake off the
news about the defeat of Poland, the Soviet Army marched into the
western parts of Poland unopposed. Millions of Polish zlotys, invested
to defend the eastern borders, were wasted. The bloody hammer blows
against Poland came from the West, that is, from "friendly" Germany.

The Soviet Army had been in Tarnopol one time before (1920).
At that time they had looked poorly and had made an unfavorable
impression. Many thought that all this came as a result of the stormy
war years, that life would normalize, and that the bad would soon
disappear. But almost twenty years had passed, and this time a well-
armed and disciplined army came into Tarnopol. The general impression was that the Soviet power would remain for good.

These unexpected events caused mixed feelings in the Jewish people. First, there was an easing of tension and a satisfaction that a Nazi occupation had been avoided in this part of former Poland. The sad news about Nazi atrocities in Germany, in occupied Western Poland, and later from Czechoslovakia, was no secret. The perceived threat from the Soviets was a different one. But this was something else. It was clear that the old order had come to an end and that a new way of life was beginning.

The old social structure, built by generations, was destroyed during a short period. The activity of different parties, organizations, and institutions in Tarnopol stopped. The old social and political leaders were removed and put aside in a corner. New, unknown faces appeared. All of a sudden the Communists, who had been known before, were out front. They declared their loyalty to the Soviet regime. The buildings of different local organizations were confiscated. The many institutions and political parties were eliminated.

Slowly the situation started to normalize. The method of Soviet power started to become clearer. The first blow came to the refugees. Entire families of former Jewish military officers, captured by the Soviet Army, were exiled deep into the USSR. True, there weren't too many of them. But this created a panic among the Jewish people.

During that time, the fate of the former Polish territories was decided. At a mass gathering of professional organizations and trade unions, a resolution was approved to establish Soviet power in the newly included Soviet Western Ukraine. A special Folks-Referendum later approved this decision.

The only remaining direct contact with the outside world was through the radio. Many listened to the BBC for London news, believing that a great spring offensive in the west would destroy Nazi Germany and reestablish the Old Order in Europe.

In the meantime, the Jews tried to acclimate themselves to the newly created conditions — the new reality. The social revolution started. New government stores were opened. The private merchants started to lose their positions.

On the horizon dark clouds started to appear. Zionist leaders were arrested in Lvov. A panic started among the Zionist leaders in Tarnopol.

Mass arrests at that time took place among Polish people as well. Many former policemen, former army officers, and government officials were exiled into Siberia and Central Asia. Those arrests created more panic in the city.

The burning problem of the day was the refugee problem of those coming from Western Poland. Separated from their homes and families, and disappointed about the gray reality, they grabbed the existing opportunity to return. There were rumors of a population exchange between the two parts of former Poland. News from Nazi-occupied Poland circulated that "life is hard, but bearable."

After a mixed commission for refugee problems was created, many Jewish refugees declared their readiness to return. It didn't take long before all illusions came to an end. The Germans refused to accept such a great number of Jews, and the Soviet authorities saw an anti-Soviet element in all those who refused to accept Soviet citizenship and who wanted to return to the Nazi-occupied territories. During the month of June 1940, mass arrests took place.

Many of the refugees were exiled and resettled in different parts of the country. All this made a devastating impression on the local Jewish population. Many considered such behavior as unjustified brutality toward the Jews by the Soviet authorities.

The order of new passports and the nationalization of private property were considered the hardest blows. Some passports carried Paragraph NR.11. Such a person wasn't permitted to reside in larger cities with industrial enterprises. Tarnopol was considered one of those cities. Thousands of Jews were forced to wander into smaller towns, where they couldn't find jobs and living quarters. The threat of being sent to Siberia was constant for those without permanent employment.

However, despite all of the negative phenomena, the great majority of the Jewish people managed to adapt to existing conditions, joining production cooperatives, government shops, and other branches of the economy. The former Jewish community leaders had desisted from any political and social activities. Thanks to this, many Zionist leaders avoided exile.

Under Nazi Occupation

On Sunday morning, June 22, 1941, Nazi Germany attacked the Soviet Union. After a short period, the Soviet army started to retreat eastward. High Government Officials and Communist party workers ran away from the Nazi onslaught. A few hundred Jews were mobilized into the Red Army. With great fear and anxiety, the remaining Jewish people saw the German army enter Tarnopol on the twelfth day of the war—July 2, 1941.

The strength of the Nazi army and its initial great victories engendered feelings of exasperation and disappointment. The great majority of the Jewish people weren't able to comprehend the tragic end awaiting them.

Many of the local Ukrainians had welcomed the Germans with unconcealed happiness, hoping that now their time had come. They associated themselves closely with the Germans, blaming the Jews for everything wrong during the Soviet reign. The Germans handed over the city administration to the Ukrainian Nationalists, nominating a Ukrainian president. A Ukrainian police was created. On the third day of the Nazi occupation, bloody anti-Jewish Pogroms occurred, which in the history of Tarnopol had never been known before.

Monday, July 7, 1941, German military units appeared in the Jewish streets. Armed with hand grenades, they cried: "Jews Out" ("Juden Raus"). Men were placed against the walls and murdered in cold blood. Others were driven to the marketplace, near the old bathhouse, on the Zacerkiewna, Ostrogski, and Lvovska Streets. Soldiers with rolled-up sleeves started to beat up the frightened Jews, ordering them to dig graves where they were to be shot. In other parts of the city, the Germans started to destroy Synagogues, burning the Scrolls. Into one Synagogue, around 500 Jews were driven; the house was ignited, and all of them perished in flames. Wild terrible cries were heard all around. Nobody could escape the inferno. Big deep cellars in large buildings were selected for the second massacre of the Jews. Hundreds lost their lives there. Some managed to crawl out later from under the piles of dead bodies.

After the "official" anti-Jewish Pogrom, which lasted a few days, the Ukrainian nationalists staged their own Pogrom. The reason given for this massacre was the fact (according to the Ukrainian Nationalists) that a few dozen Gentile bodies had been found in the prison on Mickiewicza Street. For this, the Jews were blamed, and they had to pay with their lives. Hundreds of Jews were brought into the Tarnopol prison, beaten, ordered to wash the dead bodies, and forced to do the dirtiest jobs. After these tragic scenes were over, all were brutally murdered. Some individual Jews resisted with force, reminding the bloody Ukrainian hangmen that a bitter end would be awaiting them in the future.

Stiff, dead, bloody Jewish bodies were lying all over in those days on the streets of Tarnopol.

When the Pogroms were over, tragic scenes were visible everywhere. Relatives of the murdered started to look for the dead bodies, which they couldn't even recognize. Thousands of people were seen on the streets, looking for relatives and friends. There was almost no Jewish family without a loss. Most of the victims were brought to the old Jewish cemetery, and buried there.

In those two Pogroms, around five thousand Jews lost their lives. This tragedy shattered the remaining hope for any salvation — any future. The restless anxiety didn't disappear, when the Nazi authorities declared on wall posters that the Pogrom against the Jews was over. New rules were adopted by the Nazis, isolating the Jews from the rest of the population. The Jews were placed into a situation where they were driven to do forced labor for the military establishment and civilian institutions.

In the beginning of July 1941, the Nazis ordered the teacher, Gotfried, to create a committee of sixty people. The candidates, mostly from the highly educated class, were ordered to appear for nomination near the regional building, dressed in their best clothes.

Mr. Gotfried, employed to serve and follow orders, carried out the Nazi demand. When the candidates were all in place, the German officers started to laugh. They next scolded the candidates in every possible way. Before the Jews were able to realize the seriousness of their situation, they were loaded onto open trucks and taken to the "Hitzel Mountain" (outside the town), where they were brutally beaten, and forced to dig their own graves. There, all of them were shot and buried.

The aim of this "Action" was clear: not to permit even the thought that the situation had normalized, and to eliminate all possible future Jewish leadership.

At the end of August, a civil administration was already established in the Tarnopol region. A special Referent for Jewish problems was nominated. The Nazi Falfinger brought his "specialists" from Warsaw.

Falfinger ordered the Jews to make a contribution of 1.5 million rubles, which had to be delivered within eight days to the city's Ukrainian Savings Institution. The bulk of this sum went for the repair of the Ukrainian house, "Bratstwo Mieszczankie," which the Jews were accused of having destroyed. In addition to the money, the Jews were forced to work for nothing — no pay.

Among the orders which Kreishauptman (Group Captain) Hager gave was that the "Star of David" sign be instituted. No Jew had a right to leave his living quarters freely.

In order to fulfill the German directives, the Gestapo ordered the creation of the "Judenrat," the Jewish Council. Many candidates tried their best, without endangering their own lives. So Dr. G. Fisher was nominated chairman of the Judenrat. Dr. Jacob Lipe was vice-chairman. Among the members were Dr. K. Pohoriles, Dr. S. Hirshberg, A. Klinger, M. Bernshon, J. Labiner, Dr. E. Baral, Dr. L. Dretler, F. Helreich, A. Shafkopf, and L. Exelbirt.

Only through the Judenrat could the Jew turn to the authorities. From them, they received their ration cards and personal documents. All births and deaths had to be registered there. Any permit to open a store had to come from the Jewish council. The order as to where and how long to perform forced labor was also decided there. Even the tax amount was determined there. The Judenrat dominated Jewish affairs. The most responsible duties fell on the "Labor-Forces," which were sent to perform the hardest jobs in an enemy environment from which many did not come back.

The fate of the Jews was in the hands of the German Nazis and Ukrainian Nationalists. There were no laws to protect them. The treatment was inhuman. They were used for the hardest jobs, and anybody could rob them and mistreat them brutally.

In September 1941, the order was issued to create the Jewish Ghetto. In the beginning, it included the following streets: Kazimierzowski, Perl, Lvov, Podolska, Niza, Miodowa, Sheptycki, Srebrna, Tchacki, Stara, Shkolna, and Russian.

Around 12,500 people were squeezed into this small, neglected, and poorest part of the city. The living conditions for those trapped in the Ghetto were terrible. Many people, while moving from the outside into the Ghetto, were attacked by Polish and Ukrainian *chuligans*, and robbed of their possessions.

A wire fence was erected around the Ghetto, with two entrances left open. There was a shortage of water (very few water wells), no open places, and no gardens. The conditions were an ideal breeding place for all kinds of diseases.

Over the Ghetto, a warning poster with the sign "Epidemic Threat" was hanging. The entrance of non-Jews was forbidden. The situation was designed precisely for the spread of deadly diseases inside the Jewish Ghetto.

Life on the Ghetto streets started to disappear. No laughter, no song was heard. The difference between the poor and the rich gradually disappeared. All were brought down later to the level of starvation.

Under such conditions, the Jews were forced to leave the Ghetto daily to perform forced labor for the Germans. In addition, they had to hand over gifts to the Nazis: gold, silver, crystals, garments, and other material goods.

In the Ghetto, the hunger started to grow. There wasn't even enough bread. People were starving. A typhus epidemic was spreading. The dying started. Sick people had to hide from the Gestapo. No medicines were available. Jewish doctors were mobilized to work on the Aryan side. The Judenrat had the responsibility for the burial of the dead. Suddenly, a Gestapo order came to create an ambulatory for the sick, and shelter for the orphans and the old. The main reason for the Nazi directive was their desire to get a list of the unproductive people in the Ghetto. The Nazis started a strict control at the entrance gates, with the purpose of making sure that less food reached the inside. The hunger grew from day to day. The situation was desperate.

At the end of September 1941, a fire engulfed the old Synagogue. It was clear that the Germans had set it. No permission was given to put out the fire. Many people were left without a roof over their heads. All their possessions went up in smoke. The Judenrat was punished for not having done anything to put out the fire.

The Jews also had to pay for the success of the Soviet offensive during the hard cold winter. In December, an order came to deliver all furs. Twelve people were taken into custody. The furs had to be carried to the Aryan side. The Gestapo order was a strict one. A little later, during a search in Mr. Shwartz's Bakery, a few furs were found, about which the owners didn't even know. For this "crime," five residents paid with their lives.

To keep order inside the Ghetto, the Judenrat created a Jewish police force. The orders to the police came from the Gestapo. The continued change of the police commanders was considered normal. Among them were S. Kofler, Weinstein, Dr. Rotenberg, and Grienfels. Some of the Jewish commanders followed the Gestapo orders blindly.

In the initial stage of the Judenrat's existence, the leaders tried to convince the others that by following the orders of the Nazis, it would be possible to avoid the annihilation of the Jews. With the help of gifts and hard labor, it would be possible to ensure continued Jewish existence. Nobody had any doubt that the Nazis were losing the war. The front-line news reinforced this belief. The main thing was to hold out till the Nazi end came.

The new people in the Judenrat, with Dr. Pohoriles as head (after the war he changed his name to Buczynski), didn't even try to cover up their deeds with ideological reasons. They were tools of the Nazis, whose only purpose was to save their own necks.

In 1942, an order was issued to build labor camps. Jews were forced to build such camps, and also barracks for the Ukrainian police and Nazi office workers. The camps were erected in Kamionki, on the road to Podvoloczysk, in Hluboczek Wielki, (near the stone quarry) Zagrabelia.

Young people were caught in the streets and transported to the camps. The Ghetto was asked to pay for the expenses; clothes and shoes were collected. Many people were rounded up in surrounding towns and villages and brought to the slave labor camps. The working conditions were intolerable. Hard labor, hunger, and diseases decimated the labor force. New contingents had to be brought in. Some relatives were still able to send food packages and clothes. Bribery was needed to get the stuff through.

Jewish laborers were forced to pull out tombstones in the Jewish cemeteries, split them apart, and build paved streets. From the early morning till late in the evening, in the cold and hot weather, rain or snow, the modern slaves were forced to perform their jobs without showing any signs of weakness. During the daily roll calls, the camp commander checked the physical condition of his slaves. Anybody found looking sick or weak was shot on the spot. Many laborers tried not to reveal their condition, posing as physically fit. (After the war, this slave-labor commander was caught, tried in a Polish court in Bytom, and sentenced to death.)

In addition to the labor camps, Jews were forced to work in military barracks near Janowka, helping to build an airfield. The group leader was a Polish engineer from Poznan, an exceptionally good man. He did whatever he could to help the Jewish workers. He managed to save some Jewish workers, among them a new-born child (Fam. Ginzberg), one day before the liquidation of the Jews in the camp.

In March 1942, the news reached the Ghetto that the Gestapo had taken direct power over the Jews. This was an omen that harder times were coming. And indeed, the Gestapo started to make raids into the Ghetto, confiscating heating material, wooden fences, and wooden shacks for their own use.

Hundreds of Jews were forced to work on the reconstruction of Gestapo Barracks and also in the private homes of the Gestapo and other Germans. The work load was a very hard one. Obersturmführer Miller was the commander of the Gestapo, a wild beast in human form. His helpers were Leks, Maya, Reiman, Reinish, and others — all Gestapo officers. Their Ghetto visits were accompanied with beatings, kicking, hollering, and shootings. Harsh punishment was instituted for not following orders. The former owner of a large mill, Salomon Finkelstein, was shot to death by Miller himself, because some heating material was found there. Electro-technician Lama Epstein was sentenced to death by the Gestapo, because they found in his possession a quarter of a pound of cherries when he was at work in Gaje Wielkie. He was shot, together with his wife and little daughter. The butcher, A. Keller, was shot in the Janovka Forest, because the murderers thought that he was riding too slow.

Despite the tragedy of the prevailing conditions, there were people who didn't lose the human ideals with which they were raised, doing their utmost to help others. Dr. Yehuda Friedman, Professor Chaim Hirshberg, S. Rosner and others had created a folks-kitchen, where the poor and hungry received a warm meal daily. A small committee (among them Abraham Margulies, Abraham Ochs, Moses Wall, J. Helreich) collected money to support the Rabbis and the needy.

From March 25, 1942, dates the bloodiest period in the history of the Tarnopol Jewish Ghetto: "The Mobilization of Souls."

The Gestapo ordered the Judenrat to deliver 600 souls — the old, sick, crippled, and the asocial — for resettlement in "other places." It was no secret as to what kind of fate awaited them. Some members of the Judenrat tried to foil the order but to no avail. Now the eyes of all those who still had illusions were opened. All of a sudden the German Nazis started to "care" for the old, sick, and the children. The victims were brutally thrown into open trucks, and, like lambs, led to death in Janovka Forest.

The news about this brutal massacre was impossible to cover up. This tragic event caused a bitter feeling against the Judenrat members, especially against Dr. Pohoriles, G. Halperin and the scoundrel Dr. Baral, but the Jews were helpless. Their pain and hatred against the traitors was deep.

After this brutal massacre, there were no more illusions left about the fate of the Jews. Their fate was already sealed. After this "Action" others would follow. It was clear that the Judenrat was just a tool in the hands of the hangmen, and there was no help to be expected from anywhere.

The feeling of helplessness started to spread. The behavior of many Gentiles, the lack of any sympathy for the persecuted, contributed in great degree to the disappointment and loss of hope to escape the Nazi slaughter. There was not only a lack of sympathy toward the Jews — on the contrary, many showed open satisfaction, while others helped the Nazi murderers directly. Many Ukrainian and Polish nationalists denounced the Jews, delivering them directly into the hands of the Nazis. There is not a shred of doubt that the number of Jewish survivors would have been much larger, were it not for the indifferent (and collaborationist) behavior of many Gentiles. After all, the Germans were strangers in the occupied territories. They didn't know and didn't easily recognize anybody who was Jewish. Surrounded on all sides, seeing no hope on the horizon, the bitterness and disappointment deepened in the hearts of the Jews.

No radios were available. All were confiscated right in the beginning. German newspapers were smuggled into the Ghetto. The Jews learned to read between the lines. News was brought also by Jews transporting cattle to Warsaw. Over there, more was known about what was going on in the world. The news about Nazi defeats on the front lines instilled some hope. But at the same time, the Jewish people knew that unless salvation came, it would be too late. Many would die from hunger and disease, many more would be killed by the Germans. Dr. Goebbels' propaganda and the news about the extermination camps, the crematoria, and the gas chambers didn't leave any illusions. No way out could be seen.

The measure of suffering was, however, not yet full. Before the Nazi victims were forced to leave this dark world, they had to give away to the murderers the remaining strength left in their bodies.

In the spring months (1943), some working shops were organized in the Ghetto. The Judenrat delivered the raw material for production. Some fooled themselves into thinking that, thanks to this activity, their lives would be saved. The desire to live was still so strong that it suffocated all other human feelings. No price was too high to pay in order to remain alive.

Despite all efforts, the Nazis did not succeed in demoralizing and breaking the will of all the victims, before they were annihilated. True, it was not easy to show individual heroic deeds in the Tarnopol Ghetto, but the great majority managed to preserve their human dignity. What the German Fascists could read in their victims' eyes was contempt and hatred against the Aryan masters.

In August 1942 news had reached the Aryan side of the city that resettlements approved by General Katzman, the hangman of the Lvov District, would start soon. The Gentile population was warned not to help the Jews. Anyone caught helping or hiding Jews would be sentenced to death.

The Jews started to prepare themselves, using any method available, to save their lives. The digging of underground bunkers started. Hiding places were constructed — secret corridors, blind walls, attic corners. With amazing ingenuity, everything was done in order not to fall into the bloody hands of the Nazi beast.

On a nice sunny Monday, August 31, 1942, in the early morning, the Gestapo, with the help of the army and Ukrainian police, surrounded the Jewish Ghetto on all sides. On the given order, the Judenrat and their families had to appear. From all sides they started to drive out the Jews, crying: "Jews out." The Ghetto inmates were driven into a gathering place. The Jewish police, who knew where the hiding places and the bunkers were, helped to reveal and find the people hiding.

Within a few hours, thousands of Jews were driven to the marketplace. They were forced to kneel down, and if anyone attempted to get up, the watchmen started to shoot. The Gestapo commander and his helpers controlled every Jewish work permit. Those who worked for the SS and the military were permitted to return home. During this "Action," the Gestapo commander showed his naked bestiality. Not far behind were his helpers and the Jewish police.

The Germans divided the Jews into two groups: the young, who were able to work, and all others — women, children, old, and sick — who were beaten and driven further away. The victims were loaded onto open trucks, and delivered to the railroad station. One hundred people were squeezed into a wagon designed to hold forty. In some other wagons there were already people from Zbaraz, Strusow, and Mikulince, where the "Action" had taken place two days before. They were sitting there squeezed together, having had no food or water for two days.

The transport train went through Zloczow and Lvov to Belzec — the death factory. Despite the presence of numerous watchmen, many succeeded in cutting holes in the wagon walls, and jumped out of the running train. Some jumpers fell under the wheels and were killed, but others succeeded and ran away. Most of them were later attacked by the Ukrainian Nationalists, robbed, and handed over to the German hangmen. Those who weren't caught smuggled themselves back to the Ghetto.

The fate of those transported to Belzec is known. They were suffocated in the gas chambers and later burned in the ovens.

Around 1,300 people lost their lives in the "Action" of August

31, 1942. Those who crawled out of their hiding places and bunkers started to look for their relatives, who, mostly, were no more. The murderous bloody hand had reached them.

The terrible life continued to go on. The people continued their miserable existence, having no other choice but to wait to the bitter end, from which there was no escape.

In the beginning of September 1942, the order came to shrink the Ghetto. The people who lived in the Marketplace, Pola, Berk-Yoselevich, Lvov, Russian, Zacerkewna, Doli, Sheptycki, and Bolnie Streets had to leave their homes within three hours. They were unable to take any of their possessions. The situation worsened inside the Ghetto. The noose was tightening. The people had the feeling of hunted animals, where the space kept continuously shrinking.

Very seldom was there a day without a visit of uninvited "guests." When the people found out that Storm Trooper Miller was walking around in the Ghetto, the streets looked deserted. The Judenrat wrapped itself in silence. It was not easy to find out where the next blow would be coming from. In order not to be surprised, watchmen were posted at night. People slept in their clothes. From the experience gained, hiding shelters were improved. Even children knew they had to keep quiet, so that their voices would not be heard by the murderers.

In the second half of September 1942, the Judenrat ordered that a list be compiled of people over 60 years of age. Many of the house managers started to remake the lists, knowing that they could be severely punished if caught. In my memory, a few names of those heroic Jews are left: Moses Wohl, Baruch Hershhorn, G. Kozover, and M. Kielman. They weren't the only ones. To terrorize the Jews and the Judenrat, Miller ordered the construction of a gallows on Bogata Street, near the Jewish police, making it clear that all those refusing to obey orders would be hanged. This threat achieved its aim.

On September 30, 1942, Miller's deputy, Leks, accompanied by a large group of *Shütz-Polizei,* ordered the delivery of 1,000 people. The Judenrat, as it appeared, already knew about it, because they called the police, giving them the prepared list with the names. Pohoriles, the Judenrat head, called together a few hundred Jews in the Trif's former mill. This figure wasn't enough for the Gestapo, who rounded up 750 souls, sending them to Belzec.

Just a few days passed, and the Gestapo appeared again in the Ghetto, this time in civilian dress, pulling out the surprised Jews from their houses. With such surprise raids, they succeeded, until the middle of November 1942, in kidnapping 2,400 victims. The methods of surprise used repeatedly this time were more grisly than those used before.

The criminal opportunism used by the Judenrat people was of very little help to them. In Miller's eyes, they weren't reliable enough; they were too mild. To the Jews in the Ghetto, it was clear that the last stage in their lives had arrived.

A hard, frosty cold winter started. In shabby, dirty clothes, the Jews continued, day after day, to go to work, shivering from the cold. The irony of their fate was that they were forced to unload trains of coal, at a time when they couldn't get any heating material for their own homes. Returning from work, they had to sit freezing in the dark, because the city didn't deliver electricity to the Ghetto.

In the beginning of the winter of 1942–43, Sturmführer Rokita arrived in Tarnopol. He was the commander of the Janow slave labor camp in Lvov. His bestial deeds had been known for a long time in Tarnopol. Accordingly, his arrival caused a panic in the Ghetto.

Rokita appeared in the Judenrat, ordering everything to be prepared that was necessary to organize a labor camp in the Ghetto. This meant to mobilize human and financial resources. All houses near the bathhouse and the Podolska and Niza Streets were emptied and handed over to the camp. The Jews working on the Aryan side were concentrated in the buildings around the bathhouse. A kitchen, a bakery, and a medical ambulatory were created. The death threat was imposed for any attempt to leave the camp. Rokita managed to assemble nearly three thousand people, whom he took from the Tarnopol Ghetto and nearby towns. Over the entrance gate a cynical sign read as follows: *"Arbeit Macht Frei"* ("Work makes you free"). A harsh discipline prevailed. Many times the morning roll calls lasted for hours in cold, freezing weather. All the money was taken away. The good clothes were exchanged for rags and shoes with wooden soles. The death penalty was imposed for any law violations. Those who still had some money and jewelry managed to escape Rokita's hands with bribery. The Jews were working hard, without any grand illusions that they would be able to save their lives.

From the beginning of February, 1943, the Gestapo started to systematically annihilate the remaining Jews in the Ghetto. The Judenrat and the police handed over all those who were not working to the Gestapo.

But the last chapter of the Tarnopol Jewish community was nearing its sad end. Those who still had some valuable items hidden, and who were "blessed" with a non-Jewish look, traded them for Aryan papers and falsified documents. But only a small minority of the newly baked "Aryans" managed to save themselves. Whoever aroused suspicions because of his dialect or insufficient knowledge of the Christian tradition was handed over to the Gestapo.

The silence of World Jewry destroyed the last remaining hope and completely paralyzed their belief. The victims were standing on the brink of destruction, and the world did not react — nobody rushed to help the Jews.

On April 9, 1943, the Gestapo surrounded the Ghetto, pulling out 1,000 men, who were later transferred to a camp. The younger ones were selected and handed over to Rokita. The remaining were driven through the Bridge of Blonie, toward the Petrikowe Brick Factory, and brutally shot.

However, what happened during the massacre was unexpected. The respected Professor Hirshberg got up and in sharp words condemned Nazi barbarism, predicting their bitter end. The Germans stood perplexed and silent.

The *Mezbozer* (Rabbi), behaved with great courage and dignity, refusing to remain in the camp, while his family and co-religionists were led to their death. Lev Pohl refused the Gestapo order to form four people in a marching line, protesting against this degrading task. The policeman, Katz, seeing his family being led to their death, tore up his decorations and joined the marching group.

From the 9th to the 20th of July 1943, there was almost no pause in hunting for victims. Not one family wanted to wait for death at German hands; many committed suicide. Poison caps went up in price sharply. The noose around the Jewish necks was tightening. All hope of being saved disappeared. The Nazi attempt to find the hiding places in bunkers continued at a feverish pace. Due to the great pain, some Jewish scoundrels, in moments of weakness, revealed the hidden entrances of underground bunkers. The Judenrat and the police lost complete control over the situation, the result of which was a hastening of their end. Next the Jews grabbed the only existing "life-saving" belt — Rokita's labor camp, from which they had wanted to escape a few months before. They tried to get back inside.

The "lucky" inmates in Rokita's camp looked with fear at those the Gestapo brought in from the outside. All of them were searching for relatives among the newcomers. Some chose not to separate again and shared their fate together.

A strong sensation occurred when Engineer Winter, who worked in Rokita's bakery, saw his wife and child being led to death. He joined them. Rokita, who respected Winter's technical know-how and organizational abilities, wanted to leave him in the Ghetto, but Winter refused to accept Rokita's offer and, together with his family, went to the execution place.

Not only humans were destroyed. On the orders of the Gestapo, all Jewish documents, especially birth certificates, were brought to Tarnopol and burned. The Nazis not only wanted to destroy the Jews, but also all their traces.

At the end of June, 1943, the news about the destruction at the labor camp reached Tarnopol. The remaining Jews in the Ghetto started to hide in the bunkers once more, some of which were constructed like real fortresses.

During the night of July 21, 1943, the Gestapo surrounded the Ghetto and took out around 2,500 Jews. The remaining victims were eliminated two weeks later. Thereafter, the Germans liquidated the bunkers and hiding places they had not found before.

In some of the discovered bunkers, the Germans met with resistance. On Baron Hirsch Street, the Nazis were attacked with weapons and hand-grenades.

There are no details at hand about such heroic deeds because no one survived. The resistance lasted a few days, according to our information, and some Gestapo men were injured. The bakery worker, Zelinger, took part in this uneven struggle.

Only a few individuals managed to escape, thanks to their Christian friends who risked their lives. Some did it for money. Others were guided by human conscience. It is in this way that the writer of this memoir saved his life and the lives of his family.

A few Jewish doctors working in the hospitals joined the Ukrainian partisan groups. Among the partisans were the Bandera Bands. They were open anti-Semites, but there was a need for Jewish doctors. However, when they thought that they could make it without Jewish doctors, they liquidated them brutally, without any hesitation. Many individuals and families who succeeded in hiding in the forests were murdered by Nationalist Ukrainian and Polish partisans.

From a figure of 18,000 Jews residing in Tarnopol at the beginning of the Nazi occupation, only 139 remained alive. This figure was registered by the Tarnopol Jewish Committee in the months of May–July 1944 (after the liberation of the city by the Soviet Army). Around two hundred Jews, deported to the Soviet Union, or mobilized in the Soviet Army, also survived.

After the end of the war, a few Gestapo men who had served in Tarnopol fell into the hands of the Polish authorities. Among them were the former commander of the Zaglembia Camp, Korof; the referent of the "Action" in the Lvov region, Engels; and the referent for Jewish affairs in the Tarnopol region, Rieman.

During the December 1948 trial against Rieman, some Jewish survivors from Tarnopol testified; among them was Dr. Pohoriles. Rieman threw back his terrible accusations: "You yourself collaborated with the Gestapo." All arrested Gestapo men were sentenced to death — a small satisfaction for the survivors.

The Tarnopol Jewish community was destroyed in the most inhuman, brutal way. A community that had produced people of science and wisdom, devoted social servants, successful businessmen, and skilled professionals ceased to exist. The fruits produced by generations were transformed into a mountain of ruins.

3

Trembowla as I Remember Her

Meir Selzer

Trembowla is located in the Podolian Heights, the western part of which belonged to Poland before World War II. These heights rise 400 meters above sea level. The town, which is situated on the Tarnopol-Chortkow Railroad, has a special natural beauty, and her surroundings are called the Switzerland of Podolia. The distance from Tarnopol is 30 kilometers in the northwest direction. To the south is the town of Kopyczynce, also about 30 kilometers away. Trembowla is located in the valley of the Gniezna River, at the foot of the Castle ruins.

Trembowla is divided into two parts: the old city at the foot of the castle (*shloss* in Yiddish) to the west of the river, and the new city, east of it.

The castle with the ruins of the fortress is the glory of Trembowla. A walk to the top of the hill and through the shady, fragrant pine groves, the clean air, the wonderful landscape which spreads out afar, was an important element of the *Oneg Shabbat* of the Trembowla Jews. Young and old, women and children walked around sedately, breathing the refreshing air and enjoying the peaceful atmosphere and the beauty. The castle used to inspire a special mood upon the walkers—a spiritual uplift, a feeling of purity. There was no shouting on castle heights, no noise. Its atmosphere was soothing, calming.

After the two pine groves there was a forest of shade trees which spread until Strusow in the northwest.

West of the castle there was a creek—Dmuchalec—and in the 1930's a beautiful, modern swimming pool was built there.

At the foot of the castle southward, there was a spring that was called Tarnowski Well. Jews used to come there on Shabbat from far away to enjoy its cool water.

Southward, opposite the castle, was Pokrowka Hill with the electric station.

The Gniezna Stream flows calmly through the middle of the town. On her banks are three flour mills and three bridges — two for pedestrians and carriages, and one over which the train passes. Because of the many wars that had occurred in the area, the bridges often had been destroyed and then rebuilt.

The main street is along the Tarnopol–Chortkow Road, which until the war was called Chrzanowska Street in memory and in honor of the local heroine in the 17th Century, Sophia Chrzanowska. There is a statue of her on Castle Hill. The street is also called Corso, and single people, couples and groups would walk back and forth in order to see and be seen. The main part of the street spreads from the city center towards Plebanowka. The Greek Catholic Church, the Dom Narodny, the "Sokol," the Polish Sport and Culture Center, the New Catholic Church, Fischer's Hotel, and other nice buildings are located there. The railroad station is in the alley next to the hotel.

In the center of the city stand the Magistrat (City Hall), the Catholic Monastery, the Greek Catholic Church; otherwise there are only Jewish houses: Mordechai Ploin's house where he lived and also had his hardware store, Taube Ginsberg's textile store, Rifka Rudolf's store. Opposite there was the Jewish Community Building with Silberg's Pharmacy, the Melner family's textile store, and Hirsh Weissberg's hardware store downstairs. The Kultus Klaus (*Shul*) and the office of the Jewish community were upstairs. Yitzchak Hirsh Wilner's house was the next building. The wholesale grocery was downstairs and the living quarters upstairs. Rosia Sommerfeld lived in the next building, which was one of the biggest buildings in Trembowla. Dr. Chaim Kolin lived and had his office in this building. This was at the corner of an alley which was also inhabited only by Jews.

The butcher Klaus was in this alley. Next lived Leib Kerbholz the tinsmith. Then there was the abode of Usher the rope maker. All these houses were situated along the wall of the monastery. The old part of the city was across the bridge on the other side of the river. To the right was a section inhabited only by Jews. Most of the Shuls were there. There also stood the big Shul which was burned down in the beginning of the second decade of the century (in the year 1910 or 1911).

Close to the river was the public bathhouse, which was generally used on Friday in honor of Shabbat, mainly by Jews.

In the old part of the city is Sobieski Street (as it was called before the war). Here stood the house of Rav Eliezer Leiter, the Rabbi of the town. Sobieski Street continues southward and leads to the Monastir. These are ruins of an old fortress that is located in the midst of a big forest. At the foot of the height on which the ruins are located, towards the south, the Gnieza River flows into the River Seret, which is a tributary of the Dniester River.

Trembowla is surrounded by suburbs and villages. To the east are the Sady with its fruit orchards. They are called this because of the many gardens of choice fruits — sweet and sour cherries and apples — the first to ripen are called Papirowka because their peelings are thin as paper.

Northeast, past the Jewish cemetery (which does not exist anymore) is the way to Tarnopol. There, after the railway bridge on the right side of the road, was the Trembowla soccer field. In the 1920's the local soccer team, Fortuna, used to play games against guest teams from other cities. There were only one or two goyim who participated in the games; all the rest were Jews. Its president was Salek Steinig-Ashkenazi, and among the players were Dudek Sass, the foremost soccer player of Trembowla, who also excelled in other sports. Some of the others were Yulek Einleger, Filek Schecter, Isaac Koppel, Bumba Einleger, Alexander Kotlarski (the goalkeeper). This was the first team. There were five teams. The third was the team of the young boys in which Yaakov Speicher, the mute one, played in the center.

In the thirties the soccer field was transferred to the Planty. In those days Moinio Pfefferblith, of blessed memory, was the outstanding soccer player.

The road to Tarnopol led through the suburb Krowinka, in the forest of which the most delicious wild strawberries grew. In the opposite direction — east — was the road to the suburb of Plebanowka in which some Jewish families lived. Among the other villages were Loshniov, Boryczowka, Dolhe, Ostrowczyk, Zascianocze, Semenow, Podhajczyki, Yagielnica, Darachow, and more. The towns of Strusow, Yanow, and Budzanow were part of the district of Trembowla.

The railway was a very important institution in Trembowla. It was the link that connected our town with the outside world. The coming and going of the trains marked the exact time, instead of a clock. Three passenger trains went daily in both directions, and connected the inhabitants of Trembowla with the outside world. Besides these, there were the cargo trains. The railroad was a few meters from our house. A few minutes before the train passed by, the roadblock went down and carriages used to stop before our house.

In times of war the train communication was very lively. Soldiers and war materiel were carried in them, and we could conclude from the direction of the traffic what the situation was at the front. After the destruction of the railway bridge, because of the approaching fighting, there used was a lull in the railroad traffic, and grass grew between the rails.

In the late 1930's the "Torpedo" was introduced. It consisted of two express cars on the Lwow–Kopyczynce line which shortened the trip considerably.

Another very important institution was the high school (Gymnasium). It was founded as a state school in the first decade of the century and served as a cultural factor of first importance. The Gymnasium provided general knowledge and served as an introduction to higher education. It was also a factor of assimilation to the Polish culture in spite of the Zionist spirit which prevailed in Jewish life, and it competed with traditional education. The Polish language predominated in the process of Polonization.

Trembowla is a very old city. It is a district town and, since early times, a free city, which means that she did not belong to a private person, a count or a duke, but was the living place of free citizens. She, like Przemysl, was the seat of the Ruthenian Prince. In a certain era the ruler was a Prince Danilo.

The castle served for defense against the attacks of the Turks and the Tartars, who probably conquered, more than once, the whole area. Especially famous was the war against the Turks in the 17th century in the time of Sobieski.

At that time the commander of the area was Count Chrzanowski. In his days the Turks started a very fierce attack on the castle, and the commander intended to surrender. When the commander was sitting in counsel with his comrades on the eve of the surrender, the countess appeared suddenly in the hall with a drawn dagger in her hand. She directed the dagger towards her heart and said that she would stab herself if the commander carried out his intention. Her brave appearance inspired those present with courage, and they decided not to surrender but to go on fighting. Soon after, King Sobieski came to their assistance and they were rescued from subjugation and shame. In commemoration of the event a statue of the countess was erected in the middle of the Square, showing her with a dagger in her hand in a very pathetic pose.

After the third division of Poland among the three powers — Prussia, Russia, and Austria — in the year 1795, Trembowla and the whole area came under the rule of the Austro-Hungarian Emperor, and the land was called Galicia. From then on Trembowla was in Eastern Galicia, the capital of which was Lwow (Lemberg). At the head of the City Hall, or Magistrat, was the Mayor or Burgomaster. There were some Jewish City Councilmen. My great grandfather, Naphtali Selzer, of blessed memory, was a member of City Hall in the middle of the 19th century, and therefore was called Naphtali Radnik.

The Jewish community had some measure of self-rule. The Head was President (called in German *Kultus Präsident*). After the first World War the Presidents were Yitzchak Hirsch Wilner, Professor Goldblatt, Isaac Podhorzer, and Professor Franzos (who was our last President).

From 1914, the time of the outbreak of the First World War, and until the end of the Second World War, Trembowla was an arena for fighting.

In August 1914, after war broke out and after the Austrian break-through to Russia, Jews from Kamenec Podolski and other Russian cities were brought to Trembowla as prisoners of war. I remember how shocked the Trembowla Jews were at the sight of our brethren brought as prisoners. These were received warmly and were provided with food and assistance.

The successful march of the Austrian army into Russia did not last long. Soon the fate of the war was reversed and the Austrians were forced to retreat. The Jewish inhabitants of Trembowla, fright-ened by the prospect of a Russian invasion, left the city, taking with them bigger or smaller bundles. I don't know if any of the Polish or Ukrainian inhabitants fled before the Russians. Some of the Jewish refugees reached Vienna in their flight and remained there until after the war.

The period of the Russian occupation began, and it lasted for three years. On entering the city, the Russians burned many houses in the center of the town, which was very puzzling. They did the same thing three years later while retreating; this was more understandable.

In 1915 the Austrians staged an attack against the Russians, in the course of which they arrived near Buczacz, but the offensive failed and the Russians remained another two years.

In the year 1916 we heard about the death of Emperor Franz Joseph which saddened us very much, because the Emperor was a moderate ruler and was beloved by the Jews.

In the summer of 1917 a new offensive came, this time by the Austrians with the assistance of the Germans. We were looking with great hope towards the arrival of "our" Germans. There were sporadic air raids which frightened us very much. The Russians retreated, this time for good, and the retreat dragged on for many days. All the convoys passed near our house.

One day we saw a strange commotion in the high school, which was near our house and served as a hospital. The hospital was vacated, patients and personnel evacuated, and the furniture was piled up in the middle of the yard. Towards evening the building was set afire. The fire was very big and we were afraid that it would spread to our house. All night we stood in the gate, ready for any eventuality. The next evening the railway bridge was blown up and the morning after that the Germans arrived. The Germans proceeded into Russia, and in their wake came the Austrians.

Valerian Heck, the high school principal from before the war, returned, and the high school was re-opened (in the two small buildings which were untouched by the fire). There, entrance exams were given and I was accepted as a high school pupil.

At the end of the school year, in the summer of 1918, the Austro-Hungarian empire collapsed and World War I came to an end in the West (though not in the East). Through a special arrangement, Eastern Galicia was ceded by the Austrians to the Ukrainians, who established a Ukrainian State with their own army and their own currency. School activities were discontinued; private courses, for pay, administered by Franczuk and Mazur, were established, in which the instruction continued for one half a year only, and then stopped.

The war between the Poles and the Ukrainians went on ferociously during this period, and in the summer of 1919 the Poles entered Trembowla. Again the high school was opened, this time under the principalship of Kurcz.

In the year 1920 Pilsudski led the Polish Army, "The Legions," all the way to Kiev. The Bolsheviks arranged a counter-attack and as a result of it they entered Trembowla.

The ruling system of the Communists was very strange. There were requisitions and confiscations of property, until the Polish Army, in cooperation with Petlura, repulsed the Bolsheviks, and a peace treaty was signed.

The border on the Zbrucz River became again the national border between Poland and Russia, as it was previously between Austria-Hungary and Russia.

From the year 1920 until 1939 the Poles ruled in Trembowla. There was no war, but there was suppression of the Jews and Ukrainians, and a general economic war.

In Trembowla, which had 10,000 inhabitants, there lived about 1,500 Jews. Trembowla was in Galicia, and naturally her Jews were the Galician type. They were admirers of the German culture, and enlightened and semi-enlightened people, whose language was mixed wtih German expressions taken from the language of Goethe, Schiller, Heine, and Lessing. However, in the years of the Polish independence, the Polish language of Mickiewicz and Slowacki, as well as Polish manners, became more common in Jewish life, and parents began to use the language in their contact with their children.

In the years after the death of Pilsudski in 1935, anti-Semitism gained momentum, especially under the influence of Hitler. There were anti-Jewish Pogroms (in Przytyk and other places). The Poles thought they would gain from Hitler's provocation against Czechoslovakia, and staged a drive about Cieszyn and Sylesia across the Olza River. In their foolishness and impertinence they strengthened Hitler and weakened Czechoslovakia, which could have become their strong ally against the common enemy.

In August 1939, after the Ribbentrop–Molotov agreement was concluded, the eyes of the Poles were opened, but by then it was too late. The Germans already had their base in Slovakia and from there the first bombers came and bombed Trembowla on the fifth of September; Chaim Drimmer, of blessed memory, was killed on that day.

On September 1, 1939, the Germans started their march to conquer and destroy Poland. The Russians entered the eastern part of Poland on September 17, and, without any effort and almost no casualites, annexed half of Poland. From then on Trembowla became a part of Western Ukraine.

4

Outbreak of the German-Russian War

Israel Goldfliess

I<small>T IS A LAMENTED FACT THAT</small> Eastern Poland's Jews failed to join the general evacuation of Soviet citizens upon the outbreak of the German-Russian War. I can recall that upon the German invasion of our town a total of one hundred and fifty people voluntarily retreated with the Soviets. This figure does not include people who came to live in our town during the Soviet administration, which had by then lasted for two years. I did not even know many of them at all. The list of evacuees is, indeed, quite short, but it represents more than 10% of the total pre-war Jewish population of the town. If the same percentage of Jews would have fled other cities in the Soviet Zone, another half a million Jews would have remained alive and been with us here today.

I must emphasize that we are dealing with those local residents who voluntarily fled, but not with draftees or refugees from the German Zone. People who refused to receive Soviet passports and declared that they wished to return to their former homes were picked up by the Soviets, and suddenly transported to Siberia in 1940. Not all of those exiled were able to endure the difficult conditions and the harsh life they faced in their wanderings across Soviet Russia. Many died there. I have stressed this fact in order to account for the refusal of Jews to join the Soviets as the Nazi army advanced. This refusal resulted in the destruction of a large part of Polish and Ukrainian Jewry.

The Soviets Enter Our Town

With the entry of the Soviet army into our town on September 17, 1939, relative calm ensued. We briefly thought that, safe from the German occupation, we were free people. The Ribbentrop–Molotov agreement had saved us; the war, at least for the time being, was far from us. We were made aware of this several days after the war broke out. On Tuesday, Trembowla's market day, German planes attacked the town. They came in low and, firing machine guns, sowed death among the population. Several people were killed in the bombing. Panic set in. Whoever had relatives in a village left town after this bombing. We, too, fled to our Aunt Sheyna, who lived in Malow, a village close to our town. We spent several days there.

The night before the Soviets entered we heard incessant shooting. We didn't know what was happening. No one approached our aunt's home despite the fact that the Ukrainian peasants knew that our whole family and our Uncle Leib's family, and our aunt Chana were all there. It was remarkable. We didn't sleep all night for we were recognizant of the open anti-Semitism about us. The Gentiles had business dealings with my father, who was a supplier and road builder. Their conversations were quite frank.

The village of Malow had a Ukrainian majority with a Polish minority of about fifteen to twenty families, and this was to our good fortune. The Ukrainians were settling accounts with the Poles in their village. Their underground informed them that the Polish regime had collapsed, and this night was their opportunity to wipe out Polish citizens, particularly adult males. They went from house to house searching for Poles, and they killed the men whom they found. Some were shot and died immediately, and many others were mortally wounded. Clearly, the Soviet authorities who arrived the next day knew nothing about all this. So the killers moved about freely even though everyone knew who they were. But with the Soviets, as we shall see later, everything proceeds slowly.

Only a year later did the wounded, some of whom were amputees, come to claim compensation and rehabilitation. The truth finally came to light, and the authorities learned of the events that had occurred in the interim between Polish and Soviet rule. Poles came forth to provide detailed accounts. Suddenly one night, all the suspects were arrested, and a trial was staged. The Soviets were good at this. The trial lasted several days, and I attended one session. It was held in the hall of the Polish sports association, "Sokol," rather than in the courthouse. All the accused received severe punishments — imprisonment and exile. This incident will help explain the fact that Ukrainian Nationalists later collaborated with the Germans, who promised them an independent Ukraine.

The destruction of the Jews was the responsibility of the

Germans. If the Ukrainian Nationalists acted on their own, they were called to account on more than one occasion during the beginning of German rule. At any rate, if the Ukrainian Nationalists had that night suspected that the Germans would enter our district, they would surely have slaughtered us as well. So we miraculously survived that bloody affair. It was therefore understandable that the Jews welcomed the arrival of the Soviets enthusiastically, although in the course of time many were to be disappointed.

Changes Wrought by the Soviet Regime

When the Soviet army arrived initially, young leftist Jews came out of hiding; those who had left Hashomer Hatzair and those who belonged to the Communist underground movement which had been banned in Poland. Some of them had been sentenced to imprisonment with hard labor in Bereza Kartuzka, a Polish concentration camp. Now they sprang into action. They enlisted in the Red Militia and wanted to help the new regime set up an administration in the towns and cities. Chaos reigned everywhere as attempts were made to organize the government. And the soldiers and civilians who followed in the wake of the new regime were eager to obtain commodities available in the relative prosperity of independent Poland. Their behavior pointed to the sorry state of the economy and to the shortage of consumer goods in the Soviet Union.

In stores selling clothes, shoes, fabrics, watches, and jewelry, everything in sight was snatched up without bargaining over prices. This buying panic gave rise to numerous stories and jokes.

Store owners, who had stood idle in front of their stores in the summer of 1939 and feared bankruptcy, were suddenly flooded with buyers. (In Poland the peak of the business year occurred after the harvest.) Now all the suppliers from western Poland were on the other side of the new border or had fled eastward, abandoning their factories in the process, and it was impossible to obtain new goods. The merchants were indeed flooded with shiny new hundred-ruble notes (this was the highest valued note issued by the Soviets). The authorities declared the value of the ruble equivalent to that of the Polish zloty, but the storeowners had no way to assess the purchasing power of these rubles, which they got from their energetic customers. Before the store owners managed to hide their goods, the hungry buyers pounced on whatever they found. The stores were empty again, and the store owners again were idle.

Rumors circulated that the old border with Soviet Russia had been closed. Jews who were able to smuggle themselves out brought back reports of dispossessed merchants, many of whom were in exile, far from home. These rumors and the actions ensuing from the Soviet takeover did not implant sympathy for the regime among Jews. The lack of sympathy intensified after several businessmen were put in jail. It is worth mentioning that Chaim, the son of Avranchi Briller, was imprisoned. Only with great effort and much bribery was his release obtained. I also remember the case of Moshe Landau, my friend and the son of Lajkis the teacher, who brought several pairs of socks and other items of haberdashery from Tarnopol. Apparently someone informed on him, and he, too, was jailed. His entire family, his father and sisters, for whom he was the sole provider, almost starved to death. He disappeared without leaving a trace. Every time I think of him I suffer pangs of remorse. Who knows how the poor fellow perished at the hands of the Soviets?

Understandably, these incidents did not enhance the Soviets' prestige. There were many jokes about the exaggerations of Soviet propaganda and the enormous gap between propaganda and reality in Russia. Afterwards, Russian Jewish soldiers added their own observations — at first no civilians were allowed to cross the former Polish border into the new territories. In a word, this is what they had to say: "Alas! We who looked to the West for salvation, must now be the saviors of Jews and Judaism in the West. Everything is topsy-turvy!" It seems to me that this quip reflected precisely the achievements of Jewry between the Russian Revolution and the outbreak of the Second World War, namely: minimal achievements in all facets of life.

Meanwhile, despite the setbacks suffered by the Soviets in the war with Finland that broke out several months after the occupation (which displayed Soviet incompetence on the battlefield as well), they slowly began to install their order in the Western Ukraine: the system, in my opinion, had not been functioning well there, or for that matter in their pre-war territories. This was particularly true with respect to the collectivization of farming.

The imposition of their system was aimed primarily at the residents of towns and cities who had, for the most part, been middle-class merchants and independent artisans. Since private shops were closed in our town too, government stores had to be opened, but they contained no goods. The shelves were empty. Whenever an item did arrive, it was snatched up before lines began to form. Of course, the lion's share of the arriving goods was divided up between the senior staff and the suppliers. Some of the goods ended up on the black market.

So we, by force of circumstances, returned to the barter economy that had flourished in the Middle Ages. The farmers didn't want rubles for their goods; the Russian currency had little purchasing power. Government officials whose salary consisted solely of rubles were forced to wait in line or to turn to the black market for essential commodities. Artisans began to organize along cooperative lines, while farmers with small holdings, who mostly lived in villages, retained, for the time being, their previous status.

The authorities did not manage to bring about quick changes in the status of farmers until the outbreak of the German–Russian War. Only limited quantities of their crop had to be supplied to the government at the official rate. The rest was available to them for their own needs and for barter trade. Large landholders, retail merchants, and people with capital were divested of their property immediately and without compensation. Many of them managed to sell most of their goods and moved to places where they could live under assumed names.

After the outbreak of war, numerous refugees arrived from the German side. They were for the most part Jews evicted by the Germans from the new border area between the German and Russian lines. Those who did not manage to adjust on their own, and simply stayed wherever they were, received passports with special restrictions, detailed in Paragraph 11, when the Soviets granted citizenship to all residents of the conquered territories. Holders of passports with this restrictive paragraph were unable to reside in regional capitals, and faced other limitations on their movements. These people were ineligible for government work, which they had been seeking because it provided them with a means of concealing their former identity.

Another important characteristic of the period was the nature of daily discussions. Under the pre-war Polish regime conversations ranged over a variety of current issues: employment, the situation of Eretz Yisrael (Palestine) and in Poland, anti-Semitism, and a host of other material and spiritual interests. But under the hermetically sealed Soviet regime everything was centered around the problems of acquiring food, clothing, heating, and other necessities. One's life style and even one's manner of thinking changed radically. The Soviets were intent on implementing the slogan they brought with them: *"Kto nye rabotayet, tot nye kushayet"* ("Whoever doesn't work, doesn't eat"). This, along with all the other changes I mentioned, turned out to be the case.

The plight of those who could not work grew worse, economically and socially. Many managed to survive by selling fabrics, skins, furs and other things which had been put away during the supposedly good times of the decrepit Polish regime. These items were largely worthless, but during the Soviet period their value rose considerably. A trivial item might be worth more than the average monthly wage of an office worker. What is more, work became a test of one's loyalty to the regime. No matter that the average salary of most workers barely sufficed to meet their food and clothing costs, while for several meters of cloth one might receive more than twice the average monthly salary of an office worker. A person not working before retirement age aroused the suspicion of the secret police, the N.K.V.D., as it was then known. He was considered a parasite, and an enemy of the people (*vrag naroda*).

Once I witnessed an interesting incident. Gentile workers received their salary and went to a bar near their place of work. In the course of several hours they managed to spend their entire salary. After such heavy drinking came the inevitable fist fight. The bar manager intervened and called the police to calm things down. The police came, but they did not dig deeply into the background of the participants in the brawl. They merely tried to restore order. They didn't even ask for the names of those involved. That surprised me. I reached the conclusion that almost everyone in Russia was under surveillance. This, clearly, was not the only such case.

People were afraid to loiter without working. Members of the pre-war communist organization came out of hiding in the initial stage of Soviet rule and vied for important positions. But later, fearing for their lives, they kept a low profile. Many of them were suspected of being Trotskyites. The latter were taken away from their homes in the middle of the night without leaving a trace. Their friends and relatives were afraid to make inquiries about them lest they, too, become victims of police arrest. Such was the fate of Samuel Pohorilis, an acquaintance of mine from the town of Yanow, near Trembowla. His brothers, whom I met after the liberation in 1944, knew nothing of his whereabouts, despite their having spent the entire war in Russia. They were always in constant fear of meeting their brother's fate.

For the two-year duration of the Soviet Rule, everyone looked for work. Professionals had less to fear from the changes wrought by the Soviets, and they, in fact, did suffer less. The truth of the matter is: everyone could manage to find work, even those with Paragraph

11 in their passports, or people who changed their identities, or the ones who moved from place to place and succeeded in infiltrating the ranks of those refugees from the German side of the line who had received passports without special paragraphs. Members of the pre-war Polish health insurance plan encountered no difficulties. They were not interrogated, and no inquiries were made abut their previous employment. I, too, was one of the recipients of a good passport because I had a membership card in the health plan, which I had joined while working in a school in Czortkow. The Hebrew and Zionist orientation of the school did me no harm when I had to obtain my passport. During Soviet rule, I, as a Sabbath observer, didn't work at all. Different was the fate of the refugees from the German occupation zone who were unwilling to acquire Soviet citizenship and passports. As I have previously mentioned, they were exiled one Friday night in 1940 into the depths of Russia.

The number of Jews exiled in this way has been estimated at three hundred thousand. These are the Polish refugees who came to Israel or immigrated to other Jewish centers after the end of World War II. The end result of their evacuation proved beneficial to them! They were saved from destruction in the Holocaust. Although many of them didn't survive the hardships of Russian exile, most did manage to return after the war and to reach havens of rest. The Polish Jewish immigration to Israel after the war consisted mainly of these people because only a fortunate few escaped from the jaws of the Nazi Holocaust.

And finally I must deal with one critical truth: "The future, who can foretell it?" No one was able to guess how the war would unfold. After the entry of the Soviets, a person I knew well said, as they were evicting him from his store and his livelihood, that he would prefer to live under a German occupation. He got his wish, and his only son was among the first victims killed, in an attack on an army barracks during the 1941 invasion. Within months, my friend and his wife were murdered by Ukrainian Nationalists.

5

CONGRATULATIONS
TO THE FÜHRER

THE FOLLOWING LETTER WAS written by the Metropolitan
(Archbishop) of the Greek Catholic Church of the Ukraine, Andrey
Sheptytsky, to Adolf Hitler. The occasion was the fall of the city of
Kiev to German troops in August 1941:

> His Excellency the Führer
> of the Great German Empire,
> Adolf Hitler,
> Reichschancellory, Berlin
>
> Your Excellency,
>
> As head of the Ukrainian Greek Catholic Church, I send
> your Excellency my warmest congratulations as regards the
> occupation of the capital of the Ukraine, the golden domed
> city of Dnieper — Kiev. In your person, we see the invinci-
> ble leader of the incomparable and glorious German Army.
> The aim of destroying and rooting out Bolshevism which
> you, as Führer of the Great German Reich, have made the
> target of this campaign, wins your Excellency the gratitude
> of all the Christian world. The Ukrainian Greek Catholic
> Church knows the historic meaning of the tremendous
> progress of the German nations under your guidance. I will
> pray to God to put his blessing upon the victory which shall
> be the guarantee of enduring peace for Your Excellency,
> the German Army and the German nation.
>
> > Very respectfully yours,
> > Count Andrey Sheptytsky,
> > Metropolitan*

*The Archives of the History of the Party at the Central Committee of the
Communist Party of Ukraine, fund 57, inventory 4, file 338, pp.131 – 132.

In an open address to Hitler, Yaroslav Stetsko, Head of the Nationalist Government of the Ukraine, said:

July 4, 1941

To the Führer and the Chancellor, Berlin
7/4/41, Lvov, Ukrainian Government, No.2/41.

Your Excellence:

It is with an overwhelming feeling of gratitude and admiration for your heroic army which has covered itself with new glory in battles with Europe's worst enemy — Moscow Bolsheviks — that we are hereby sending Your Excellence, on behalf of the Ukrainian people and its government which has been created in liberated Lvov, our heartfelt wishes for complete victory in your struggle.

The triumph of German arms, will enable you to extend your planned construction of new Europe also to her Eastern Part. You have thus also given an opportunity to the Ukrainian people as one of the full and free members of the family of European nations to take an active part in the implementation of this great plan in its sovereign Ukrainian state.

> On behalf of the Ukrainian government,
> Yaroslav Stetzko,
> Head
> (Seal of Ukrainian State)*

---

*Captured Nazi War Document no. 145. Translated into English. Courtesy Soviet State Archive, Ukraine SSR.

Part Two

Memories

Of The Time

And Events

July 3, 1941

"We saw trenches 5 m. deep and 20 m. wide They were filled with men, women and children, mostly Jews. Every trench contained some 60–80 persons. We could hear their moans and shrieks as grenades exploded among them. On both sides of the trenches stood some 12 men dressed in civilian clothes. They were hurling grenades down the trenches . . . Later, officers of the Gestapo told us that those men were Banderists."

From an article by Otto Korfes, former Nazi general,
Mittei Lungsblad, No. 11, 1959

6

I REMEMBER

Moshe Briller

SOME TIME AGO I HAPPENED to come upon two pictures. One was an old one, acquired long ago. It was a picture of a "Kvutza" of Hanoar Hazioni in Trembowla, with my sister Clara, Fancia Horowitz, and a few other girls, some of them our close friends. The other picture was given to me just recently. It was a picture of my older cousin, Chanusia Horowitz. What sad memories! What painful thoughts they evoked!

A generation gone and lost forever!

One has to look at these faces, to read in their eyes a drive for self-expression, a desire to live and to drink to the full from the cup of life. If life is a stage and the people its actors, then life is also a dream of varying intensity and of changing character. It is filled with suspense and excitement, with disappointments, and sufferings. It gravitates between comedy and tragedy, between hope and disillusionment, between joy and despair. But the lives of these young people in the pictures were cut short, their hopes never materializing, their disillusionments ending in the greatest tragedy our nation ever experienced.

Trembowla. To us, born and raised there, it was not only a town, it was a world in itself. It was a place where every stone spoke to us, where every house carried some memories and meaning, where every street told a story. Most of all, it was a town filled with people, old and young, everyone with his own problems, his own worries and his own outlook on life.

It was a town, and a town it still remains.

But there were people in it, our own brothers and sisters — and they are gone — gone forever. There must be some life in this town, but I am afraid that if I visited it now it would make on me the impression of a ghost town, bereft of its soul, of the life that gave

it a meaning, of the laughter that perhaps in the stillness of the night
still resounds over its emptiness. For we were an integral part of this
place, our roots deeply implanted, our lives a part of the general life,
our joys and sorrows intertwined with that of the rest of the population.

I remember the town. It rested sleepily between hills and
mountains of a Podolia country-side. A small river ran lazily through
its center, dividing it into an old and new town. In the spring this
river would rise from its half-year slumber, swell with the rising waves
of water, thunder with the ice chunks it carried on its rebellious
shoulders, scare the fearful with the noise created by this spring
awakening, and present the brave, daring and curious with a spectacle
of unforgettable beauty. In the hot days of summer, the same river
would swarm with a multitude of bathers, its banks covered with men,
women, and children clad in an endless variety of bathing apparel.
There would be chatting, laughter and gossip. Mostly these (men)
would be the perennial idlers, living from day to day, from month
to month, hoping for employment and a steady occupation, dreaming
for a miracle in a world filled with stagnation and hopelessness. On
other days, the same idlers would be seen standing on one of the
bridges or sprawling on the river's grassy bank, dreamily observing
a bough, a few leaves or a broken board slowly drifting over the
smooth surface of the river.

What did they dream about? What happened to their dreams?

Another unforgettable thing of beauty was the "Zamek" (the
fortress, or castle). Built on the top of a high, fairly steep mountain,
it kept vigil over the town itself, the surrounding villages with roads
leading to them, and over another mountain; the Pokrovka. Who,
born in Trembowla, would not have sharply outlined in his memory
the shape of this Zamek? Winding approaches brought one to its top;
the wide, strong walls and turrets had once, centuries ago, served
as a military outpost in the wars against the invading Turks. Who
would not remember the statue of the lady who, with one outstretched
arm pointed to the east, while in her other hand she held a dagger
directed at her own heart? Legend or historical truth, it was an
imposing sight. No wonder so many people liked to have their pictures
taken at the feet of this majestic and martial Venus. But the Zamek
also offered some other features of interest; something akin to a
beautiful park with wide alleys running between trees; benches lined
up along the alleys, and the open spaces; wide areas of green lawns;
resting places; an open, valley-like area for concerts, dances and shows
of various character; lovers' lanes; a fir forest stretching for miles,

and leading to a neighboring town, Strusow.

Saturday was the day for the Jews of Trembowla to walk up to the Zamek and to enjoy the cool, fresh, unpolluted air, together with the natural beauty of the park. Groups of people could be seen everywhere. They assembled by families or groups of friends. Children could be seen running around, rolling down the little hills, chasing one another or playing hide and seek. Their young laughter, their high-pitched voices, would fill the air with sounds of play, joy, and happiness. Their mothers and fathers watched them with eager, loving smiles on their lips, always ready to supply them with a fresh, crisp cookie, a piece of strudel, a knish, or some other delicacy—and in the process of doing it not forgetting themselves. At other places one could see young people engaging in the game of socializing; the boys trying to impress their girlfriends, the girls using all their inborn charms to attract their beaus. Laughter and giggles were the only louder sounds coming from such groups.

I myself, I remember, loved to wake at sunrise in the summer, dress, take a book along and venture up the Zamek. Lying on the grass on my belly, with the book in one hand as an alibi, I would pick handfuls of berries and direct them into my mouth. How good it was to dream on such mornings! How beautiful the world looked! How far—in one's imagination—one could be carried away! I saw myself crossing oceans, visiting foreign countries, listening to the most beautiful concerts, participating personally in the creation of music, and in general experiencing all the wonders and delights for which my nature craved. How good it was to be young and to daydream, even if reality was a nightmare and even if one realized that such dreams would never come true.

Yes, life was difficult but it had its rewards.

In the absence of big-city recreation, and being too poor to acquire our own objects for play, games, and entertainment, we created our own toys, our own entertainment. Luckily, nature and Trembowla's scenic beauty supplied us with ample means for self-gratification and self-expression.

Yet—and this is the sad truth—we lived in an ocean of hatred! At that time we did not realize it, and if we had no one would have believed it. What was fated to come was too inhuman to be believed. Only the devil could have thought of a crematorium, gas chambers, shooting squads: *Einsatzgruppen* and all the other inventions of the modern "age of progress."

Surely our people, the Jews, led a quasi-normal life. One cannot call it otherwise, even if in reality it was not normal. A people constantly squeezed out from its positions, constantly pointed out as the country's parasites, driven from occupations, bereft of almost all the avenues of livelihood, persecuted and victimized, cannot and could not regard life as normal. It was difficult — especially for the young generation. It was hopeless and impossible. Yet, with our inborn tenacity (to succeed, progress, and never to surrender), we kept on striving to better ourselves. Against impossible odds we tried to emigrate to other countries and to build our life on a new basis. Few succeeded. For the far greater majority it was only a mirage, never to be reached; an impossible dream. The doors to other countries were tightly shut. Pious expressions of sympathy for our bitter fate did not help us. Persecutions and oppression remained, in the leaders' words: an "internal national affair."

No need to delve deeper. By now it is all history, a generally known fact. As usual, we were standing alone, and there is no need for apologies, not even our own apologies. The explanation is simple; we were a convenient scapegoat in international politics. All accusations, all explanations are useless, in fact, ridiculous. If we were not better than our neighbors, then we were surely not worse, but if it can help our neighbors to still their consciences then let them go on with this myth of our alleged faults and sins. They are welcome to it.

Our youth was resourceful, idealistic (in most cases) and, despite all misfortunes, misery of life, and perennial poverty, optimistic. Before the war there was no despair.

On the contrary, most of our glances were directed towards a far corner, the land of our national birth, of our ancestors. We ardently believed in the great teaching of Herzl. To rid ourselves of our bitter fate, we would have to become a nation again. We would have to rebuild our land, settle on its soil, turn its sandy, rocky wastes into fertile fields. No wonder that so many Zionist youth organizations flourished in Trembowla.

I myself belonged for years to Hanoar Hazioni. I still remember the serious faces of the youngsters that made up its ranks; the speeches of the leaders, the lessons in Jewish history, the study of Zionist theories and aims, of the geography of Palestine, etc. The evenings after school and after the completion of work were spent in these organizations. It was work, serious work, but also fun. An integral part of our gatherings were discussions — *pogadanki*. There we broadened our minds, there we learned to live together with others, to cooperate in a spirit of *kvutzot*. We sang Hebrew songs and even old Jewish songs. They often expressed our longings for a better and freer life, our nostalgia for a return to the land of our fathers. They had in them the simplicity of warmth of our own home life; they also contained notes of defiance, of a willingness to fight it through, to go on despite all difficulties and despite the animosity in the midst of which we lived.

I remember and I still hear it. In the stillness of the night I often hear these songs, only by now they have grown into powerful symphonies that express the whole misery of a nation doomed, the anguish of the mothers and fathers who soon would hear the despairing voices of their children brutally torn from their mother's bosom and then witness their death. They might even hear themselves crying out and then, broken spiritually, surrendering to the butcher's knife. Maybe their outcry of despair even reached heaven, knocked at its broad portals, but all in vain. There would be no response — not even an echo. All would be lost, irrecoverably lost!

Or those dances — the horas. Wild, exuberant. Feet hitting hard against the floor, bodies interlocked in a powerful rhythmical motion that carried them around in an uninterruptible circle. Songs and dances that provided the rhythmical frame for the feet in motion. Joy and restlessness. An expression of youth, of hope, of optimism.

The older generation was God-fearing, industrious and enterprising; deeply devoted to their families and their way of life. Their existence was a constant struggle for survival — mere survival. Despite the myth of Jewish wealth, there were only a few families who lived above the level of poverty. On a Western-World basis they were paupers; in comparison with the rest of the Jewish population in Trembowla, they were well off. The majority lived on the verge of poverty. Life was difficult, competition keen. Jobs were almost non-existent — especially for a Jew. Except for the few professionals and artisans, a Jew could engage only in business, small retail business. For most it was a hopeless task.

They were sustained by their deep religious faith — a faith that was also a way of life. They lived from Sabbath to Sabbath, from one holiday to another. All week they could survive on a piece of dry bread, but on the Sabbath it was different. The Synagogue was the place where they could meet other Jews, discuss current happenings, speculate about their future, and, for a while, a Jew could forget his troubles and take a respite from his daily worries. There too, he could pour out his heart to the Almighty God, feeling and hoping that God would not forsake him in time of danger.

Perhaps at this point I should mention some of the names of the men and women, youngsters and the elderly, who, during their allotted time on earth, strolled the streets of Trembowla, who regarded the town as their own place. After all, a human being even by International Law has a right to his birthplace. But, their appropriate name could be "million," in fact, "six million!" Let it suffice to mention the names of my own family: My parents, Israel Abraham and Chana Briller, my sister Klara and my brothers Max and Milek, of blessed memory. God keep them in peace — God keep all the millions in peace.

We owe it to these martyrs — we owe it to our Trembowla. We owe it to the children whose lives were cut short by the brutal arm of the Nazis and their helpers. Let us remember — we cannot and should not forget. It is our holy obligation.

7

BETWEEN CRUELTY AND DEATH

Janett Margolies

AFTER A BRIEF STRUGGLE, the Nazi army marched into Tarnopol on July 2, 1941. The population was taking cover inside their apartments. Very few people dared to walk the streets. The Jews were afraid to leave their shelter and kept their doors closed.

In the evening, when it started to darken, a group of Germans showed up near our gate. It was raining very hard. They knocked on the gate, but the neighbors decided, after a brief consultation, not to open. They tried to storm the gate with rifle butts, but didn't succeed. With fear and anxiety, we sat in the house all night.

In the morning, when nobody was outside, we opened the gate. The streets were filled with soldiers. Military trucks were traveling wildly, and a civilian crowd was emptying the stores.

A disquiet broke into the air at noon. A rumor started to circulate that dead bodies had been found inside the prison and that the Jews had been responsible for it — which was untrue. In the evening, the Germans called the Ukrainian Nationalist Committee together for a meeting where the technicalities of a Pogrom against the Jews, already in preparation, were discussed. Taking part in this meeting were, among others, the druggist Bilinski and the teacher Chomowa. The house watchmen were ordered to show who was living where. The crowd had to start a panic among the Jews, robbing and plundering.

Friday, July 4, 1941, at 9:00 a.m., machine guns were posted on street corners. Death's Head SS detachments in black uniforms appeared in the streets. Near each house a (Gentile) watchman pointed to who was living where. People were taken (allegedly to work) outside and shot on the spot. Mass executions took place in many parts of the city.

While the bloody Pogrom took place in the Jewish quarters, the

Jews living in other parts of the city did not know anything of what was going on. Also, we knew nothing until the machine-gun noise was later heard and the first bodies were seen. The gate was closed right away, and we started to hide wherever possible. Not being able to force the gate open, the Germans knocked out the windows, forcing their way inside and plundering whatever they could. Searching the cellars and attics, they couldn't find us. It isn't hard to imagine what we went through in those horrible hours.

In the evening, the women went down to lock the gate. The men remained hidden inside. Through the window, a grisly picture appeared before our eyes. A group of murdered bodies — their heads smashed, bloody, and mixed with dirt (after the rain) — were lying on the streets. Cars and trucks passed through, between the dead bodies.

In the morning of the next day, the Jews were ordered to bury the bodies because the stench poisoned the air. In the afternoon, the massacres started again. On that day, Saturday, July 5, 1941, my father was murdered in the prison.

On Sunday, wall posters appeared stating that it was forbidden to kidnap and kill people. "Law and order" would prevail in the city. Violators of public orders would be severely punished. Not suspecting anything bad, the Jews started to crawl out of the hiding places. When the Jews were back in the apartments, the Ukrainian Nationalists started to come into the houses, assuring the Jews that the killing was over and that they were now only taking people to work. Many agreed to go. But after they finished their jobs, they were taken to the city prison and other places, and brutally murdered. Only a few returned alive from these jobs.

On the same day, a mass execution took place in a nearby house where 37 people were massacred.

The SS men, who forced their way into our house, found all the men hiding inside, except my husband. They were ordered to carry heavy boxes with ammunition. Among the men outside was my only son.

Disregarding any threat, I ran after the group, begging the Germans to permit me to help my son at the job. He chased me away, threatening to shoot. Suddenly, the street was closed, and I had no choice but to return home.

During my absence, my mother was pulled from the house and forced to carry away the dead bodies lying on the streets. Having returned from trying to help my son, I saw my mother pulling a dead body, the face all red. I ran forward to help her. Suddenly, terrible cries were heard all around. A young woman was being attacked by two Germans. Her two small children nearby were crying bitterly. Seeing me, the Germans let the woman go, and started plundering.

After the Germans left, I spotted a group of Jews, with their hands up, at the house where my mother was installed. I was afraid to check out what was going on there. Suddenly I heard a machine-gun burst. After a few minutes, the Germans left. Talking to each other, one of them said that all of them were *"Hin"* ("dead") there. I understood that my mother was no longer alive.

My desperation was endless. Yesterday, my father, and today, my mother; my son, in the meantime, was also not around. But after one hour, I heard a voice say, "Mama, I am here." I threw my arms around him. Not everyone had returned, but I was so happy with the appearance of my son that I simply forgot about everything else.

Our neighbor also returned, and my husband came out of hiding. Of all the residents in the house, only two families were left. My son and the neighbors were ordered twice, the next morning, to go to work.

Inside the house it was dark. We, that is, the two families, sat down to discuss what should be done next. Should the men go to work, or hide? Our neighbor was for going. I was against it. After long arguments, it was decided that they should go. All that night I was lying down, dressed. My husband was lying across the end of the bed.

We got up early in the morning. I prepared something to eat, but nobody could swallow anything. My husband and son shaved. They dressed in new underwear and suits, getting ready to go.

Before they left the house, I went outside, near the place where my mother had been killed the day before. A horrible picture appeared before my eyes. A large open pit full of dead bodies, and on top of them, was my poor mother, kneeling with her face down, all stiff. From one side of the pit, some Germans took a picture with their camera. Assuming that I was not Jewish, they asked who did it. Not being able to control myself with the pain I felt, I threw it in their faces saying: "You and yours alike."

Bewildered from what I had seen, I ran back home, and started to cry hysterically. Both my husband and son also cried with me.

Our neighbor started to insist upon going to work. My husband and son wanted to avoid saying goodbye. I decided to accompany them from behind.

The gathering point was in front of the prison. The men were ordered to stand in line, to exercise. I stood among a group of Christians who were watching the show. When the men were led inside the prison, a very bad intuition overwhelmed me. I wanted to do something in order to save them. Wherever I went, I met indifference or helplessness. Seeing that there was nothing I could do, I ran back home.

The time passed slowly. In the evening our neighbor returned alone, without my husband and son. I understood that they were no more. I blamed my neighbor for insisting upon going to work and pulling them to their death. But what was the use? It had already happened. I started to cry, hitting my head with my fists, and banging my head against the wall. I wanted to commit suicide. My neighbors were watchful. They tried to overcome my desperation with whiskey. It didn't help. Corpses, corpses.

At exactly the same time, a relative of mine, my sister-in-law, arrived from the village Gaje Wielkie with the very sad news that all Jews there, including my father-in-law and brother-in-law, had been murdered. The dead bodies lay in the forest, not buried. My pain had no limit. I saw everything around me crumbling. I was left almost without relatives — six dead among the nearest. I stopped eating, and lit the candles for the dead souls. I didn't go outside. People started to come into the house to tell me stories that my husband and son had been seen somewhere. I ran and searched for them everywhere. All those stories were designed to instill some hope in me, to pull me out of my deep depression.

After one week of continued Pogroms, which lasted from Friday, July 4, until Friday, July 11, 1941, things quieted down a little. During that bloody week, 5,000 Jews were murdered, among them 800 women and children. During that week, the Jewish intellectuals were eliminated, the people who had been told they were being chosen to create the first Judenrat. This is how it happened:

The Germans called Mr. Gotfried, a teacher, and asked him to gather a few dozen prominent Jews, in order to organize the Judenrat. He went from house to house, assuring the candidates that the proposition was a clean one and that nothing would happen to the candidates. The meeting place was the Regional building. When the delegation arrived, they were loaded on trucks, and transported to the brick factory. There they were all shot and buried. Gotfried himself was careful enough and did not appear. (A rumor was circulated that they were transported to work.) A few weeks later, their bodies were found.

In the meantime, new orders against Jews were proclaimed. All males had to appear at the employment office, where they were directed to perform hard labor. For the price of 100 zlotys they had to buy a special sign with the Star of David, and were forced to wear armbands with the same sign. Under the threat of death, they were ordered to hang the paper sign on the door of the house. Dr. Fisher, a lawyer, was ordered to collect from among the Jews 1.5 million zlotys, under the threat that hostages would be taken, locked in the Synagogue, and burned alive if this sum was not collected in a few days. A panic befell the Jewish community. The people didn't have such a large sum of money. They were forced to sell whatever possible. The Christian businessmen took advantage of the situation and bought things very cheaply at bargain prices. Despite all efforts, Dr. Fisher was not able to collect the requested sum in such a short period. Some good Christians, like Dr. Beneszowicz and others (anonymously), helped the Jews. The money was delivered. But money alone wasn't enough. The Germans asked for jewelry, crystal, leather, and other material goods — without an end.

Suddenly, the news spread that for a certain amount of money the Germans would permit the dead bodies to be exhumed. I did succeed in getting such a permit. I came with a group of women to dig my mother out in the presence of a sanitary commission. The stench coming from the pit was so strong that it was impossible to work. After we dug the bodies out, the sanitary commission stopped the digging. They did it for two reasons: Too many spectators had gathered all around, and the stench was intolerable. I managed to transfer my mother to the Jewish cemetery.

I felt sad and bitter. With little food, I continued to visit my mother's grave, where I met many more people like me. Returning to my dark apartment, I met friends who tried to avoid me, in order not to meet eye to eye. Even my cousins stopped writing. I was left all alone with my pain.

Thinking about my situation, I started to believe that I had a special mission to fulfill. And it looks like I remained alive thanks to this. My mission was to find the bodies of my dearest ones, and rebury them in Israel. All my energy turned in this direction. I started to wander, to wherever a mass grave was opened, in order to search for my dearest ones.

After a short time, I was able to find out how my husband and son were killed. They had been forced to carry out the Ukrainian dead bodies from the city prison to the cemetery. While my husband was working on the (horse) wagon, my son and other Jews were pulled down, chased around, and beaten with wooden sticks or planks. My son allegedly cried out, "You have no right to beat and maim us. We aren't guilty. Kill us, but stop torturing us." As a reply, he was beaten to death. My husband, seeing his son dead, lost consciousness. The Germans noticed that he stopped working, and they started to beat him murderously, until he stopped moving and they later pumped a bullet into his body.

This story broke me down again. I felt that I was on the verge of losing my mind. Day and night I saw before my eyes this terrible picture. Physically, I felt the blows.

Ten weeks after this tragedy, a mass grave was opened at the cemetery. The bodies were already decomposed, some in shirts only, some with hands and feet tied with barbed, thorny wire. That day I did not find my dearest. At night I saw my son in a dream so clear that I felt his presence. In the morning I again went to the cemetery. The bodies were transferred to a funeral home in the meantime. I went inside. Suddenly I recognized a pair of slacks and a shirt with a familiar belt. My son, my only dear son.

While standing still, crying, I was called and told that my husband was also found. He had the documents with him. I had looked at the body a few times before, but could not recognize it at all. It looked so different.

In the dark, I buried one near the other—my husband and my son. Now the job was left to find my father. Despite all efforts, I could not find him.

The Ghetto

Events continued on their course. The creation of the Tarnopol Ghetto started. The organizer was a Jew from Bendzin, Firstenberg. He lived in the house of Samuel Kopper, and was also given the job of organizing the Jewish police, advising strongly to join its ranks. Kopper managed to create the first police detachment. He also organized the Warsaw Ghetto. In agreement with the Judenrat, the construction started. A commission drew the borderline, and we had to be locked into the Ghetto until the end of September 1941.

The roundups continued. The Jews were driven to the Ghetto. It was terribly crowded. Also here, the difference between the rich and the poor was quite visible. Some got used to it after a while, having a lot of foodstuff. The others lived in overcrowded conditions, dozens in a room, starving from hunger. True, a folks-kitchen was created, supplying warm soup daily. But all those who benefited from it, or received any other support, were the first candidates in every "Action." Many people, swollen from hunger, avoided the kitchen like fire, being afraid to pay with their lives for a little soup. The second plague was the cold, which the poor suffered from terribly.

Were it not for the continued search, the life in the Ghetto would have been monotonous in 1941. I started to think about social work. A few meetings of teachers took place, during which children were registered. The parents disagreed, being afraid for the children to be in one place together. Small groups of five to eight were created, being taught privately.

In the meantime, the Judenrat organized a department for social security and a hospital. Donations were collected for the poor, the orphans, the old, and the kindergarten. The hospital was in Maika's house at the old market. The orphans were located in a school. The children slept on wooden "beds," suffering from hunger. Prof. Joachim Hirschberg was the head of the orphanage. The old-age home was in a Synagogue. The situation of the old was terrible. The kindergarten had not managed to start functioning when it was transformed into a prison, located near the Jewish police.

The Jewish people started to look around for some income. Some opened a teahouse, others a repair shop. Children were selling cigarettes. Others were baking for the stores. Those who went outside the Ghetto smuggled in food products.

In the Ghetto there were also some "doers" who were engaged in illegal business. Among them were Koppler, the Commander of the Jewish police; Fleishman, who was associated (connected) with the Gestapo; Baral, the Camp Doctor; and Eisner and Rosa Schwartz, co-workers in the Labor Department. The house of the drugstore owner, Froidental, where the top Jewish Brass resided, was called "The Palace." The Gestapo visited the house frequently with their girlfriends. There they drank and ate, playing cards and concluding different "transactions." A leech of a different kind was Mr. Labiner, provision boss of the Ghetto. We received 70 grams of bread daily, and from time to time a little marmalade. The rest, except for the meager portion given for social needs, disappeared into Labiner's pockets. An exception was the Judenrat people, who received food packages. All this was done at the cost of the poor, while the rich could help themselves to make ends meet. Dr. Baral classified people for the labor camps. The rich bribed themselves out, and the poor were sent to hard labor in the camps.

Rosa Schwartz managed the women's department. This *heina* wasn't satisfied with a one-time bribery. The poor Ghetto slave girls were forced to serve her personally.

The First "Action"

In the beginning of 1942, a rumor circulated that the Germans were asking for "blood donations" from one thousand Jews. After trans-actions with the Gestapo, it was decided that the Judenrat would perform the job with the help of an element from the police. They made a list of those sentenced to death, and Dr. Dratler approved it.

Despite the Judenrat's attempt to keep the whole thing secret, the people felt that something was underway. The date was not known. One day, the police and the officeholders were called together and divided into groups of three. Each group received a partial list of victims, which, under different excuses, had to be brought to the old Synagogue. The "Action" started at 2:00 p.m., and should have been over at 5:00 a.m., the next day. The Germans didn't take part in the action. When the "contingent" couldn't be brought in by 4:00 a.m., Dr. Baral's orders were to catch people in the streets of Podolska, Wirza, and Niza (sections of the poor).

It was a cruel night. The hollering and cries went sky-high. "Mother, don't cry, I am going with you. Don't be afraid, your daughter will not leave you alone."

At exactly 5:00 a.m. in the morning, the victims were taken from the Synagogue and driven outside. They were loaded onto open trucks, thrown one on top of the other. The top layer was covered with a large truck cover, and on top of the victims' bodies, SS men and Ukrainian policemen were standing and stomping the people with their boots. Machine guns were loaded on the trucks, and all were brought to the Janow Forest, where the "Baudienst" had already prepared the mass graves. All had to undress, and neatly put aside their clothes and belongings. Men were ordered to stand on one side, and women and children on the other. The first shot were the children, with the fathers and mothers watching.

After this action, the bitterness increased in the Ghetto. What right had the Judenrat, people cried, to decide who should live and who should die? People pointed to other cities where Judenrat leaders chose suicide, refusing to follow orders. But some shared the opinion that the murdered couldn't outlive the Ghetto anyway, and that it was necessary to sacrifice the barn to save the house.

This "Action" taught the people a great deal. The most important thing was not to fall into the hands of the police, but to hide from their eyes. A hasty activity of constructing hiding places and bunkers started in the Ghetto. The noose was tightening.

The first Passover was a very sad one. The Judenrat didn't permit matzos to be baked. The people started to bake privately. The Rabbi gave them the O.K. to eat buckwheat, peas, and beans. During the holidays, a large group of inmates were taken out to the Janow camp, where they were shot. Such actions started to take place regularly.

People started to talk, saying that all Ghetto inmates without any distinction, between the ages of 14 and 60, would be forced to work. The "Employment Office" would provide the jobs, and give them armbands with a number and the letter "A," inside the Star of David. These rumors were proven to be right.

Without such an armband, nobody was permitted to move around in the Ghetto streets or stay outside the front door. It was strictly forbidden to move outside the Ghetto. (The aim of this strict order was not to permit any contact with the Christian population.) Even the Ghetto officials weren't permitted to move around without armbands, unless they had permission from the doctors. The Ghetto looked like a ghost town until 5:00 or 6:00 in the evenings. Only after that did people start to show up in the street, running for food products and water.

Suddenly, news started to circulate that one thousand women and girls would have to go to a camp to work in "Koksagiz Plantation" (plants containing rubber). Very often women were caught in the street, going to and from work. They stopped showing up in the streets. At that time a few thousand women were taken out of their rooms and hiding places and transported to the camps. After the accomplished task, the women were transported to the Belzec crematoria ovens.

In July 1942, a rumor was spread that all labor cards had to be stamped. Those without a stamp, as they were saying, would go into the "Sky-Command." The family members of the owners of such stamped cards were allegedly saved from being caught in the streets.

A "stamp panic" started. Mr. S. Kopper, a former police commander, delivered the stamps. When he showed up in the street, people surrounded him, begging him with tears in their eyes to give them the stamp. He helped many, including his friends.

In the meantime, the news about the August "Action" in Lvov

reached Tarnopol. The stamped cards increased the panic.

Every minute we had expected that the "Action" would start. The famous "Roll-Brigade" was supposed to show up here. They were traveling around in the towns, rounding up people and transporting them to Belzec. Every day people were running around in great fear, trying to find out if the wagons had arrived at the railroad station.

The August "Action"

On August 29, 1942, in the early morning, I heard a voice that said, "Lolek, get up, it started." Through the window I saw the Ghetto surrounded with Gestapo men in the marketplace (our window faced the market). We quickly went into our hiding places. It was a room with a movable wall and covered entrance. From the window in the room, we could see what was going on in the market.

The place was full. Trucks were continuously arriving. People were forced out and loaded onto the waiting trucks. Watchmen were standing with machine guns. The trucks went directly to the railroad station. The heat was terrible. People fainted from thirst. We heard screams and shoutings, mixed with shouting from a distance. The police were dragging people on all sides. In another location was the *Umschlags Platz* (collecting place), at the horse market, near the Targowa Street where the Judenrat had its "office."

The Germans were in our house twice that day, and they miraculously didn't find us. In this "Action," almost one thousand people lost their lives.

The Ghetto shrank. Orders were issued to leave the Pola Street, Lvov and Berek-Joselewicz Streets, and the market side.

A large "Action" was predicted for October. Day and night people were thinking of ways to hide from the nearing disaster. Already at that time, some managed to cross over to the "Aryan" side. Weinstein delivered the needed false papers. He was caught later and shot. "Aryan" papers started to be a dream. But few could acquire them, much less use them, since an "Aryan" look, Christian friends, and the proper accent were necessary.

On the Road to Death

On November 8, 1942, when I was busy carrying my belongings to another house, I noticed that there suddenly was a panic and shooting. Understanding that this was an "Action," I ran into another house with other neighbors to hide in the cellar, which had a special hiding place. The entrance, however, was badly masked, or camouflaged. I had a feeling that it would be very dangerous there, but it was too late to find anything better.

After a short time, the Germans forced their way in, and together with the Jewish police, chased us out of the cellar, taking from us our rings, watches, and money. "It isn't needed anymore." I was severely beaten up, and later found myself near Kazimierzowska Street.

There were already many people there. More victims were continuously brought in. Dead bodies were lying on the streets. Shooting was heard all the time. The staff of the Gestapo, headed by Miller, stood in the wheat mill on the Baron-Hirsch Street. In a small area in the mill, one thousand people were squeezed together, one close to the other. Suddenly we were told to sit down, which naturally, was impossible. But when a few received blows to their heads with rifle butts, and the blood started to flow, all dropped to the floor, one on top of the other. This position was intolerable. The watchmen continued the beating. The dead and the living were mixed together. People were sitting on dead bodies, and walking over them. The watchmen kept changing continuously because they could not stand the stale air.

We were forced to sit this way for two days without water or food. In the meantime, the Judenrat members and the police pulled out their friends, replacing them with other victims. The figure had to be exact. At the end of the second day, we were led outside into the street, divided into groups of ten, and led to the railroad station. I said goodbye to the known streets, to the visible cemetery, trying to walk fast, in order not to get hit over the head. We were surrounded tightly by the Jewish and Ukrainian police, with the Gestapo and the SS, led by Storm Trooper Miller himself. The Christian people were standing on the sidewalks, looking eagerly toward the marching crowd. Their looks were indifferent, often even smiling. We were talking quietly, concentrating. Everybody said goodbye to the city, remembering better times in the past.

On the way, a policeman came close to me, whispering quietly into my ear to join the younger ladies in the wagon. When we arrived at the railroad station, the men were separated, and we were pushed toward the railroad cars. I did observe where the young were concentrated, joining them in the wagon, which was closed and sealed.

A Jump into Life

We were eighty women. The small windows were high up, with bars and thorny wire. Once inside, we found out that somebody had smuggled in a file to cut the bars. I started to organize a crew. Standing on top of the others, we started to work. The train continued to run. When the job was finished, and the bars cut, each candidate, in order to jump, had to stand on the shoulders of the other, with legs through the window, then hold on with their hands, later with only one hand, and with a strong swing, jump into the direction of the running train.

I stood watching the jumping. Most of them were killed on the spot. Some were killed by trains coming from the opposite direction. Others were shot by Gestapo watchmen. Those who succeeded were later caught by special railroad watchmen. Of all the Tarnopol train jumpers, I think that I was the only one left alive.

It took quite a while to decide to jump, or not to jump. I realized fully, how hopeless the situation looked. O.K., I will jump, and if I succeed in reaching my home, then what next? I would be caught again, and the story would be repeated. I did look through the window, seeing an endless darkness. Then I noticed that of the eighty women only a few were left, and I wondered what would happen to those remaining after their discovery.

I decided to jump. Already hanging outside the wagon, I got tangled up in the thorny wire. Being scared, I cried out loudly, feeling that I was falling down. A shot was heard over my head. It was a watchman. Luckily he missed. At the same moment I noticed a locomotive running straight toward me. With my last strength, I rolled over downwards into a depression. All this lasted just a few seconds. I was saved, but badly injured, bleeding from my head and hands. I tore out a little frozen grass, putting it on my wounds. I succeeded in stopping the bleeding. Later I wiped it off my face, bringing myself to order.

Managing to just get on my feet, I noticed two Ukrainians standing near me. "Oh, a Jewess, come to the Gestapo," they hollered. I did ask them how they knew I was Jewish. They replied that only Jews were jumping from trains. I started to criticize them, explaining who the Germans were, and who they were fooling and misleading, Ukrainians as well. One of them, it looked to me, was a nice guy, who said to the other one: "Let her go." He, however, asked for money. I told him that I had only twenty zlotys (which wasn't much), which he took. Before their departure, they clearly explained to me where I was, 14 kilometers from Lvov. They showed me two roads: one through the forest, the other, the highway. I chose the highway.

On the "Aryan" Side

It was still early morning and cold. (I was in a summer overcoat.) Suddenly I saw before me a village. On its edge, near a barn, a gentile lady was milking a cow. I came closer to her, saying good morning, asking at the same time if I could buy some milk. I noticed that she was observing me suspiciously. It's not good, I thought. I must find a story to calm her down. I told her I was a business woman from Lvov, and that I was touring with products through the villages in order to exchange the products for food. I told her the driver had robbed me, taking everything away from me and throwing me out of the car, and that I could have been killed. Now, I would have to return home empty-handed. It looked to me that she believed me, because she invited me inside, and in addition to milk, she gave me some hot soup.

I had been without food and water for three days, so I ate the soup with an appetite, finishing it all. At the same time, I kept thinking about the victims left behind, who must surely have reached their destination, and wondered what they were going through. I couldn't believe that I was sitting here quietly, near a soup bowl.

After the meal, I felt very tired. I begged the lady to permit me to take a nap. She agreed, and I did lie down on the hard bench, and fell asleep.

My nerves did not permit me to sleep long. I got up, washed myself and fixed my socks and torn overcoat. The lady gave me something to eat. She told me that in the evening, a truck would be there with which the Germans would pick up laborers for work, and that I would be able to return with them. O.K., I said, thinking that this was bad. However, until the evening, there was plenty of time. I started a conversation, in order to find out if I could stay overnight. A bed, with straw underneath, was prepared. When I lay down, I felt that a miracle had happened to me.

The next morning I made a deal with the homeowners for them to take me to Lvov with their horse wagon. It is clear that I paid a good price for everything. The lady of the house loaned me a large scarf, which I wrapped around myself, and got up on the wagon.

During the trip, I kept thinking about how to ask the coachman (*Kutcher*) to help me find employment in Lvov, among Christians. I asked him if he was a good Polak, a patriot, and if I could trust him with a secret. When he nodded his head affirmatively, I felt that he was an honest person. I told him a story that I was Polish, working in the underground in Tarnopol, where the Germans caught me. But I succeeded in running away. Now, I was forced to hide temporarily in Lvov, because they would look for me in Tarnopol. I did mention different priests (clergymen) as my friends, who would pay, and help those who helped me. The farmer started to think. I noticed that my story sounded good, and that he wanted to help me. He suggested an apartment with his relative who would surely agree to keep me, if the payment was right.

We arrived at the designated place. The farmer went inside to talk it over with his relative. I was still sitting in the wagon, waiting. After a while, both of them came out, inviting me to come inside. Two women greeted me, one the relative's wife, the other younger, heavy-set and with a lot of make-up. Turning towards me, she said: "We thought that a Jewess was sitting in the wagon, but now I see you." I had a short conversation with the homeowners about the financial problem, asking them if they knew where I could find a doctor to take care of my wounds, My hand was swollen, covered with black spots.

I sat at the table near the younger lady (a sub-tenant) of Ukrainian nationality, from Buczacz. During the supper, I asked her to send a telegram to Tarnopol, to an Aryan address, stating that I was alive. She didn't stop staring at me, and at last she said: "Don't be afraid, I know you are Jewish, and I assume that you must have jumped from the train. You have played your role well. I am also Jewish, but I already have 'Aryan' papers. I'm registered and they call me Julia. I'll help you. We will tell the neighbors that a friend of ours arrived from the region to see the doctor. In the meantime, lie down and take a rest, and keep yourself strong." After those words, I felt a warmth in my heart, and a feeling of security predominated.

A new chapter started in my life, not a less difficult one but less tragic, because who else did I have to lose?

Despite the changed situation, the struggle between life and death, for just a small corner on this godforsaken earth, still continued. I was again surrounded by open and hidden murderers watching everywhere. Wherever I turned, I saw death threats around me, death and death, a sea of humanity and egoism without a drop of human kindness or readiness to help.

So, life continued with terribly long days and nights, until finally, the day came. The artillery duels and the bombings over Lvov stopped. All this was a sign that the end of our tragic ordeal had finally arrived.

Tired, broken, orphaned, I reached the shore of life.

8

From the Depths

Salomea Luft

THE WRITER OF THE LETTER published here, Salomea (Musia) Luft, was born in 1912. After finishing school in Vienna, Austria, she returned with her parents (Salomon and Chana) to her home, where she finished her education at a music school. Later she taught music in the Tarnopol Music School. In 1937 she married David Ochs, Doctor of Philosophy, a gymnasium (high school) teacher. They spent the summer months of 1939 in Tarnopol, where they remained until the outbreak of the war.

She handed this long letter over to a Gentile Polish friend, who hid it in a tin can in the cellar. When the Soviet Army liberated Tarnopol, he gave the letter to her brother Bubi, who was hiding in Tarnopol. He brought it to Israel after the war.

For a while, the writer of this letter managed to hide with Polish people. But on July 4, 1943, they denounced her to the Germans. She was imprisoned until July 20, the day she was murdered by the Nazi hangmen.

The names, Cily and Bubi, mentioned in the book, are her sister and brother. Cily died. Bubi emigrated to Israel after the war.

Tarnopol, April 7, 1943.

My dear,

Before I leave this world, I want, my dear, to leave you a few lines. By the time this letter reaches you, I and the others will not be here anymore. Our end is coming nearer. It is felt, and it is known. We are already like dead, all innocent, indefensible Jews, sentenced to death. Those still alive, left from the mass killings, are next in line, in the near future (days or weeks).

It is horrible but true. There is no way out for us to escape from the cruel, terrible death.

I could tell you a lot, but how is it possible to describe the tragedy and pain. It is impossible. No pen can draw a picture of the tragedy of our people on this blood-soaked earth. The pain, the refined method of degradation, humiliation, hate and cruelty, until the annihilation. First we were squeezed like a lemon. Our blood was sucked to the last drop, then thrown like a piece of garbage. We were robbed of all our human feelings and instincts, transformed into mechanical labor-animals, and later mass-murdered. No, you will never be able to comprehend this. You will never be able to feel what we went through. A normal thinking person cannot believe that it is possible to endure such punishment, that one can outlast such cruelty in the 20th century. I will try briefly, to describe the story of our fate from July 1941.

Right at the beginning of July 1941, around 5,000 men were murdered, among them also my husband. David left the house on July 7, 1941, and never returned. He volunteered for the Judenrat (Jewish Council) which had to be created. I tried to dissuade him from doing it. But, as a Rabbi, he considered it his duty to serve the Jewish people. Six weeks later, after a five day search, I found him among the dead, which were brought from the Brick factory (where they were murdered) to the Jewish cemetery. From this day on, my normal life stopped. There was no more purpose for it.

In my girlhood I could not have wished for a better, more devoted boyfriend. Only two years and two months we were happy together, exactly two years and two months (May 7, 1939, married—July 7, 1941, the parting). There is no sense in telling you about my suffering. My heart was bleeding. With my own hands to bury the loveliest person, who understood you so well, who was devoted and loved you, to bury the person with my own hands. How can I describe this, when I was so tired from searching, that I was already "happy" to find him among the other dead bodies, to find your "own." Is it possible to describe such scenes, can such inner feelings be told in words?

During one day, one woman lost her husband. Another her only child. The third lost all, her husband and her children. Can so much pain and suffering be described? This was the fate of thousands.

David is no more. How satisfied he must be. He has everything behind him and doesn't have to witness the two years of cruelty. We are still waiting for the bullet. In the beginning I was convinced that I would not be able to endure his death. I thought that I would not be able to live without him. But what kind of endurance a human being has. I continued to live. How, it isn't easy to tell. The blood wound was impossible to heal. How sad it was to be left so alone, being used to a peaceful, satisfactory and quiet home. But, I continued to live.

In September 1941, we were sent to the Ghetto. Imagine, we were separated and isolated, not permitted to walk onto the Aryan side without passes, which were only given to the workers. A large gate, guarded by German or Ukrainian police, was the "Border." Food products were smuggled into the Ghetto with great difficulty, fear and combinations. In September 1941, I got a job as a secretary typist, with a German company. It was interesting to note that the office was in our former apartment. The kitchen was transformed into an office. In the place where the piano stood, was now my writing table. Instead of playing the piano, I am now playing on the typewriter machine. I cannot complain, I had a very good job. My boss, and also the co-workers, are very good people. All treated me as a human being, and not as a Jewess. My father, and Bubi, got a job at the same construction company.

The Ghetto made a very bad impression in the beginning, but slowly we also got used to this way of life.

The winter of 1941–42 was a very hard and cold one. It wasn't easy to hold on. Many people were dying from hunger and cold weather. Despite all "robberies" and searches, cold and hunger, we continued to live. All the time we continued to sell something, clothing, shoes, underwear, etc. So we managed to last until March 1942. Then it started again.

March 23, 1942 was a night to remember. The Judenrat was ordered to deliver a "contingent" of "700 Pieces" — people to be liquidated. What, you don't want to believe it, it isn't true? Yes that's the way it was. Our own brothers, our policemen, were leading people to their death. The Synagogue was the gathering place of the victims. Over there it was already warm, so the "poor" did not freeze before they were to die. They were given bread and marmalade, loaded onto the trucks and driven to Janowka. Everything was prepared with all conveniences in advance. The dug-out pits were already waiting for the victims and the machine guns were ready. How terrible a night that was. All this was only the beginning. Then, for some time it was "quiet." Quiet, with a continued fear of being taken to a slave labor camp, and endless fear of what tomorrow would bring. We continued to live in fear and in misery.

In July 1942, Cily (my sister) arrived at the labor camp in Jagielnica. She didn't have it too bad.

On August 31, 1942, a large "Action" started. The Germans

asked for 3,000 victims. How many left this world, we don't exactly know — 2,500 or more. At that time we lost our dear, good, devoted mother.

This time a new trick was used. Those working with their families received from the police a special stamp on their documents, which would exclude them from this "Action." The "Action" would also this time (as in March) include the non-working, and the children. Again our Jewish policemen started to search for victims in the apartments and hiding places. Bubi and I went to work. My mother and father remained at home. They had the "Life-Saving Stamp." We weren't permitted through the border gate. They led us to the gathering place. We were convinced that we would not come out alive. We didn't stay there long. We simply ran away, and succeeded for the time being. Many were shot on the spot. I managed to return to the office, where quite a lot of work was waiting for me. I was sitting in the office, and outside thousands of people were waiting for death. Oh, how can I describe all this? In the afternoon, I found out that my father and mother were seen at the gathering place. I had to continue to work. I had no other choice. I couldn't help myself. I thought that I was losing my mind. But you don't get crazy. In the evening our German co-worker came, who saved forty people in our company, including my father. My mother he couldn't pull out. Housewives, not working women, were impossible to save. I didn't know if I should cry because I had lost my mother, or whether I should be happy my father was saved. Normally, how could one stand such pain? No, nothing happened to those remaining alive. Only the victims were eliminated.

It was a terrible August 31, 1942. Thousands were squeezed into cattle cars — women, children, men, old and young, all were loaded and transported to the slaughterhouse, Belzec. There, allegedly, the people were poisoned with gas; others said that electrical current was used. Exactly how the people were eliminated isn't known. I just want to mention that all of David's family perished long before. It was the same everywhere. In large cities, in small towns, in villages, it was almost the same. An order was an order — everywhere. We continued to live without our mother — how we missed her everywhere.

In October, Cily returned from the labor camp in Jagielnica. In the meantime, the struggle for life and future existence continued. We had to resettle again. The Ghetto was shrunk, because the houses of the murdered people were empty. We moved, this time to the Szeptycki No. 22. The three houses (20, 22 and 24) belonged to the Ghetto. We continued to live. November 3–5, 1942, the "Actions" started again. People were pulled out from all hiding places, all underground bunkers, and led toward death. Young, useful people were again pulled out by our police, and thrown to "waste." Entire families, households with all inhabitants perished from the surface of the earth.

November 1942 was on a Sunday. Unxpectedly, at 11:00 a.m. in the morning, the "resettlement" started. The Ghetto was surrounded, and the same story was repeated again. At that time I was unexpectedly lucky. Not foreseeing any "Action," I went outside just ten minutes before the Ghetto was surrounded, to join the last transport.

After the "resettlement," the Ghetto shrank again. With the passing of time, people got used to the newly created conditions. The human feelings were dulled. When close relatives were lost, there was almost no reaction. People stopped crying. We were no longer humans, just like stones, completely without feeling. Arriving news made no impression. People were marching to their death calmly. The people at the gathering places, the victims, kept their self-control and dignity.

In January 1943, we were transferred from the company to a labor camp. We were put into barracks, women and men separated. Only in closed labor formations could we walk outside, accompanied by a policeman, and only in the "Aryan" part of town. We were transformed into labor prisoners.

My father and Bubi were in the men's department. Cily was in the women's department. I dragged my father into the camp with a bad kidney inflammation. I wanted to be together with them, to march together toward death. So we continued to live in the camp. Many people we knew ran away to other cities with "Aryan Documents." Many were caught. Maybe some managed to save their lives.

From January until April 1943, it was quiet. We continued to live with all the inconveniences, with the daily line formations, etc.

In April 1943, it started again. In groups of twenty and fifty, people were taken out of the Ghetto and shot.

April 26, 1943.

I am still alive, and I want to describe what happened from the 7th until today. It is assumed, in general, that "everything" will be going now. Galizia will be completely *Judenrein* (free of Jews). First, the Ghetto will be liquidated until the first of May. In the Ghetto, there are only 700 people left.

During the last days thousands were shot. Now a new method is being used. The people are "officially" led to death. Before it was called *Ansiedlung* (settlement) amd *Umsiedlung* (resettlement). Now, no more. What happened next was sheer cruelty. The gathering place was in our camp. Over there are the human victims which the Jewish police dragged out of their hiding places. They were selected, and led toward death. We were able to "observe" through the window in the camp, the scenes going on, the pictures we have seen — how can I describe it? We are not human anymore. Sons brought out their parents toward death. Fathers brought their children. Mothers left their children at the gathering place, trying to escape. In other cases, children joined their parents marching toward death together, even when they could have continued to work for a while in the camp. It could be seen how the gathering place was getting crowded with more and more people going to their death. This time, the mass graves were already prepared in Petrikow. The victims had to leave their overcoats on the spot, in the camp. The men were left in their undershirts, and like a bunch of animals led to their final destination — death. The pits weren't far away. Why use gasoline for trucks, why bother with railroads? It was much simpler to get rid of the surplus element on the spot. When people were loaded into cattle cars before, some still managed to escape. So, this chance was taken away. I think that this way death was easier. To travel two to three days, with the knowledge that you were traveling to your death, must have been something terrible. Here it went much faster.

At the pits the people are forced to undress completely naked. They must kneel down on their knees, and wait for the bullet. The people wait to be next in line. In the meantime, those still alive, waiting, must neatly place the dead bodies in the mass graves, so that they lay one close to the other, and save space. All this procedure doesn't last long. After half an hour, the remaining clothing of the thousands killed is back in the camp. It's getting a little too much. The nerves cannot take it any longer. If anybody would have predicted, and told me that I'd be able to live through such cruelty, I would not have comprehended it. Where can one acquire the strength to hold out, and for what, when it is known that every effort is useless? There is no redemption. There is no sense in deluding ourselves that it will be possible to avoid the cruel mass killing. We have no hope anymore; we're living from day to day, from hour to hour.

On April 9, 1943, 1,500 people were murdered; then again, two to three days of quiet, and it starts all over, without an end. Now there are only 700 Jews left in the Ghetto.

I would just like to mention that after the "Actions," the Ghetto received a bill of 30,000 zlotys to pay for the "used bullets." Interesting, not true? We in the camp are forced after finishing the job to go into the rooms of the murdered and take all items left. It's so painful, so cruel, dreadful. Those mountains of items, the leftovers of a whole nation. The empty apartments, the silent streets, the "dead city," how painful it is; why has it to be like this? Why can't we cry; why can't we get weapons to defend ourselves? How is it possible to see so much blood streaming and say nothing, do nothing, and wait for death, until one day, you are next taken? Oh, it's terrible. You think you'll explode, but you don't. You continue to live, if one can call it "life." And all the world knows that we are being annihilated, and nothing is happening. Nobody wants to help us, nobody wants to save us. Left all alone, without any pity, we are forced to go under. Do you think that we want to die this way—No! No! we don't, despite everything we lived through. On the contrary, the self-preservation instinct is even stronger now; the closer to death, the will to live grows stronger. We would like so much to continue to live, to see the revenge for so many millions of victims, for so much suffering without an end.

Sadly, we will not live to take revenge. My dear, you must take revenge, you must do something to pay back, to take revenge for so much injustice, for such inhuman barbarism.

In general, there is no revenge. No matter what happens in the future, it will not be enough, nothing in comparison to our fate. What was done with us—it is impossible to comprehend.

Oh, I cannot continue, I cannot write more. I could smear more and more pages, and you will not understand it anyway, I'm concluding.

My dear! David is lying in the Jewish cemetery; my mother, I don't know where she is. She was transported to the extermination camp, Belzec. Where I will be buried, I don't know, in Petrikow, Zagrabla, or Zarudin, I don't know. If you ever come here after the war, maybe you will find out from known people, where the camp transports were sent.

It isn't easy to say goodbye, to part forever. But we are going, laughing, toward death.

Live well, you shall have it good, and if you will be able, then take REVENGE.

Meine Teueren! Ihr müßt Rache nehmen, ihr müßt was tun und zumindest so viel Merkwürdigkeiten solche unmenschliche Barbareien zu rächen.

Eigentlich gibt es überhaupt keine Rache. Was auch geschehen wird, ist viel zu wenig, nichts gegenüber unserem Schicksal. Das was mit uns gemacht wurde ist nicht zum Begreifen.

Ach, ich kann nicht mehr, kann nicht mehr schreiben. Könnte noch mal Bogen hinschmieren, und Ihr würdet es sowieso nicht verstehen. Will Schluß machen.

Meine Lieben! David liegt am jüdischen Friedhof, meine Mutter weiß ich nicht wo, sie wurde nach Belzec verschleppt, wo ich begraben sein werde, weiß ich nicht ob in Petrikov, oder Zagrobela, Tarnobin, ich weiß es so nicht. Wenn Ihr vielleicht nach dem Kriege herkommt, dann werdet Ihr bei Bekannten erfahren, wie die Transporte des Lagers eingerichtet wurden.

Es ist nicht leicht, Abschied für immer zu nehmen, aber wir gehen schon bewusst in den Tod.

Lebet wohl, lasset es Euch recht gut gehen und wenn Ihr könnt dann nehmt einst

Rache.

Facsimile of letter

Salomea Luft

פֿאַקסימיליע פֿון בריוו

→ *TARNOPOL STORY...*

9

FRAGMENTS OF MY
HOLOCAUST EXPERIENCES

Israel Goldfliess

The Suddenness of the Blitzkrieg
and the German Invasion

IN THE EARLY MORNING HOURS OF Sunday morning, June 22, 1941, we were awakened by the noise of airplanes flying east and west continuously. Near our house lay the road from the municipal barracks, which were not far from the main road, to Tarnopol, Czortkow, and Zaleszczki. Right at our corner the street turned into this main road via the Planty, which led to the new bridge. As soon as I went out into the street, I came across large posters printed in black and white and put up on the front wall of the house. I don't remember all the details on the notices, just the gist of what was written.

The Soviet authorities informed us that the Nazis had violated the peace treaty signed two years before by Ribbentrop and Molotov. Without delivering an ultimatum, they had attacked our troops and were invading our territory. Predictably, the famous ending of such notices was in place: We shall thrash and defeat them, long live our outstanding leader, "The light of humanity," etc. Of course, the situation was quite different. I didn't stand outside for long before seeing vehicles streaming from all sides and moving in one direction: to Planty and the bridge in order to reach the main road to the east.

I got the impression that the Russians were fleeing in the same manner as the Poles had two years before at the outbreak of the war, with one exception. The Poles fled primarily southwards in the directions of Czortkow-Zaleszczyki and the Rumanian border. But now this region, too, was under Soviet rule; the Russians had annexed all of Bukovina to the Ukraine just one month before the fighting. So all the traffic now moved in one direction — eastward. The local population, particularly the Jews, were perplexed and did not know what to do. People returned to their homes, and whoever had a radio set it to one of the European stations to find out what was happening.

We listened to the broadcasts of Western European stations, especially to those from England. Free radio stations from all occupied European countries transmitted war news daily, from England.

The disorderly flight eastward lasted much longer than a week. In the middle of the second week, many civilians joined in the exodus. One Tuesday, July 1, 1941, in the early morning hours, the remaining Soviet government officials fled. My brother fled the same day but returned towards evening because of the confusion of the retreat. It was a veritable "Tower of Babel," a situation in which people did not understand each other's language, and no one had a clear idea of where to go. Trembowla that day resembled a ghost town because those who decided not to flee locked themselves indoors; they feared the anarchy that might erupt from the power vacuum.

I well remember what my neighbor, the Hebrew teacher Abraham Lederman, said to me then: "You see — he turned to me — now there is no government *(bez kolewia)* and everyone fears the outbreak of a riot or a Pogrom although no one, for the time being, is harming us. I wish this situation could last till the end of the war. But my heart tells me that when the Germans come, things will be much worse. We will yet long for the current state of affairs which seems so chaotic."

Much to my regret, he knew of what he was prophesying, for his prophecy was fulfilled. I have recalled, on more than one occasion, his accurate and telling comments throughout the war. He did not live to see the outcome of all his predictions.

Quiet prevailed until the Sabbath, four days later, when the Germans entered our town.

The Entry of the Germans and the Ukrainian Nationalist Pogrom

On Saturday, July 5, 1941, at twelve noon, three motorcycles appeared on the main road. A rumor quickly spread to us on the other side of the Gniezna River that there were already three Jewish victims who had been run over by the German motorcyclists traveling at lightning speed who signaled the arrival of the German Nazi occupation.

We saw no signs of war: neither the thunder of cannon, nor the rumble of tanks, nor even soldiers armed with light weapons. These were only to be seen at certain spots where the wedges (called *klins,* a term set aside for this type of warfare) were fixed. At any rate we moved imperceptibly into the German Nazi occupation. This stage lasted several days, during which there was complete quiet. We did hear that the Ukrainian Nationalists hoped to be bosses, selecting Jews for work. Everyone, of course, hid, especially the men, but a few individuals were grabbed for temporary jobs in the barracks and elsewhere.

On Thursday, July 10, 1941, several people were picked up for work at the barracks, and they didn't return at the end of the day, nor the next day, nor later. Only a few who succeeded in escaping from that inferno lay in hiding and frightened for several days, and no one managed to meet them. One of the survivors was my cousin, Dudye Goldfliess. It was only several days after he returned that we managed to squeeze a few words out of him about that night. It seems that twenty people were slaughtered after being severely tortured. Among them were his younger brother, my cousin Yeshayahu; the three sons of Abraham Briller, the hunchback, who was called little Jew *(Koce Zyed)*; Abba Briller; Moshe Lazarus; my father's cousin, Baruch Weismann, and others.

After this incident, quiet set in. Periodically rumors spread that the Germans were looking for workers, and the men hurried into hiding. Six weeks later — that is, in the beginning of August notices appeared in German announcing that all of the pre-war Polish territory would be incorporated into the Government-General and be subject to its laws. In other words, the territory of occupied Poland would constitute one judicial unit, and the Polish state was henceforth known as the Government-General.

So the Ukrainian Nationalists were to suffer complete disappointment. Their hope for "independence" under German auspices remained unfulfilled. This area, after its conquest from the Russians, was transferred from the Ukraine to which it had been annexed in 1939, back to Poland. Such was the situation of the Polish and Ukrainian populations.

The Jews were not considered part of the local population. Their sole boss was the S.S. and the Gestapo in Tarnopol. The situation of the Jews was different. Besides issuing an order in the first few days of the occupation that required Jews to wear armbands with a Star of David, a curfew was also imposed — no Jew was allowed out of doors at night.

It became clear that the Jews were placed outside the pale of the law, and they were now under the jurisdiction of the Gestapo and the S.S., who appeared as angels of destruction, ordering the establishment of a Jewish council, the Judenrat. Only the head of the council, the "Obmann," was to be the contact between the Gestapo and the Jews. Nobody really knew what the role of the council head entailed. One thing must be made clear: with the arrival of the Germans the ties between localities were severed for Jews. No one knew what was happening in nearby towns. No Jew was permitted to travel without permission, and any traveler might easily disappear. Therefore, we knew nothing about the nature of the institutions being planned by the Germans.

And yet, there were some who understood what was in store for the Jews. Many refused to cooperate with the German authorities and were under no circumstances willing to serve on the council. Among those was my brother. In spite of the many appeals to him, he did not on even a single occasion accept the offer of joining such a council or any of its affiliated institutions. I will discuss the Judenrat in an objective manner, for I took no part in its activities, and I will do so before describing in detail what happened to us under the German occupation.

To this day the Judenrat has a negative image, although that is not a fair assessment in every case. At first, attempts were made to recruit members of the Zionist Council and former members of the Jewish Community Council, but very few of these people agreed to accept the assignments. Eventually, a council consisting of many members of the former community council was appointed. I don't recall the exact composition of the council, and for this I must ask forgiveness of the Almighty because I have forgotten some details over the years. I have no lists from that period and none from earlier periods. I have only my memory to draw upon for recollections of our town's Jews. But I remember the basic facts clearly, and I hope accurately.

The Judenrat and Its Initial Activity

The local council chose the Rabbi's house as its meeting place. The rabbi had no objection and set aside one of his rooms for this purpose. It is quite possible that the members of the local council chose the rabbi's house on the mistaken assumption that what had occurred in the first days of the occupation was the work of the Ukrainian Nationalists and now correct relations would be established with the Germans. Everything affecting Jews would be transmitted through the regular channels including the Jewish council.

But events unfolded quite differently this time (precisely in relation to the German occupiers). We were simply placed outside the fold of the law from the start. We were in every way unprotected, and without the protection of the law it is impossible to speak of regular channels of authority.

After the initial murders on the day the Germans entered and the Pogrom perpetrated by the Ukrainian Nationalists in the barracks, it seemed that the relations with the authorities would somehow stabilize, and we would pass through this awful period.

True, snatching people for forced labor did not stop, but most people tried to find jobs which accorded them immunity from the work gangs, jobs in agriculture or in institutions and plants contributing to the war effort, which was the label the Germans placed on every plant they were in need of. Naturally, the Jews were accepted only as simple workers or in their pre-war specialties — engineers, doctors, technicians, pharmacists, etc. In these places of work they tried to be inconspicuous and to avoid contact with high officials, who were either Germans or *Volksdeutsche,* that is, residents of Western Poland, near the German border, who declared themselves to be German after the outbreak of fighting and volunteered en masse for service with the Nazis.

At the lower levels of administration were the pre-war Polish government officials and even a few Soviet officials who did not have time to flee back into the Soviet Union or did not choose to do so. I must emphasize that the latter group was small, for most Soviet officials fled back into Russia when the Germans advanced.

The Jewish council received its orders directly from the S.S. staff in Tarnopol. All the Jews were under its authority; the local institutions could not intervene for or against the Jews independently. If any Ukrainian dared to undertake an action on his own, and word of this reached the S.S., the Ukrainian would be punished. I remembered cases of Ukrainians who killed or maltreated Jews and were later put on trial and handed stiff sentences.

The German Civil Administration

A civil administration was set up, headed by a military governor, and the police consisted of Germans or *Volksdeutsche.* Aside from carrying out the orders of the governor, who bore the title *Kreishauptmann* (Group Captain), the police undertook their own initiatives, searching

Jewish homes and taking what they saw fit to take.

Once they raided several Jewish homes, stole whatever was in sight, and, in addition, threatened to kill anyone uttering a word in their presence. Our home was one of those raided. They emptied out the wardrobe, taking all of my suits and my brother's suit, and they paid particular attention to removing all the many German books in the bookcase — books like the Brockhaus Encyclopedia, Schiller's and Goethe's writings, etc. In a fit of rage they shouted in German: *"Bei euch verfluchte Juden gibt es deutsche arische Bucher,"* meaning "What are you damn Jews doing with German Aryan literature?" This didn't prevent them, several months later, from using these books to fuel their stoves in the police station, which was set up in Marindorf's large new house, after all the tenants had been expelled, irrespective of their nationality. I know from a reliable witness, my brother, of blessed memory, who went to the Burki slave labor camp, and I, too, after returning from the camp, worked there several times and heated the stoves with these books.

This, in fact, was the work of the Jews: cleaning the rooms and bringing inside stolen items to be used as firewood. These raids, particularly the ones aimed at Jews, who were to live in their homes for more than a year, were the daily fare of the police. Some of the policemen were rotated but others served for the duration of the occupation, including Shklarek, Namislow, and Chrust. One could tell a great deal about their misdeeds, but that would take too long, and I do not want to go into these details.

The "Contribution"

The first decree issuing directly from the Gestapo in Tarnopol ordered the Jews to bring to the Judenrat without delay all their valuables: gold, silver, precious stones, jewelry, furs, and foreign currency. Anyone hiding anything in his home would, if caught, face the death penalty.

The rumor about the "contribution" — so was it called by Jews who remembered the indemnities imposed by the Russian occupation forces during the First World War — struck the Jews like lightning. But they slowly adjusted to the idea, and for a short period fulfilled the quota that was assigned to the Judenrat for collection by a certain date. So were our affairs conducted without further shocks until after the holidays. The High Holy Days of 5702 in the autumn of 1941, and the Sukkos holiday passed relatively peacefully.

There were services in private homes but not in the synagogues, and, as I recall, there was even shofar-blowing. Meanwhile, the German army was advancing deep into European Russia. Kiev had been captured some time before. Kharkov, Leningrad, and Moscow were facing severe sieges. And all the huge plants in the Don lowlands had been conquered. But the Jews in their undue optimism daily envisioned the German defeat. Such was the state of affairs until the end of October 1941.

Recruitment for the Labor Camps
in Stupki and Borki Wielki

During November there was a rumor that a quota of laborers for labor camps in the vicinity of Tarnopol would have to be raised. The Judenrat must have already known. It was, by then, organized and in control of the Jewish population.

The Judenrat issued orders through spokesmen and representatives, who were appointed immediately after its establishment and were called *Ordnungsdienst* (military orderlies). Informally they were known as the Jewish Militia. So on one fine day these messenger policemen went out to distribute special invitations to many individuals who were asked to make an appearance at the Judenrat offices. I was one of those invited. There were more than sixty of us. I don't remember exactly how many of the group came. But I do remember that many of those who did come consulted with a number of the council members in their office — that is, in a room in the rabbi's house — and shortly thereafter these people left, one by one.

Finally twenty-two of us were left in the Judenrat office. In a brief conversation, the group was told by the Judenrat members that it was being sent to a labor camp. Neither the location nor the character of these labor camps were revealed.

I am not certain whether the members of the Judenrat knew exactly where we were being sent. But one thing became apparent after we left. The Judenrat well knew the quota they were expected to fill and perhaps they also knew the general destination. They handled the recruitment in such a way as to be in a position to accept bribes from those who wished to buy their way out of the labor camps. The Judenrat needed the money to meet periodic German demands.

I wish to point out that only the first transport to the labor camps was conducted in an orderly manner. When the conditions in the camp became known through the bearers of the food parcels that the

Germans allowed the local Judenrat to organize for camp prisoners in 1941–42, no one voluntarily came for recruitment to the work camp. People were simply seized by the representatives of the Judenrat, the *Ordnungsdienst*. In these actions, the Ukrainian militia also participated and sometimes agents of the Gestapo as well.

An Orderly Departure for the Camp

I must say that our orderly departure for the camp may well not have taken place in any other community. When we got to the camp, I was told by people from other communities that most of them had been abducted and had not come in an organized fashion. This was true of the hundred already there and of those who came later from the many communities in the Tarnopol district. I remember people from Skalat, Buczacz, Kopyczynce, Borszczow and many other towns in the southern part of the Tarnopol district. Since we had left in an orderly manner, no one attempted to escape en route to Borki Wielki.

There was another advantage to our organized departure. Few communities attended to the needs of their prisoners as did the Trembowla Judenrat, not even communities closer to the camp such as Skalat, Grzymalow, Podwolotsisk, and others. I must note, in praising the Trembowla Judenrat, that almost every week a wagon loaded with food parcels came to the camp. The wagon was sent by the Judenrat with food from the families of prisoners or from other volunteer families.

These parcels enabled us to hold out in the camp despite the dreadful conditions that we found upon arrival. And things got worse as time went on. We, the first inmates, did not suffer as much as the following groups who replaced us and those who later were abducted to fill camp quotas.

Before I tell how I left the camp and what followed, I shall briefly describe the camp in which I spent three whole months. It is worth describing camps of this type, for too little is known about them. I will therefore draw a sketch of this camp in memory of all my brothers who were beaten, tortured, and suffered martyrdom there. I will present it in its everlasting abhorrence for future generations.

The Burki Wielki and Stupki Slave Labor Camps

All the camps in our vicinity in the district of Tarnopol were originally supposed to be labor camps, unlike camps in Poland such as Belzec, Treblinka, and Auschwitz, whose purpose was that of extermination. But when the policy of total destruction was decided upon, these labor camps also liquidated their inmates from the end of 1942 until the middle of 1943.

We left for the camp at the end of November 1941. I think that the Judenrat provided us with wagons for the trip to Tarnopol and from there soldiers — not S.S., Wehrmacht — took us on foot to the Stupki, Burki Wielki camp compound. The two were adjoining camps. The luggage was transported by wagons, and we walked. Throughout the trip the soldiers escorting us told us that we were going to a fine place, a veritable convalescent camp, and that we would not lack a thing, a true earthly paradise.

So did they soothe us with comforting words until we reached the camp. The barbed wire surrounding the camp and the yellow patch displayed in front and on the back of the poor human beings running about the yard in despair terrified us even before we passed through the gate. At that moment we understood that all the soldiers' chatter as they were leading us was typical German deception, camouflage for their despicable actions, which were to be revealed a short time later. The true picture became clear to us as soon as we stood at the threshold of the narrow entry gate, which was surrounded by a spiky barbed wire fence, packed tightly.

At the gate stood German sentries with large thick clubs, raining blows on the backs of the newcomers with wild shouts of *"Los, los!"* ("Let's go, let's go!")

After receiving murderous blows from which some people suffered injuries, we entered the camp and faced elongated huts. There we were told to pick bunk beds arranged in three decks.

At last we were greeted in the huts by human beings as well. These were Jews from Lwow and its environs who were seized in the streets and brought here. They immediately stretched out their hands in supplication and begged for a slice of bread. They hadn't eaten during the few days that they had been here. Of course we shared our food with them.

Several hours later the soldiers who escorted us appeared and, cognizant of how we had been welcomed, brazenly asked us how our reception was. To my question whether this was the paradise they had promised us they replied briefly: "Apparently you didn't behave well, otherwise they wouldn't have welcomed you that way."

I am describing this "welcome" in detail in order to demonstrate that not only the S.S. but also the Wehrmacht soldiers had a hand in Nazi treachery to the same extent as the others. It may well be that there were Germans who were unaware of what was taking place, but most of the German people, and not only the Gestapo and the Nazis, took part in the work of extermination. I will not dwell at length on the work regimen and food in the camp. They are well known from all the stories and works written on the Holocaust, with each situation differing only slightly from the others. The camp commanders and organizers, with their individual characters and whims, were in a position to make a small impact for better or worse on the overall patterns.

Let me just mention a number of events and facts that testify to the attitude of the Germans towards the Jews and not only the Jews but also towards other prisoners and local residents. If one probes into the motives of the Germans in setting up all these camps, one can, I believe, draw the conclusion that these camps were set up for one reason: to exploit the physical strength of the prisoners until it was completely sapped, and they were unable to resist any measures taken against them. The attempt to paralyze all thought and independent initiative was a permanent feature of German conduct during the occupation. This tactic was a factor in the success of their diabolical deeds.

In my opinion there was little of practical value to be gained from the labor of the camp inmates, perhaps nothing at all. This was not their object. Their conduct did not display the characteristic German efficiency which we learned about from our parents: don't waste energy and exploit labor to the hilt. Actually, the sole activity of the camps in our area—Stupki, Burki, Kamionka, Halowotsk, and many others—consisted in changing the gauge of the railroad tracks from the one the Russians had installed when they conquered this part of Poland to the gauge used in all of Western Europe. The workers were also occupied in maintaining the roads going from west to east through which supplies and war materials were sent to the fronts in the depths of Russia.

But the execution of these projects was careless and lacking the effective technical supervision that our parents had come to recognize in pre-World War I German work.

I conceived all of these tasks in terms of the image used by the Polish writer Zeromski in describing the 19th-century Russification of Poland: "*Syzyfowe prace,*" Sisyphean labors, an image familiar to us from Greek mythology: it means pouring water into a bottomless barrel.

And, indeed, on many occasions the previous day's work was ruined by different commandants whose tour of duty began the following day. In fact, much of the dismantling was not completed by the time the Germans turned back in retreat.

Much depended on commanders and supervisors. I remember days when murderous supervisors pounded the workers until they bled. On more than one occasion a single day's toll of the injured reached forty out of one hundred workers. We can assume that these rearguard troops exerted every effort to avoid being sent to the Russian front or the Western front, which was then seemingly quiet.

As time passed and particularly after the decision on the Final Solution had been reached, these camps came to serve another useful purpose: safe assembly points which were escape-proof. Implementing the mass extermination required a minimum of operational forces, and, as I have already mentioned, they simply diminished the victims' power to resist and seek refuge from the Germans' overriding aim — genocide.

As to specific instances of brutality which I witnessed let me just mention one that occurred two days after we arrived. This was late 1941 before the decision on the Final Solution. That day one of the workers had an accident in which his foot was smashed. I believe that he was one of the first men brought to the camp who were from Lwow. They had been starving for several days because no one had organized the kitchen, and there were no food supplies, not even bread. They had been abducted in the streets and came to the camp without a thing. Apparently, as a result of his hunger, the prisoner got dizzy and the injury to his foot occurred.

We all went to work as soon as we arrived. As was customary, the camp commandant and his staff personally went out to see the new arrivals at roll call. Our first commandant was a member of the Wehrmacht. This was so because the camp had previously served as a prisoner-of-war camp for Russian prisoners, and the guards had to be army soldiers and not S.S. personnel. I will never forget the words of the commandment during that roll call. After briefly describing what happened, he said: "You will now be witnesses to what happens when a prisoner is injured and cannot go on working. We," he continued, "recognize two types of people: workers and the dead. Since, after his injury, this prisoner is no longer capable of working — he must die." And in front of us he led the injured man aside and shot him. This was a Wehrmacht officer, not a member of the S.S. or the Gestapo.

I should add a comment on the general abuse of camp prisoners. Every morning before going out to work, the prisoners lined up for a roll call which lasted an hour. There was a check for missing prisoners. If someone ran away, all the remaining inmates were responsible. For such a terrible deed everyone would have to suffer. The punishment could easily end in the death of a number of prisoners, although that didn't happen while I was there.

There was also the possibility of a roll call to search for money, gold, or foreign currency. I was present at one of them.

I don't know what aroused the commandant. At any rate, someone hid several dollars during the roll call and was caught. It would be impossible to describe the beating he received.

Sometimes, there was maltreatment for its own sake, running the prisoners around the camp to wear them out. Clearly, after such maltreatment labor output was very low, but, after all, the Germans weren't interested in efficiency and productivity. Their sole aim was to confuse and break us.

Here is another type of abuse. We were told to stand and were asked different questions. Once a German asked us who spoke Hebrew. I, in my innocence, responded affirmatively. I was immediately taken out of line and showered with sentences in German which I was to translate quickly into Hebrew. I performed satisfactorily. I was not, to my good fortune, tongue-tied; I translated everything quickly. He was surprised, and he returned me to my place in line after dismissing me. But for the next few days he observed me closely during roll call, and when I tripped once while running and was forced to step out of line, he called me over and proclaimed aloud: "Even a Hebrew speaker trips. Be so kind as to remove your coat," and he thrashed me soundly on my behind, a thrashing I felt for several days. From then I fully understood the saying "Silence is Golden," but I was not the only one to be so thrashed. Each time they invented another reason for these whippings.

Earlier I mentioned the treatment of Russian prisoners. While working outside along the tracks, we saw at some distance from the camp a large field with many wooden crosses. After making inquiries — a task that was not easy due to our having no contact with the local residents or outsiders — we learned that, before our arrival, the huts had been put up for prisoners of war from the Far East: Uzbeks, Kirghiz, and other Soviet minority Nationalities.

These prisoners had spent three months in the camp and had starved to death. They came from far away and were unable to make contact with the local population. Even if they had, it would have been to no avail, because no one understood their language.

I was unable to ascertain the exact number of war prisoners who had been confined in the camp, and to this day I have no idea. A rumor claimed that there were more than a thousand. But I can remember vividly the thoughts this discovery evoked in me.

If this was the way the Germans dealt with non-Jewish prisoners of war who, according to international practice were entitled to humane treatment and Red Cross supervision, but who were instead lying under crosses without anyone knowing what had happened to them, how then could we hope to leave the camp alive.

I Am Officially Discharged from the Camp and Return Home

My torment did not last indefinitely. Everything depends on luck, circumstances, and time. Thus, after we spent some time in the camp, our relatives began to complain on our behalf. Why was this group of Jews, which went voluntarily, being made to suffer without respite while other families did not share the burden at all? It seems that the members of the Judenrat decided to rotate prisoners.

Discharge Document from the Labor Camp at Burki Wielki

The camp director who had been receiving parcels from the Judenrat apparently agreed to the proposal. Though I do not know all the details of the negotiations, they bore fruit, and a third of the prisoners were released, without being replaced, after the director received a generous payment under the table.

Some prisoners from Buczacz, too, were released, but I was not included among the third of the prisoners sent home. This fact became known to the members of the Trembowla Judenrat, who, during my stay in the camp, kept in close contact with us by means of the parcels that they sent. My family and the townspeople made a commotion about my continued detention because according to the agreement, I, too, was to have been included among the returnees.

One of the active townspeople, a woman whom the commandant liked, agreed to come to the camp a week later to negotiate the release of another prisoner. And with the assurances she received she did come a week after the first group was released and obtained my legal release, authorized by the camp commandant. He even gave me a discharge document with an S.S. stamp. I have the document to this day.

This activist was Zusia Angel, née Edelman. I used to visit her home regularly because I taught her younger brothers, Munio and Izyo, Hebrew and Judaism. She had been to the camp before because her brother Izyo was also one of my group and was one of those released. She, too, was fortunate to survive and today lives in Australia. She once visited Israel, but I did not meet her. I found out about the visit from our mutual friend, Arola, of blessed memory, only after she left the country.

I am going into this incident in great detail simply to underline the role of blind fate during the Holocaust. How right were our Sages in saying: "Man's feet are his guarantors; they take him wherever he is required to go." Who knows if—had I not been among the first to go to the camp almost voluntarily—I would be writing today about the events in Trembowla. This early stay in the camp saved me in town for a long time thereafter, as my narrative will later make clear. I must stress that I was the last to leave the camp in this manner, without causing grief and harm to others.

After I left the camp the commandant was replaced, and his successor, whose name was Minkus, would agree only to prisoner exchanges but not to unconditional discharges. And, indeed, several people were exchanged not long afterwards, but this was to occur just once because the situation constantly deteriorated until the bitter end. The exchange stopped, but occasionally people were abducted, if not to Burki then to Hlowocek Camp.

My brother was among those carted off to Hlowocek. Miraculously, he left the camp and returned home after coming down with typhus. He was to have been shot, as was the practice in the camp. My brother was saved through the efforts of Yehuda Leisner, a member of the Judenrat, and I shall never forget this kindness of his. My brother did indeed perish later, but he was not shot in a camp because of illness.

After returning home and wandering about without work for several weeks, I began to work in a quarry managed by the Lange firm from Germany and located in the village Zaszczanocie, which was several kilometers from town.

I was not afraid of being forcibly taken to a camp. The rotation system was in effect for half a year, and I had just come back. I was protected since the Judenrat was responsible for the rotation, and they would not select me again. But someone else who returned from the camp said to me: "Be aware that your immunity is not permanent; despite your release, your turn may come up again. And take care not to be abducted." It was true; changes were in the offing. There were rumors of a population transfer which I shall refer to shortly.

The work in the quarry was backbreaking, but it had one advantage. We returned home every day. The work took place without foremen to goad us on. We worked together with several non-Jewish workers whose status differed from ours in the following respects: they received a fair wage, and they were also used to this work, having been quarry workers before the Germans took over the management. I worked there several months until the middle of the summer. I don't remember exactly when I left, but I do remember working in a forest in August, arranging firewood. We would make piles in the forest in units of a cubic meter so that they would dry by autumn. Then, the forest management sold the firewood on behalf of the municipality.

Rumors of a Population Transfer

During the time I worked in the forest there were rumors that several times, at night, trains passed with coaches full of Jews in the direction of Tarnopol, that is, northward. Understandably, Jews began to make inquiries. There was as yet no Jewish Ghetto. Jews continued to live where they had lived in the past. They maintained contact with their Christian neighbors, but the latter, too, did not know what was happening. Some of them said — in the wake of German lies and the widely spread falsehood that Jews were a harmful element — that Jews were being resettled in a center where they would be trained for useful and productive labor.

Yet it was strange that the wailing of babies could be heard coming out of those railway cars, that they were very crowded, and that cattle cars were being used instead of passenger coaches. Rumors increased. They began to unsettle the Jewish population.

No one knew where the coaches were going, but instinctively we understood they meant something worse than abduction to the camps. Word spread — particularly after Mrs. Lampe received a message from her brother, who lived close to Belzec, where a camp had been set up — that no one who entered the camp would ever leave. There, what was known as a "population transfer" was being turned into mass murder.

How? We did not know until after the liberation. Clearly, we heard nothing about places like Auschwitz, Treblinka, Ponar, Sobibor, and others until after the liberation. They were too far away for word to reach us even through our Christian neighbors. But what rumors there were made many of us apprehensive. How could we hide ceaselessly, how could we abandon our little remaining property and leave? How long would things go on like this? There were indeed optimists, who saw a Russian victory in the offing, but most people did not deceive themselves and realized that victory, even if it was to come, was still far off. Obviously, work no longer was a source of interest, and many people went for days at a time to sit in the forests since it was still summer. Even at the end of that summer in 1942, there were clear beautiful days. I continued to work in the forest; so, in any case, I was not at home all day.

There were also other optimists. They had heard about the railroad cars passing through the station, filled with Jews from the towns south of Trembowla as far as the Rumanian border, who were being taken northward to Tarnopol. But they believed that we would somehow be overlooked.

Some said that resistance was the order of the day: "Don't move, pounce and destroy whoever tries to take you." Others were opposed. By resisting we would bring about our complete destruction and lose the chance of salvation that seemed to them quite near.

The debates ended when the order to set aside a special neighborhood for Jews was announced after the Jewish holidays in the fall of 1942. Its boundaries were the middle of Sobieski Street, from Itzi Briller's house until the Kepfel house, and all of Podzamcze and the surrounding area. All the non-Jewish residents were to be moved to the other side of the city beyond the river.

The Jewish residents of the towns of Strusow, Janow and Budzanow, which were part of the Trembowla district were ordered to move to this neighborhood. In Strusow there had already been an "Action" even before Jews were sealed off in Ghettos. Strusow was not unique in this regard. All the villages in the district were subject to the same edict which forced Jews out, although few of them remained in the villages. When the Germans came, many Jews were killed, and others fled in fear of the Ukrainians. During that period chaos prevailed and Jews had no legal protection.

The Desecration of the Cemetery and Removal of the Tombstones

The rumors intensified, but in town people went about their business. Demands for workers continued to be made of the Judenrat. One day there was an emergency call for workers. After the group assembled, they were taken to the cemetery and ordered to remove the tombstones and grind them into gravel for roadpaving. And the gravestones were to be used to pave the sidewalks. Even after the liberation one could find many places in which the paving stones were cemetery gravestones with large Hebrew lettering.

This vandalous act was trivial in comparison with the many brutal deeds committed by the Germans and, yet, it left the Jewish community in a state of grief. I can recall my state of deep depression on the day the desecration of the cemetery began. If the Germans would not leave a trace of the dead, what would they do with the living? This order together with the rumors of population transfers flung me into real despair. Our Christian neighbors, too, saw the Jewish population as a group of condemned prisoners waiting for the execution of their sentence, with no possibility of reprieve. They said this on more than one occasion in conversation with their Jewish friends and acquaintances.

Meanwhile we had to comply with the order to create a Ghetto in the limited area which I described earlier, and we had to include the Jewish population of the three towns, Janow, Strusow, and Budzanow. Obviously, many people would have to be squeezed into a single room because this small area could barely contain the Jewish population of Trembowla alone. And the evacuees from the three smaller towns doubled the population.

Ten people on an average would have to be assigned to every small room and double-deckers had to be placed in many rooms. But what was the saying? "We stand cramped, but bend down easily." The conditions didn't dampen our spirits; they were not our main concern. What worried us was the ultimate aim of the evacuation. Common sense suggested that there could be only one aim: making life easier for those involved in the terrible work of destruction.

I shall never forget the picture of the Jews from Janow, Budzanow, and Strusow pulling all their belongings in wagons harnessed to half-dead horses, which had been rented from Gentiles. The Jews were plodding along, asking for addresses of friends and acquaintances. The Judenrat was working at full steam to try to keep order and ensure that no one would sleep in the streets because he was unable to find his assigned lodgings.

I have read many books on the Holocaust and Nazi atrocities, but I have yet to find descriptions of these scenes which were the lot of many cities and towns in Poland. Nor have I heard of painters commemorating these scenes.

I remember talking to these Jews because I was not busy moving.

I lived in the Kepfel houses, which fell within the boundaries of the Jewish district in Trembowla until the final liquidation. We did somehow manage — sitting quietly, packed together — waiting for the bitter end.

The First "Action": November 5, 1942

The fateful day made its inevitable but slow approach. Every day in the conditions of the Ghetto was longer than a day in normal times, filled with work and regular activities. Everyone, from his own niche, scanned the territory for a hiding place in case we were caught inside our houses when Gestapo thugs suddenly surrounded the district and sealed it off for an "Action." Where could we hide and remain undetected by a Nazi search party?

Even before we had put our remaining possessions in place, the feverish activity of building bunkers began. This was the name given to the hiding places which were tunnels lying beneath the cellars in every house. Their entrances were carefully camouflaged. Thousands of cubic meters of earth were removed and carted far away so that nothing would suggest the digging of tunnels in the immediate vicinity of a house.

Whole sections of attics were closed off in such a way that one could not distinguish between a hiding place and the end of a house. Nights were filled with sleepless activity. We knew from experience that the Germans would not dare to enter the cellars and search for hidden, camouflaged tunnels. And not all the Ukrainians dared to do this. If a hiding place remained undetected at the end of an "Action," the group in hiding could emerge and continue living in the house. After every "Action" the routines of Ghetto life were reestablished. We would go up, get on with our lives, and wait for the next "Action." But in the duration we might be saved.

In the Kepfel houses too, tunnels such as these were dug out. But the tunnel right below our apartment was camouflaged extraordinarily well and was not detected even after we left the house and the area was declared *Judenrein*. I saw it after the liberation when I returned with a group of people who were looking for gold that they had buried in the cellars. They did not, in fact, find the gold, but the bunkers farther on were still camouflaged and shut tight.

Our bunker was meant to contain thirty people at most, but during the Second "Action," which happened suddenly, more than fifty of us were saved in the bunker. More about this a bit later.

I believe that our town was one of the last in the Tarnopol district to be subjected to a "population transfer." It took place as late as November 5, 1942. I wasn't in town when this "Action" took place, and the bunker I described had not yet been prepared. We dug tunnels between the First and Second "Actions." Despite the fact that work in the forest had long since stopped, I, in my customary manner, used to go out with Meir, the son of my teacher Pinchas Arak, not in the morning but rather towards evening, to sleep in the forest. We went there as if we were continuing our work in the forest. I can remember what my mother said to me towards evening on November 4, 1942. My mother, may God avenge her, escorted me part of the way. I did not see her after that.

I must mention that just that day a farmer met us on the road as we reached the Castle, which was on the way to our work in the forest. Apparently, this farmer heard or knew something about the "Action" and asked where we were going now that everyone was on their way home from work. I don't remember our exact answer. I think we said that we were in fact, returning home from work, but we had lost our way. He told us that we were going in the opposite direction. But he didn't bother us. We continued into the forest, and he went towards town. After a horrible night spent wandering around, we heard at dawn the crack of gunfire and explosions in the distance, in the direction of our town. We realized that we had managed to escape from the inferno. We stayed in the forest all day, and we said, to the few Gentiles we met, that we had come to finish arranging the firewood.

That is how we spent the whole day and the following night. Only on the next day, Friday morning, did we dare approach the Castle on our way home. The Gentiles we passed knew everything that had taken place the previous day. They relayed to us the terrible news that there had been an "Action" in the city the day before. Many people had been brought to the train and were then sent away.

When I came home I met my brother, and he told me what had happened. They took away all the Jews that they found in the houses and bunkers and led them to the square near the synagogue, facing the kiosk of Mendele Fogelman's family. These Jews were forced to sit on the ground. Armed guards, some Ukrainian and others German, were positioned near them. Our relative, Dr. Stern, the head of the Jewish National Fund in town for many years and, at the time of the "Action" a member of the Judenrat, did not obey the order to sit down and was shot on the spot. The same happened to a number of other people who disobeyed the guards' orders and stood up. And they also shot those who refused to leave their houses.

It was estimated that more than twenty people were killed before everyone was brought to the assembly point. One of them was Abraham Shenhaut from the Husyatin prayer house, who was called Abraham Zishyes. They finished assembling at nightfall.

Fifteen hundred people were seized that day and brought to the square. From there they were taken to the train station and loaded onto cattle cars for transport to a destination unknown to them — to Belzec.

My brother told me more. A bunker in an attic was discovered because of a child's wailing behind the wall. Everyone hiding in that bunker was taken out. My brother was saved by a bribe of several dollars that he took out of his knapsack and gave to a guard who let him slip away from the group. Since evening was drawing near, he stayed there, and no one else approached that spot. He was thus the only survivor of the group in the attic, which included my mother, my Aunt Hannah, and her whole family. Her grandson, Kohut, the son of Ita, was the baby whose crying gave the bunker away. As I have said, the "Action" took place on Thursday and I came back on Friday. I remember the Sabbath after the "Action." I could think only of the event we had just lived through. I thought about the way in which fifteen hundred residents of the Jewish quarter were sliced off as if this had been done with a sharp knife. And this "Action" occurred only several days after the camps had been set up to facilitate the implementation of the enemy's monstrous aim — genocide!

Life Returns to "Normal" After the First "Action"

Life, it seems, is stronger than even a terrible "Action," which shakes one to the core and induces extreme despair and indifference. A few days later the survivors began to snap out of the dreadful despair into which they had sunk. But many stopped working and began to plan. Where was there a hiding place which would provide safety until help arrived? Living to see our salvation was the common wish in all our hearts.

Optimists saw in the siege of Stalingrad, which was then beginning, the victory at the gates of the town. Others, who weren't so optimistic, fully understood that until we could be rescued, if at all, this demon would manage to destroy the sorrowful worn-down remnants of our people who were lacking in willpower, without determination, panic-stricken, unable to plan any course of action.

Despite the loss of one-third of the population, the crowding was making us miserable, for the size of the Jewish *district* had been reduced accordingly. All of the side streets from Itzi Briller's house up to Kepfel's house were placed outside the Ghetto, which now consisted of a half of Sobieski Street.

A typhus epidemic struck the town, and it claimed victims daily. A quarantined area in the house of Mr. Miller, a Christian teacher, was turned into a hospital. In the pre-war period its two rooms had been part of the municipal school. But this makeshift hospital did not do much good.

I resumed working in the stone quarry administered by the Fritz Lange firm. I had a pass allowing me to go out of the Jewish quarter and leave the city on my way to work. Although the Jewish quarter was not a sealed-off Ghetto, once it came into being we could not freely move about the city without a pass.

Typhus struck our house, too. My mother's cousin Bluma and her husband Leibish Weiser fell ill and died. And my Aunt Chana, my mother's sister, also died of typhus. Our Aunt Etye recovered from the illness. And finally I, too, became infected with typhus, but I began to recover. All winter we worked feverishly to build and conceal a bunker. I have already mentioned the help of Joseph Chaikin, who was living in our house. He came to us with the evacuees from Strusow. The other members of his family had perished in the "Action" at Strusow; he was now alone.

It was a very difficult winter and cold and illness were everywhere. But these maladies did not crush us. Most of the remaining population withstood the hardships. But the Second "Action," on April 7, 1943, in which most of the Jewish quarter perished, took us by surprise.

The Second "Action"

In the course of the Second "Action," not only the Jewish population was destroyed but also its illusions. In my eulogy for our town's martyrs on the thirty-fifth anniversary of the Second "Action" I said that it was this "Action," bringing to light the German system of deceit, which shattered all our illusions. We saw that it was only a code for the word "destruction" (*Vernichtung*), which they did not wish to proclaim before the whole world. We saw that the Germans' sole aim was our physical annihilation, since events were pressing down upon them, and they no longer had time for niceties. In addition, they wanted to save the manpower they were assigning to the transports and inside the concentration camps.

The cynicism of this demonic people grew with its appetite for murder. Why use workers when the victims themselves could prepare their graves? To this end some Jews were taken to dig pits outside the city. No one knew the purpose of these pits. On more than one occasion we were forced to do torturous work whose purpose was not made clear.

In our case the place was Plebanowka, a village two kilometers from town. A number of houses on the outskirts of town merged with those of the village. At five in the morning before dawn, I was awakened, as if by a thunderbolt, with the news that the Germans and their Ukrainian helpers had surrounded the Jewish quarter and were sealing it off. It was even impossible to escape from our home in the Kepfel house, which was near the edge of town and quite close to the forest.

Our only refuge was the bunker that we had prepared during the winter. Of all the bunkers in the Kepfel houses, which contained many tenants, only those who hid in ours were saved from the Second "Action." All the other bunkers were discovered, and the people hiding in them were taken to the assembly point. This time it was the market square. I, of course, wasn't there, but witnesses told me that the people were forced to take off their upper garments and run, half-naked, to pits prepared several days earlier. They were lined up in rows at the edge of the pit and shot. The firing squads did not even bother to check whether they had struck their victims or not, so the living and the dead fell on top of each other. There were even more people who had not been injured. They lay silently among the mass of bodies until nightfall, and then they managed to crawl their way out and escape.

I don't know how many people, if any, survived this slaughter and lived to the end of the war. But there were such survivors from similar "Actions" in the Tarnopol district. They were widespread in our area, but I am not familiar with the situation in other districts of the Government-General.

I had not yet completely recovered from my bout of typhus. It was several days after the crisis, but I summoned up all my strength and went down into the bunker. It was meant to hold thirty people, but my guess is that about sixty people squeezed in. I cannot recall the exact number. My friend Joseph Chaikin, who energetically helped to dig the bunker had made sure that everyone who came to us entered the bunker, but he himself remained outside. My brother did not notice that he hadn't entered, nor did we notice. He stayed at the entrance to the cellar crouching in a niche in the corner, but after several searches he was discovered, and so he perished with all the other martyrs of the Second "Action."

I was miraculously saved in this "Action," which was the only one in which I hid in a bunker; I was still very weak from typhus. Needless to say, I had difficulty breathing in the congestion, but I held out. When it got dark, the sounds of soldiers' boots, which rang in our ears all day as they marched back and forth, ceased.

I thought that the "Action" was surely over although there was no sure sign. The camouflaged entrance to the bunker was opened, and I went out—at my own risk. I reached the point immediately above the bunker, which lay under the apartment of our neighbor, Jonah Ochs. We had begun to dig the bunker under the cellar beneath our apartment. The area beneath his apartment lay just ahead, and it became the core of the tuennel. As I came out, an armed Ukrainian policeman stood before me. He had apparently come to loot the houses or was ordered to make a final search at the end of the "Action." He immediately asked me where I was coming from, and how I had gotten here, but he didn't lower his rifle or cock the trigger. He told me to go away quickly, and so I was again miraculously saved.

I know of many who died this way. Despite having been in a safe hiding place during the "Action," they came out too early and were led away to be killed. I remember that on the day following this "Action" I went outside with Mrs. Sommerstein from Janow, the mother of Mr. Frankel, who now lives in Haifa (he was one of the refugees in Russia). We looked around. It was a clear spring day. We talked and came to the conclusion that there was no way out. Sooner or later this would be our fate too. She was a clever woman, sharp and energetic in business, more so than her husband. I can well remember her three daughters, Hadas, Becha, and Zosia, who were all saved with us but later perished in the forest on the way to their town Janow, after it had been declared *Judenrein.*

10

A Shelter in the Forest

Israel Goldfliess

After the Second "Action" we understood that there was no escape for us in town. The forest was our only hope of refuge. Whoever survived this "Action" sought a hiding place with Gentile acquaintances. Those who had no Gentile acquaintances — or those who didn't trust their acquaintances, suspecting that the latter would eventually turn them over to the Germans — went to the forest outside town. Most people had stopped working by now although the abductions for work in the labor camps continued.

Before the Second "Action," a new camp was set up in Tarnopol. Its commandant was a Nazi named Rockita. He promised us that work in this camp would go on and that we would be protected. There were some Jews who had earlier sought refuge in his camp, and after the Second "Action" others followed.

We decided to go to the forest. With the help of a Gentile acquaintance, Strylecki, we found a remote, well-hidden spot. We decided to dig a camouflaged bunker for ourselves and wait there until we were rescued. As long as it was still possible we would occasionally go to town, and after the area would be declared *Judenrein* this farmer would serve as a middleman and procure food for us from town.

Since May 1943 was approaching, we could remain out-of-doors until autumn. By then we might be rescued. Now after the defeat of the German army at Stalingrad, the prospect of surviving grew, and there was already a basis for hope that, by autumn, the war would end.

My brother and I argued. I maintained that even if we were to hold out in the forest until autumn, there was no way for us to get food. Before then we would die of starvation and not live to see the liberation. But my brother maintained that if Hitler did not kill us by autumn, then neither would starvation. This was the simplest problem. Throughout the summer we could live on what could be collected in the fields at night and plucked from trees; no one would interfere. The farmers locked themselves in at night and would not risk going out.

He was right. True, we suffered. We lived on bread and water, but none of us died of hunger. Some probably did, because, according to an estimate I made after the liberation, when our town was declared *Judenrein* more than two hundred people fled to the forest but few of them survived.

There were indeed sworn optimists who believed that after the Stalingrad debacle most of the surviving Jews would live to see the complete downfall of Hitler and his army. But many of us understood that Stalingrad was quite far away, and it would take a long time until the enemy retreated from our region; salvation was nowhere near. The enemy would still manage to wipe us out before then. I was one of the sworn pessimists, but I did not believe that we would spend the coming winter in the forest; help would surely arrive before winter. But even my pessimistic view proved to be an underestimation of the length of our ordeal.

A full year was to pass from the surrender of the German army at Stalingrad until the German retreat from our area. Their withdrawal was very slow, particularly from the viewpoint of the few survivors, huddling in the forest bunkers or hiding with Gentiles. That year seemed endless; every day was an eternity.

But let us return to our chronological account of events. We followed our plan. As soon as Passover ended we moved to the forest, to the bunker that we had already prepared. We took enough supplies to last us for some time. Now and then we went to town for bread and other items such as matches and salt.

Once we went to sleep in our house, and, precisely on that night, people were seized for the labor camps. We were almost caught. We managed to hide in our bunker which had been undetected during the Second "Action." We then decided not to return to town at all. We kept in contact by means of the farmer Strylecki and our cousin Esther, who was supposed to join us. Things remained this way until June 3, 1943, when the last "Action" took place.

We did not know much about what was happening in town after we left. Our cousin Esther remembers that, by chance, my brother was in town that day, and they both got back to us in the forest with the help of our contact, Strylecki.

On June 3rd, we once again heard the sound of gunfire early

in the morning. This time we were deeper in the woods than during the First "Action." The shooting didn't last long. We received precise details from my cousin, who managed to reach us with her little sister. Her parents remained in their home but did not perish together with the five hundred people who were rounded up and brought, as before, to Plebanowka. But this "Action" wasn't yet over, for two days later, that is, on June 5, 1943 Trembowla was declared *Judenrein*: any Jew found anywhere was to be immediately handed over to the German police to be executed. This is how the Trembowla Jewry was finally liquidated.

In The Forests of Trembowla, Krowinka, Strusow, and Slobodka

We were in the forest from the beginning of May 1943 until December 12, 1943 — the day my brother perished — a total of more than seven months. I cannot describe the flight from town to forest as a move "from the frying pan to the fire," but neither can I describe it as a step into "wide open spaces." In the forest as in the city we were frightened by the sound of a falling leaf. We were without weapons, and defenseless. We could not purchase arms. We didn't even know where to acquire them, and we had no means to do so.

As I mentioned before, I, in my deep pessimism, expressed the opinion in all our debates that even if the Germans did not get their hands on us, we would starve to death. We had no money for purchasing food from the Gentiles even if they were prepared to supply it. My brother held a different opinion. Whatever happened, we would not starve to death. But we could not materialize our dreams of joining the partisans. Our region had few forests and there weren't many partisans.

True, as the front moved westward, the Soviet army landed a group of partisans nearby, but our group did not know about this. I only became aware of these partisans recently, in the course of reading memorial books which were published by people from the localities in our area.

I do not wish to depict the period spent in the forest, which constituted almost a quarter of the time I lived under Nazi occupation, in the same detail I devoted to the previous phase, to Trembowla before the town was declared *Judenrein*. My experiences in the forest were more personal, and they do not deal with Nazi rule, a description of which was my purpose in writing these recollections on the Holocaust. The story of my rescue is similar to that of other individuals or groups who were saved. But I do wish to say something about the attitudes of Gentile neighbors and also include some general comments on German activities. And I particularly wish to commemorate a Ukrainian family, the Jackiw's of Trembowla, true Righteous Gentiles, who were so few in number during the Holocaust. This family saved almost ten Jews through its own initiative, without asking for remuneration or a reward for their deeds. But quite understandably they have been receiving their just due since the liberation.

They took maximal risks. If the neighbors had found out, someone might have informed on them to the German authorities, and they, too, could have been executed if caught harboring Jews. We were with them for only three months, but they kept the family of our neighbor, the teacher of religion Rosenberg, in a hiding place in their home for an entire year, and it is quite impossible to overlook such acts of heroism and self-sacrifice.

As I pointed out, we built with the help of farmer Strylecki a camouflaged bunker in the forest, which we first used before Passover. Another bunker was dug out close to us. We didn't know anything about it at that stage, but after Trembowla was declared *Judenrein,* we sensed that there were other Jews in the vicinity. We only found out about this other bunker after it was destroyed.

To this day I don't know whether it was liquidated because the Gentile Strylecki informed on us, and the Germans were in fact looking for our bunker and mistakenly stumbled upon the other one; or because other farmers told the Germans after Trembowla became *Judenrein* that many Jews were roaming about the forests. (Strylecki, our contact, was said to have served two masters, and when the Soviets returned, he was immediately arrested. But my cousin Esther Shweiger [Stern] testified on his behalf.)

It was true, according to my estimate, that one hundred and fifty people sought refuge in the forest after managing to survive the Third "Action" on June 3, 1943. They were no longer able to stay in town because on the fifth of June, it was declared *Judenrein.* Any Jew found alive was to be turned over to the German police, who would kill him. (We must bear in mind that the local population was forbidden to kill the Jews, since anyone found with weapons was liable to execution.)

The raid on the nearby bunker occurred on a Sabbath several weeks after Trembowla was declared *Judenrein.* We heard shouting and gunshots at close range. I do not recall whether we left our bunker and hid under some trees in the forests or remained there until the noise stopped, or whether some left the bunker and some remained. In any event, the scare lasted several hours until there was silence. At night we went out to see what had happened. I believe that my pupil Isaac Staub, who survived the onslaught on the other bunker, came to us and provided all the details. He was, not surprisingly, very depressed and in a desperate mood. In the other bunker a large portion of his family perished, his brothers and sisters, who had survived all the "Actions" and also an aunt who came to them from the town of Yegolnice during the occupation. He told us that his aunt had kept several hundred dollars well-hidden in the clothes she was wearing. He refused to go back alone, so I volunteered to go. We took candles and matches.

I don't recall whether Staub himself went to the bunker with me or someone else escorted me. I do remember going down into the bunker alone. I found all the corpses killed by the bullets the German fired into the bunker (they didn't dare go inside themselves). I went from deceased to deceased. I knew practically all of them, and I particularly recall having come across Nachum Shecter, the watchmaker. It was a while before I found my aunt's corpse; I hardly knew her. She had not been a resident of our town. I looked for the money in her clothes for some time but found nothing. Then it dawned on me that I ought to check underneath the belt around her waist and I felt what seemed like rustling paper. I took the belt off, and along its edges I found one hundred dollars in several notes sewn into a rag. Afterwards I gave the money to Isaac Staub, and he handed me ten dollars for my efforts.

I must admit that after the liberation I constantly mused over my strict observance of the inheritance laws, about giving all the money to the relative who, I believed, deserved it.

During this period, we continued living in the forest. For a period of time our contact Strylecki brought us bread in return for the money which we gave him, but he never found us a bunker. We wandered around without a bunker of our own for a month or more.

During that interval we were attacked, premeditatedly or otherwise, by either Banderovtsi, Ukrainian Nationalists, or plain robbers; we didn't know how they found us. They conducted searches, but when they found nothing of value, they left us unharmed, although they did have weapons. They came again a week or two later and conducted another search. This time they found a whole loaf of bread which had been brought to us from the city just that day. It made their blood curdle, and they beat us viciously in order to make us tell them where we had hidden our treasures of gold or silver. They claimed that on the previous occasion they found only small thin slices of bread, and, therefore, they thought that merciful peasants whom we knew must have given us scraps, but no peasant would give us loaves of bread for nothing, and certainly not during wartime. So they now assumed that we were paying for the bread in gold, and they insisted that we give them the gold. They shouted, became enraged, and took my eyeglasses from me. But in the end they let us go and went away.

We saw that a miracle had again saved us, but if we continued to stay where we were, these people would come again and again and eventually kill us. So we decided to move to another part of the forest. There we were safe from their harassment.

We stayed in the shadows during the day and hid at night. We gathered twigs and lit a fire to boil water. Once a day we ate a slice of bread that did not weigh more than 200 grams. We continued doing this for several weeks. At night we also picked stalks of wheat and corn which were already ripe in the month of June. We took out the kernels, boiled them in water for several hours, and ate them as if they were a delicacy. The first potatoes were coming out of the ground at the beginning of July, and we picked them too, at night, from fields at the edge of the forest. Fruit was also ripening, particularly apples. In our region there were many varieties of apples which ripened at different times. We prepared a large stockpile of them.

I remember that during those few weeks it rained for one entire week. I believe that one of those days was the fast day on the seventeenth of June. We couldn't light a fire because the matches were all wet. We lay there, soaked to the skin, and kept our loaf of bread from getting wet, in whatever way possible. The slice of bread was an essential element of our diet.

But our stay out-of-doors came to an end in its turn. One day at the end of the month of July my brother saw someone observing us from a distance. We were apprehensive and discussed the matter for several days. We didn't know what to expect, but we did not leave the area. Several days later—I remember that it was on a Sabbath afternoon—we suddenly heard gunshots. We were exposed in a forest clearing. We couldn't tell from which direction the shots were coming, and since the Ukrainian bandits had stolen my glasses, I couldn't make anyone out from a distance. I got up and began to run aimlessly. We all ran—I, my brother, my cousin Esther and her sister Bronya. Everyone ran off in a different direction. I ran until the echo of the gunfire tapered off. I found a safe spot in a thicket and lay there until nightfall. I fell asleep.

The next morning I got up to look for my brother and cousins, and as I was picking myself up off the ground, I felt a dull pain in my shoulder. In the excitement earlier I hadn't felt anything. I touched my shoulder and realized that the coat was wet. I took it off and saw that the upper part of the sleeve was full of blood. There was a wound in my shoulder from a bullet that had made a deep scratch in it. Obviously I had nothing with which to bandage my wound. It bled for some time and then it healed by itself. I still have a small scar there to this day.

I returned the next morning to where we had been sitting the day before, and I did find my brother safe and sound, but Esther's sister Bronya, was lying there lifeless. She had been struck down by bullets. Esther was nowhere in sight, and we did not see a body, so we assumed that she had survived the attack. We didn't know what to do or where to look. We kept hidden a supply of apples that we picked at night in some small orchards. We were able to pick them at night without much danger because no farmer dared to go out and see what was happening in his orchard, despite his dogs barking. During wartime an outing at night could prove costly. It wasn't worth risking one's life for apples.

On the fourth day we were reunited with my cousin Esther. Our Gentile contact Strylecki brought her to us. She had lost her way while fleeing from the gunfire and ended up at the edge of the forest. Unwittingly, quite remarkably, miraculously she found herself at the house of our former contact. He then brought her back to us in the forest. So, when he was arrested by the Soviets, after the liberation, Esther testified on his behalf, after having been the beneficiary of so much help from him. He really did save her and brought her back to us, and he did not inform on us. We have no way of verifying what others say. . . . To our joy, we were finally reunited with our cousin, but it was mixed with sorrow, for we had lost Bronya, Esther's sister.

After a brief discussion we agreed that there was no purpose in staying where we were. We found out from someone — it may have been information that Esther relayed to us from Strylecki — that Isaac Staub and our cousin on our father's side, Bronia Kelman, who had survived the massacre at the neighboring bunker, were now in the forest in the vicinity of Zelawia Slobodka and were not suffering from any harassment. We decided to send someone at night to find traces of them in the forest.

We solved the problem of procuring food in a manner which I suggested. We had a gold watch that had belonged to my aunt Chaye, the wife of my Uncle Leib Goldfliess, and a number of other valuables that we managed to save. Needless to say, we didn't keep them on us; they were buried in the ground not far from our first bunker in the forest. We decided to take them out little by little and sell them one at a time, as the need arose, while leaving the remainder buried.

It turned out that a number of other people perished during the shooting that injured me and killed my cousin at the end of July. Among them there were members of the Brust family who had been hiding in the forest. Once they passed not far from us at night, loaded with sacks of flour which they were bringing from town. It dawned upon me that they must be getting all this with the help of their neighbor, the blacksmith. His smithy was located not far from Pokrowka Hill, and his house lay in the small orchards at the edge of the forest.

We had to go to his house at night and notify him that the entire Brust family had perished. Perhaps he would consent to sell the gold watch and buy us food with the money he received for it. We would come for our food at night. I argued that we ought to try and speak with them. I said simply that the Brusts were not relatives of Jackiw the blacksmith, just good neighbors. If he were willing to do this for neighbors, he might not refuse us, as well. We only wanted him to buy and sell for us. They were known to be a good and honest family and Father, of blessed memory, had had business dealings with him, too. He fixed wagons and shod horses when Father came to supply gravel for the roads.

I said that I could not go because I did not know the paths and might lose my bearings. "You go!" My brother and cousin consented. One night they went and met with success: the Jackiw family agreed to provide us with food in exchange for the money or valuables that we would give them. It was clear that the Jackiws could not supply us food for nothing. They were not rich.

This is how we lived during the months of November and December 1943, and January 1944, a cohesive group of fifteen people. I, my brother, and my cousin Esther formed one trio. Staub, his relative from Warsaw, Elimelech Zilberstein, and my cousin Bronia Kelman formed a second trio; the family of Yoske Drimmer, including his wife, his sister, and his sister-in-law constituted a foursome. I don't remember the others.

Each group obtained food on its own. We sat hidden beneath

the trees all day. No one at all visited this section of the forest. We heard the voices of village youths from a distance, moving their cattle back from pasture in the stubble fields; it was already autumn. To our good fortune, after a very rainy summer came a completely dry fall. Once a week we sneaked over to the Jackiws. We continued eating our meager bread. We had enough water from the springs in the forest; there was no need for rationing. Once, between Rosh Hashona and Yom Kippur (the Jewish New Year's Day and Day of Atonement), we stealthily returned to our first hiding place, the bunker, in order to take out the valuables we had hidden nearby. And we did find all of them, untouched. Time passed uneventfully.

I had a prayer book in my possession. I could not put on my Tfillin (phylacteries) because the Ukrainian bandits had removed all the leather straps, thereby rendering the Tfillin useless. I devoted considerable time to prayer and to reciting Psalms. I also had a one-volume copy of *Ein Yaakov* (a collection of Midrashic literature), which my friend Yosef Chaikin had brought to our home. I took this book to the forest but did not manage to spend much time studying it. I had no patience; I was preoccupied. Winter was on our doorstep, and, according to Jackiw, who kept us abreast of all the news, in addition to supplying us with food, the Russians were indeed getting closer; the Germans were retreating on all the eastern fronts, but the withdrawal was very slow and might last all winter.

How could we hold out? My brother was more sensitive and delicate than I. I had boots, but his light shoes were worn out, so I gave him my boots. I wrapped my feet in rags and lay in one spot without moving about too much. But we did not have adequate upper garments, and what we wore was in tatters.

Now, as I write this down, it seems that all our efforts were superhuman. A description today cannot do justice to the reality of yesterday. No one can imagine conditions in which people live in the same clothes day and night for almost an entire year without even a change of underwear or a clean shirt. We did not manage to bathe in the forest, with the possible exception of one or two occasions in the early part of our stay there. Thereafter, there were no opportunities. Lice and worms literally ate us alive. We sat for days on end in the summer removing lice from our garments, but to no avail. The next day they were full of the vermin.

In such circumstances it is extremely difficult to maintain human dignity and not go out of one's mind. I am not speaking of the indifference and despair into which one sinks helplessly. There were many people who were unable to survive in the forests. They died of their straitened circumstances and not from an enemy bullet. Spiritual heroism of a very high degree was necessary. Only very few were able to withstand this difficult trial.

After much deliberation we decided to consult with the Jackiws. Our plan called for two women in our group to hide in the Jackiw household—either in some attic or in the barn—and for the rest of us to remain in the forest and hope that we could hold out.

My brother and cousin went to him that week and proposed our plan. And the wonder came to pass. The Jackiws agreed, and the next time we had to contact them the women were to go along and remain in hiding there until the liberation which was drawing near.

But fate determined otherwise. On December 12, 1943, we got up in the morning and heard noise and movement in the forest. It was a bitter cold but dry day. To our good fortune not only had rain not fallen that autumn but it had also not yet snowed that winter, which was quite exceptional. December usually saw a large snowfall. The days were the shortest days of the year, but the sky was bright all the time.

What was the reason for the movement in the forest that day? To this day I do not know for certain. Some of us thought that the Germans were looking for a Soviet plane that had been shot down or that was planning to land in the vicinity. Others felt that the Germans were out hunting. There is also the possibility that they were looking for organized bandits, Banderovtsi, or Ukrainian partisans who roamed the forest. At any rate, it is almost certain that they weren't looking for Jews, because six months had passed since the town was declared *Judenrein* and so few of us had survived. They did not know of our existence in the forest. They must have been quite sure by now that there were no traces of Jews in the forest.

I remember that precisely the night before we had paid our regular visit to the Jackiws in order to pick up our supply of food, and on that very visit they promised to provide shelter for the women. They also informed us that liberation was close at hand. So, in the morning we got up and wished each other *"Le'chaim"* ("To life!") with a glass of water or some other drink that was brought from town to celebrate the departure of the women from the forest. Before we had time to enjoy the good news, the non-stop clatter of gunfire rang out. Frightened, we scattered off to whatever hiding place we could find. I, alone, stayed where I was because I had no boots; I wrapped rags around my feet and lay on the ground. I was in complete despair and apathetic, and I thought to myself that it made no difference where a bullet caught up with me. Salvation was indeed close, but I apparently wasn't worthy of seeing it with my own eyes. So I decided not to move, but my instinct for survival overpowered me, and at the last moment I picked myself up and began to run. I caught up with my brother and quickly passed him. I told him to run along with me because the sound of gunfire was coming from the opposite direction; my hearing was much more acute than his. I continued running without taking notice, from the start, of whether he was near me or not. A short while later the sound of gunfire weakened and finally subsided.

After I'd been sitting motionless for two hours, the sun began to set in the west on this short day and I retraced my steps back to the place where we had been sitting. I met one member of our group, and we continued walking together. We approached our previous spot and before me lay a lifeless corpse. It was the body of my brother. Apparently, he had been struck by a stray bullet shot by the marksmen, who were aiming in every direction. I don't know how it happened, to this day. At nightfall the entire group returned to that spot. Only two were missing: my brother and Isaac Staub from the second group. Someone may also have been missing from the Drimmer group; I don't remember now. The Drimmer group perished several days before the liberation.

That night the cold intensified, and the temperature dropped to more than ten degrees below zero. We stood there, desperate, not knowing what to do. Finally, we made a decision! Since the two people who had been killed were members of our group, which had been reduced in size from six to four, we had no other option but to go to Jackiw and tell him what happened. He had promised to take the women into his home anyway. There were only two men left: Elimelech Zilberstein from Warsaw and I. If he were willing to take us, we would stay there; if not, we could return to the forest that same night. Perhaps after all that had happened he might take us in as well.

We spread out to look for Staub's body. We wanted to know what had happened to him. Maybe he was wounded and could not move. It took us a long time because darkness was setting in. We finally found him dead, but we could not bury the victims because we did not have a shovel, and the cold was becoming so fierce that it was quite difficult to move earth without the proper tools. So, after discussions which lasted several hours and in tears and pain over the victims, we left the forest before midnight, and the four of us went in the direction of Jackiw's house.

At midnight we arrived there. The women knocked and entered according to a pre-arranged signal, and we stayed outside for some time. After a brief conversation they came out again and said that the family had agreed to let us stay with them, and they were setting aside a section of the attic in the barn as a hiding place for all of us. The very spot that they had prepared for the women was large enough for all of us, and they told us not to be frightened upon seeing another person who had been in hiding there for several months. He was a Jew from Lwow who had an uncle in Trembowla, one of the Podhorcers. His sister was staying with relatives of the Jackiws. She pretended to be a Christian and had Aryan papers. She had found the hiding place for her brother, who as a male would have had great difficulty passing himself off as an Aryan.

The Jackiws came out only to see me, for this was the first time that I had come to their home — as I have already pointed out, I could not find my way very easily at night, so I took no part in the trips to their place for food. I remember that when Mrs. Jackiw saw me, she was stunned and cried out in pain: "Oh, he looks like a dead man. Who knows if he will hold out? Why, this is the shadow of a human being, not a real human being." As to food, they could not promise an abundant supply, but they would do whatever was possible. They could come only once a day, just before morning, to give us something to eat, because at that hour they went out to feed the cows. Their presence in the barn would arouse no suspicion.

When they brought us food, they also changed the pail which we used to relieve ourselves. Aside from this morning meeting, no one came in contact with us all day or night. We were conscious of the fact that we had to be still in the attic without uttering a sound. It was quite possible that if we indiscreetly raised our voices, someone on the other side of the wall might hear us and disaster could ensue for us and the Jackiws.

I had only the prayer book, which, on that fateful day when my brother perished, had been lying on the ground as I picked myself up and ran away. It was riddled with bullet holes when I came back. But who had patience to peruse it?

We hid there for more than three and a half months and our daily schedule was fixed, as I have indicated. In the morning we were able to exchange a few words without fear.

I shall mention a fact which proved the spiritual greatness of the Jackiw family, whose equals were few and far between. They saved ten Jews, who accounted for a high percentage of the Trembowla survivors. I doubt whether the number of Holocaust survivors in Trembowla reached fifty.

In addition to the five in the attic and the sister of the fellow from Lwow, who was passing herself off as a Christian, the Jackiws hid a family of three people for almost an entire year in a bunker beneath their house. Aside from the nine people in hiding, they kept, as one of their family, the son of a Jewish dentist, Dr. Kelber, who together with his wife, joined the Ukrainian Bandera bands. They thought that they would be saved this way, but they were eventually murdered. The boy grew up in an orphanage in Poland and came to Israel at the age of fifteen. He completed his studies here and later raised a family. The Jackiws did all this without receiving any money in advance. There were other people who insisted on receiving money before hiding Jews, and, afterwards, killed them. And I must stress that even after the liberation, the Jackiws did not ask for compensation of any kind. When my cousin retrieved a cow and gave it to them, and when I too, gave them what I could, they always protested: "Why are you giving us these things? What did we do for you?"

I am moved to tears whenever I think of the way this family treated us. I cannot forget what this noble family did on our behalf, and while recording these events, I have received some small satisfaction at the opportunity to extol their deeds. This is a small portion of the reward I owe the Jackiws. The financial recompense which our group has tried to give them is nothing compared with the greatness of their deeds. And to throw into proper relief these "Righteous of the Nations" I shall recount two facts that bear testimony to the magnanimity of their spirit and their piety. For they did not merely share their bread with us.

I remember that we came to them in December 1943, a month which ends in Christian holidays. Even then they did not forget us. They gave us excellent food, what they themselves ate.

An argument between me and the boy in the attic erupted for the following reason. When I came there from the forest, I had a slight cold and was coughing, which was to be expected if one takes into consideration the clothes I wore and the nourishment available in the forest. One couldn't hear my cough at a distance; I did my best to suppress it because one loud cough in the attic in the course of a day, when neighbors were around, could have brought disaster. So, when he heard me cough, he charged at me and shouted that I would bring misfortune to us all. It would be best if I went down and handed myself over to the Germans and not endanger everyone else. His fear grew from day to day.

I understood him and tried to overcome the cough, but I didn't always succeed. Finally, I told him: "You are right—but your idea could only complicate matters without providing a solution. On the contrary, it might be harmful. As things are now, it is possible that no one will hear the coughing, but if I give myself up to the Germans, they might torture me into telling them who else is hiding." So, in my opinion, we had to consult with Mrs. Jackiw when she came in the morning. When she came, we told her about the argument, in a whisper, of course. After hearing what we had to say, she did not even bother to consult with her husband (she was Polish, and her husband was Ukrainian) but said briefly and to the point: "There is no danger in coughing during the day because people are always coming in and out of the barn and the storeroom and anyone might be coughing. The situation is worse at night, but there is a simple solution: If he coughs as you claim, we must give him milk which will stop the cough." So, at one stroke, she removed his grounds for complaint. I couldn't conceive of such a solution. It was appropriate only for one of the Righteous Gentiles such as she.

I shall end with an account of the second incident which highlights the great piety of this family. On the day of the liberation, March 22, 1944, we wanted to leave our hiding place right away, to taste the freedom we had so yearned for, immediately. But she insisted that we wait another day and refused to let us go. We understood that she was worried about our safety and wanted to be 100 percent certain that we could really leave without facing any danger and that the Soviet authorities were in full control of the area.

This was clearly a reason for her caution, but something else was lurking in the background. When we went outside the next day, she brought us into her house to show us to the family that had been hiding in the bunker. They had been complaining about her nightly visits to "these Brusts." (They knew only that the Brusts were their neighbors, but the family was not aware that the Brusts had perished in the forest.) They feared that the contact with the other people might lead someone to their hiding place in her house. They did not even know that the Jackiws saved five other people by giving them shelter in the attic of their barn.

May the Jackiw family be forever enshrined in the book of the "Righteous Among the Nations."

A Letter from Liberated Galicia

Here are parts of a letter from me, telling what happened to the Jews of Trembowla. The letter was received by the Imber family in Israel in 1944.

Trembowla, May 10, 1944

My Dear Sister and Brother-in-law,

Seven weeks have passed since the Red Army liberated us. What I have to tell you is not vain talk but the naked truth. To my sorrow, a pitiful few lived to see the liberation. It is with great difficulty that I write to you — my precious treasures, the only people still alive in my whole world. I did not know how it would be possible to hold a pen in my hand and write about what happened to us. I am indeed able to inform you of the good news that your brother is one of the few survivors, or, more accurately, one of the few miserable individuals who was fated to live through the torment of Hitler's Seven Departments of Hell and remain alive. But when I remember all our suffering — the terrible shocking tragedy! — it is so awful, savage, dreadful that there is no prophet or writer who ever described, even in his imagination at its richest, such a horrible reality.

Lying before me is a small notebook, all that remains of my books and my writings. Exactly eleven months ago when I was in the forest I began to write a farewell letter to you. I was able to record then, the date, the place, the forest I was in, the names of the people with me, and nothing more. I was overcome by a terrible state of despair, and I was unable to continue writing although at that time my brother David was still with me. When I think of the tragic death of our dear brother a short time before salvation reached us — how can I tell you all this? My dear sister and brother-in-law! Believe me, in order to write these words I must strain my meager powers, of which so few are left, to the utmost. I am only a shadow of my former self, your brother Israel. When I left the forest and met an acquaintance who, for years, lived near us — he did not recognize me, I had changed so much.

But none of this should have affected me so strongly were it not for the tragic death of my brother in the forest. It shattered me more than anything I witnessed during these terrible years. Even the tragic death of our dear mother and all our other relatives did not depress me in such a way because cold, calculating logic perceived that there was no refuge for my family from the systematic, thorough destruction implemented by Hitler's dogs. But I cannot come to terms with the tragic death in the forest of my brother David. He shared my lot for three years in all their afflictions and cruel tortures. We were at the gates of deliverance. The Red Army had already reached Zhitomir and was approaching our area. I was completely shattered. There is not a moment when the memory of him does not pursue me and torment me.

As I write these words tears are once again welling up in my eyes, and it is difficult for me to continue. How can the news of my survival gladden you when I describe to you all the suffering and bitter memories which my relatives and I experienced. Out of our ramified family only a few individuals have survived.

This time I will provide you with no further details; writing is difficult for me. I hope to have another opportunity to tell you everything and perhaps to do so face to face because it was our great hope, through all our misfortunes, to meet you, God willing, and only this hope — so I believe — made my suffering worthwhile, for without the hope of seeing you, what meaning would my life have after I saw and heard about the slaughter and killing of thousands and millions of Jews, the destruction of the cream of world Jewry.

We remain here, naked and barefoot, without any means of living. My one possible consolation would be to join you, to live together, and to use our holy tongue, Hebrew, which is now seven times as precious to me. Leave no stone unturned so that this consolation will come to pass. In the meantime, the men here are being taken to the army. I feel extremely weak, exhausted, and depressed, and I doubt whether I shall be found fit for military service. I don't want to worry too much, God will help!

Here in Trembowla there are sixty to seventy Jews left, almost all of them young men. Most of them will join the army.

[The letter contains several items of information about the fate of Zloczow and a number of personal matters.]

From your tormented brother who looks forward to seeing you,

(Israel Goldfliess)

11

FOR MY DAUGHTER'S SAKE

Sabina Herbst

MY DEAR HUSBAND HAD BEEN one of the first victims of the Nazis, in 1941, and I had been left alone with my child who was three years old at that time. By the end of May 1943 there were about 1,800 Jewish people in the Trembowla Ghetto, many of them from the neighboring smaller towns and villages. Jews were walking in the Ghetto streets like shadows, sad and depressed with only one thought in their mind—where to run and where to hide.

A Pogrom by the Nazis was expected, any hour, any minute. I took my daughter, Ziunia, and went out secretly from the Ghetto to find a place to hide. I went to a few Gentiles, who once were customers in our store, and begged them to find some shelter for me and my child in their house. Everybody refused. We spent the night in the woods with many other people. We returned in the morning to the Ghetto; it was still quiet. Everybody was asking, "Do you have a place to hide?" I was tired to the point of exhaustion. Ziunia was crying, tired, thirsty and hungry. She told me, "I don't want to know about anything—just give me something to drink and put me to sleep."

Since the age of three, she had been running with me to shelters to hide, in hunger and fear, but she still could not understand why we had to hide. I explained that we were in danger of being killed, but she didn't know what it meant and asked, "How does it look when someone is killed?" I explained to her exactly what it meant—that the Germans were hunting us with guns and when a person is shot, the blood runs, he dies and he is buried forever. "No Mommy, I want to live. I will be quiet." I taught her that lesson when she was three and a half years old.

We felt like hunted animals, filled with fear and anguish. People kept asking one another, "Where is America; where is the whole civilized world? Are we all condemned to die?" That same night came the attack. Every house in the Ghetto had made caves under the furniture or hiding places in the attic, to hide from the Germans. We went into a cave, which was prepared in advance — the same place people had been previously taken out of by the Nazis for extermination. Among the people in the cave were my older brother, Moshe, his wife, Fania, and their 15-year-old daughter, Genia. My brother's older son, Zalmen, age 18, was taken in 1941 to Belzec to the gas chamber. In the cave was my sister-in-law, Henia, with her child; Wolf Rosenstrauch's wife and children; and approximately sixty other people. Before we managed to close the cave, the murderers came in and started to pull out all the people. I was sitting with Ziunia in my arms in a corner and heard the cries of the victims. I have no words to express that feeling, expecting to be taken out at any minute. I saw a Nazi come down to the cave and take my niece, Genia, with Rosenstrauch's little five-year-old girl. Genia begged to be left and asked if it was possible to run away. I can never forget the sight of my beloved niece begging for her life. My brother, Moshe, was lying on the ground of the cave unconscious, and as soon as he gained consciousness another Nazi came in and grabbed him. It was a miracle that they didn't see me with my child, my sister-in-law, Fania, and my sister-in-law, Henia, with her child. (The rest of Henia's family — husband, sister, brothers and father — had perished in the previous "Actions.") The Germans threw burning straw in the cave and when no sound was heard, they thought that nobody was there and left.

We went to another house, where we found a few other single people without families — depressed and disgusted with no more spirit or will to live. I did not know what to do or where to go. The Germans were liquidating the Ghetto to make Trembowla *Judenrein* (free from Jews). I gathered all my courage to go out to other houses of the Ghetto, hoping to find someone to join us to go somewhere together. Henia left with her child. . . I didn't know where she went. At that time, the Ghetto consisted of only a small number of houses in Sobieska Street (called "Koplowka"). I was walking through the gardens and bushes in fear, filled with anxiety. The houses were empty. I saw the corpses of people who once were my neighbors, a sight I will never forget. Overpowered by fear, I started to return to the house, to the house where I left my child sleeping and my sister-in-law, Fania, waiting for me. Fania was completely apathetic. She said she didn't care any more; she had lost all her dear ones — husband, children, sister and family; she had nothing to live for. While I was walking back, I noticed that Sklarek and two other Nazis were walking to the same house. Sklarek was a German gendarme stationed in Trembowla. He was always walking in the company of a big black German Shepherd dog, watching that no Jew escaped from the Ghetto and that no one brought any food into the Ghetto. He was also the enforcer of every new law and decree issued to the Jews in the Ghetto. Everybody feared him. I ran quietly into the house to be with my child and thought to myself, "Now comes the end of everything." Sklarek approached me and said in German, "Come to work." I answered, "I have a small child." He said, "You don't want to," and took out his gun to shoot. I was motionless. At that moment, the sound of a whistle was heard and the voice of the other Germans who were telling him they found more Jews. Sklarek put back the gun and told me, "You can go. I don't need you." As soon as the Nazis left with a group of Jews, I gathered a few necessities, took my daughter and sister-in-law and started walking to a nearby village, about 10 kilometers from town.

Podhajczyki

The name of the village was Podhajczyki. On the way, we were attacked by bands of Ukrainians who were collaborating with the Nazis in killing Jews. They took whatever we had. Ziunia was crying. Some gentile women were looking and said to the attacker, "Leave them alone; look at the crying child." Luckily, we were left alive, and we went on our journey to Podhajczyki. Upon our arrival in the village, we came to the house of a farmer who was once a customer in our store. When the war broke out, we had given him merchandise from our store to hide. He had a wife with two little girls and was a religious Catholic. Many people who were running from the Ghetto at that time were being killed by the Ukrainians or Germans. We were sheltered in the attic of the farmer's house. The wife gave us food to eat, but told us that they had no room for us. I begged her with tears to save our lives. "Do it please for the sake of my child; I do not care for myself." After talking the matter over with her husband, she came to tell us that they had a hiding place underground. We also found out from the farmer that all the people from the Ghetto had been taken to Plebanowka, a suburb of Trembowla, and all — men, women and children — were shot by a German firing squad and buried in a previously prepared mass grave. Some people were buried still alive. I listened in horror and disbelief, but in spite of all that, I didn't want to die, and looking at my child, I was willing to go on.

Fania was completely passive, but didn't want to die by the hand of the Nazis.

Late that night, the farmer took us down to a vegetable garden on his premises and next to the foot of a big tree there was an entrance to a hiding place, covered with a big square stone plate. First Fania was lowered down. Then he handed her my child and I was last. When I heard the sound of the closing of the entrance, I thought to myself, "Now we are buried alive." The cave was about 8 feet long, 5 feet wide and 8 feet deep. It was dark, damp, and dreary. We had some rags to cover ourselves. I was filled with anxiety and fear, that we would die here of starvation, a most terrible death, looking at my starving child. We could not go out by ourselves. We depended completely on the mercy of the farmer. I could not share my thoughts with Fania; I didn't want to frighten her. She had enough of her own tragedy. My daughter asked me, "What will we do here? . . . It is dark and cold." I was trying to comfort her and reassure her that in the morning it would be different; that now it was night and we had to sleep. Every hour seemed an eternity. Finally, we heard the sound of the opening of the stone plate at the foot of the cave and being lowered down on a string was a bottle with tea and a pot of food and spoons to eat with. I was overwhelmed with a feeling of hope.

We started to eat eagerly. It was pitch dark and Ziunia got very impatient. I was telling her stories, making all kinds of promises, but the anxiety grew. Every hour was endless, and I felt that it was impossible to stay here. In the evening, the farmer opened the cave again and asked how it was inside. I answered that we had lost the spoons; it was pitch dark and we needed some light. He brought down a kerosene lamp, but it could not burn because of the lack of air. He then made a couple of holes in the ground above the cave. We could see daylight, hear the bells ringing in the church and became a little more hopeful. The next day, there was a rainstorm; it got dark; there was thunder and lightning and the water was pouring in through the holes. The water reached our ankles. I was holding my daughter in my arms and thinking that maybe it would be better to drown her and all our suffering could be over. Suddenly, we heard a sound and a voice from above. It was the farmer who had just come from town. He asked, "How is it in there?" "The cave is filled with water," I answered. "Give me the child quickly," he said. Fania handed him my daughter. I could not reach so high. Then she helped me to climb up, and then the farmer pulled Fania out. We felt relieved to get out of the cave, went into the house, washed ourselves, got something to eat and were put into the attic again. The next day, we were told to go because they had no place to hide us. I started to beg them to have mercy and find something for us. After many tears and long persuasion, they told us they would try to find a hiding place.

The next night, we were taken to a nearby barn, in which they had goats, chickens and rabbits. Our hiding place was made between the slope of the straw roof of the barn and a straw wall that was made especially for us. The space was about seven feet long and three feet wide. We could sit there, but my sister-in-law could only lie down, being too tall to sit. Through the cracks and corners of the roof some light came in. During the days when there were no Germans in the village, we crept out of the hole to straighten up and do some exercise, which was some recreation for Ziunia. We also spent time outside the straw wall. We could all sit down and talk. My daughter could play with the rabbits, which had been brought up to the attic, by feeding them leaves, which were thrown to them almost every day in the summer. The biggest treat for my daughter was a sunflower. She ate the seeds and the rest she could feed to the rabbits. Many times, they threw leftover food and pieces of moldy bread into the attic. Ziunia grabbed it. I cleaned it up and gave it to her to eat. At the same time she was worried that the rabbits would be hungry. We were given a small loaf of bread for three days; hot water in the morning and evening and some soup for lunch. Sometimes they gave us a tomato, a carrot and a scallion fresh from the garden. It was enough to keep us alive. I made up countless stories to tell my daughter to keep her interested. She complained that there was nothing to do. I told her to braid my hair and tell me some stories she had learned. All our talks were in a whisper. My sister-in-law was mostly lying down, quiet and depressed; I tried to make conversation with her and asked her to serve us the meals we got.

"Tell Me Why"

One sunny summer day, Ziunia looked through the cracks of the roof and, seeing the bright sun and children playing outside, she said. "Tell me, Mommy, why do we have to hide here in the dark without Daddy and without food, and other children can play in the sun and have their father?" I had no answer. I was choking, trying to suppress my painful emotions, but tears were running over my cheeks. My daughter patted my face with her little hands and said, "Don't cry Mommy. Daddy will come back and we will be together again." I had no such hopes, but at the same time I didn't want to believe that I would never see him again.

Our clothing was falling apart. I asked Mrs. Rajski to give me a needle and thread, and I tried to sew the holes together. She gave me a skirt and an old jacket from her husband. She was a religious woman, and whenever I found her resentful for our being a burden to them, I used my religious persuasion which helped a little. We gave the farmer all the valuables we had. I had sewn them into the vest I wore and luckily this had not been taken by the bandits. I found out that they were hiding another Jewish family, the Einlegers. They later left them, but they knew about us, which was to our benefit. That farmer belonged to the Polish underground and used to have meetings in his house. In the winter of 1943–44, German soldiers were stationed in almost every house of the village, but the farmer knew how to avoid them by pretending that his family was sick, so the Nazis stayed away. At that time, we had to be especially careful not to make any sounds. At night one of us was always awake when the others slept, to keep guard. We heard their singing in the evening and picked up certain verses that were amusing to my daughter. I tried not to run out of stories. I told her that the war would end soon and we would be free; we would go to America. She had Uncle Leo and Aunt Martha there who would teach her to play the piano. We would have plenty of food. I would cook big pots of good dishes. I would bake big loaves of bread as big as a table. She would be able to shout and sing. There would be no more whispering.

At this time, I would like to mention that my younger brother, Leo, with his wife, Martha, were in Vienna when the war began. My sister-in-law succeeded in leaving for the U.S.A. in 1939 on a visa from my aunt, but my brother could not go because he did not have Austrian citizenship. He got a permit to go to Cuba. In May 1939, he boarded with several hundred other Jews who were fleeing from Austria. When they reached Havana, they were not allowed to land. They tried other countries, but they were refused everywhere. They cruised for six weeks on the ocean, and finally France let them in. My brother was interned for three months. In the meantime, Hitler invaded France. My brother was in the Pyrenees for eight or more months and after many hardships, he came to the U.S.A. in 1941 on a visa from our relatives. At that time, I received a telegram that he had arrived in New York.

All through the winter in the attic, we covered ourselves with straw and an old coat which I had with me. The entrance to the attic was covered with a straw mat, which made it darker. The waiting seemed endless. We could not wash or change clothing. There were times when there was much shooting and burning, and I was always afraid that the barn would catch on fire. Sometimes, I could not believe that this was happening to us. Only my child gave me the strength and courage to endure all that suffering. I was trying to fight off the moments of despair and told myself that I must be strong. I could not break down. I have my child to live for. I must go on. We need each other. We were in the attic for ten months.

Finally, in March 1944, we were told by the farmer that we could step down from the attic and that we were free. The war was still going on. There was a loud thundering of bombs as the Germans were fleeing, and the Russians came. We got a ladder to come down. I could not believe that it was true. We were still filled with fear. We were weak, undernourished and could hardly walk. We got something to eat and started to walk to Trembowla. On the way, we met Russian soldiers. Some Gentiles invited us to their house and gave us food. We did not rejoice. Our spirit was broken. We felt alone, unwanted, betrayed by the whole world. My daughter was crying. She could not walk, and I could not carry her. She had been whispering for weeks; she couldn't raise her voice. I encouraged her to shout and promised to teach her to sing, but I had to wait in anguish, afraid that she had lost her voice.

In Trembowla, we met more survivors; my sister-in-law Henia Selzer came with her daughter, Musia. They were the only survivors from their family. We embraced each other, but we had only tears in our eyes. More survivors started coming out from their hiding places, about twenty to thirty people. We all gathered in the house of Dr. Sass. It was shocking to learn that so few of us were left. We felt physically and spiritually broken to pieces. There are no words to describe the pain we felt when we were faced with the unbelievable reality. My sister-in-law, Fania, said, "I wish I would have gone together with my family. What do I have to live for?" It is strange that after going through all that hell, everybody felt the same way.

The war still was going on, and there were rumors that the Germans were coming back. We started to run again, closer to the Russian border, until we came to Podwoloczysk. We found a few houses there with survivors in a crowded room. Many houses were demolished from the bombs. Suddenly, an epidemic of typhoid fever broke out and almost everybody got sick. We were taken by buses to a nearby village, Kaczanowka. The abandoned houses were turned into hospitals. Bundles of straw were used for beds. There was a nurse, a Jewish girl, who had previously been working with the Germans in disguise as a Gentile. She helped us greatly, but there was very little medication. Many of the survivors died. My daughter and I were released after three weeks, but my sister-in-law Fania had to stay on. I didn't know where to go from the hospital. I was walking from house to house begging people to take me in with my child. My offer to them was to sew dresses, blouses, etc. Finally, a woman with two children invited me to stay with them. She allowed me to use her potatoes and vegetables to cook soup, and I brought some of it to the hospital for my sister-in-law Fania. After her release, we had to leave the village because the woman refused to house all three of us.

We went back to Podwoloczysk, where I met my sister-in-law, Henia, with her daughter. They lived in a very crowded place, but invited us to stay with them. After being there a few weeks, we went back to our home town, Trembowla, which was occupied by the Russians. They were occupying my father-in-law's house when I arrived, but they returned it to me. I struggled to make a living; went through a lot of hardship and fears. I remembered the address of my aunt who lived in the U.S.A. and wrote her a letter, so that she would know about our survival. She notified my brother, Leo, who was in the U.S.A. by that time and saying Kaddish (prayer for the dead) for us. I started getting letters and packages from my brother and sister-in-law and was filled with new hopes of putting together my shattered life.

On May 7, 1945, Germany surrendered and the war in Europe ended. I will never forget that day when a friend of ours came knocking on our window to tell us that the war was over. A parade and music were going on in the streets and Ziunia wanted to go out and see it. Soldiers were parading. Some were hugging and kissing, rejoicing with their friends and family. My daughter looked on and said to me, "Maybe I will find my Daddy here." The tears were choking me and running over my cheeks, and I only had one question in mind. Where would I go and what would I do? I felt so lonely and forlorn that I had to go home and sit down and cry. I have no words to describe that feeling. We subsequently left the house in Trembowla and went to Bytom, a city in Poland. From there, we went on to Austria, with the help of the *"Haganah."* We were stationed in Ebensee, in a camp which was once built by the Nazis as a death camp for the Jews. We found machinery from the gas chambers and other equipment of that concentration camp still there. After being there three months, we were transferred to Germany, to an area occupied by the Americans, and after two years in a camp for displaced persons, we arrived in the U.S.A. in 1948.

12

THE ANNIHILATION OF THE TREMBOWLA JEWISH COMMUNITY

Joseph Einleger

ON JUNE 22, 1941, WAR SUDDENLY broke out between Germany and Russia, and on July 5, the German army entered Trembowla.

I remember that Sabbath day, the fifth of July, when at approximately eleven o'clock in the morning the Ukrainian population gathered in the streets to see the Germans who were arriving from the north by way of Krowinka village.

The Jews stayed in the houses and were not to be seen in the streets, while the Ukrainians greeted the Germans with a Nazi salute.

That night Joseph Mester, the first victim, was shot and killed. They said that a neighbor denounced him as a known Communist. Another victim fell that day—the head of bookkeeping at Drummer's windmill. This is how it started. The Ukrainians began to organize; a militia and local government were formed. There was a big parade in the streets of the city with flags and a band. Everyone was marching toward Pokrowka. The Castle, as is well known, was a symbol of the Poles; but Pokrowka was the Ukrainian rallying point. There were rumors of an independent Ukraine with Lwow as its capital and as the seat of a Ukrainian government. Several days later the Germans announced that the districts of Lwow, Tarnopol, and Stanislawow would be henceforth known as the district of Galicia and would be attached to the Government-General in Poland, headed by Dr. Frank in Cracow. The district governor of Galicia was Dr. Wachter in Lwow.

A German newspaper—*Lemberger Zeitung*—was published, as well as a Ukrainian newspaper. The Poles kept silent, but they secretly listened to foreign radio broadcasts.

Seizures for work camps took place. The Ukrainian militia was organized to help the German authorities. Its headquarters were in the home of Leib Scherzer on Sobieski Street. The Ukrainian

Nationalists would enter Jewish homes and take everything they could put their hands on. They also took men and women away to clean the German and Ukrainian offices and the floors and windows at the Ukrainian center. One group cleaned the clay floor of the cellars and the storerooms at the center and also moved sacks and crates around. Jews were also taken to work in German army camps around Trembowla. Once the Ukrainian Nationalists caught a group of Jews and took them to the empty barracks and tortured them. They didn't return alive, except for Gedalyahu Tunis, who was released thanks to the intervention of the priest Mochanacki. Among those who died were Samuel Herbst, Abba Briller, Moti Brief, and Masyo Lazarus. I don't remember the others. The headquarters of the local administration was at the courthouse in "Dom Narodni" (The People's House). There, a group of Jews was once arrested, including the photographer Schneelicht. It was said that they were taken out of the city to the forest and shot.

The *Landeskommissar* set himself up in the building of the prewar subprefecture as the administrative authority. It was his job to steal all valuables such as furs, cameras, gold, etc. His name was Gaukler. He strutted about in an S.S. uniform with a skull and crossbones on his hat. He came from Stuttgart.

German gendarmes in green uniforms also arrived. They lived and worked in Mariendorf's house on Sobieski Street. The Ukrainian Militia was subject to the authority of the gendarmes and the Gestapo, and they in turn were under the command of the Gestapo in Tarnopol. The gendarmes were between the ages of 35 and 45. They included some typical murderers but also people who were helpful and who even saved a few lives.

There was a murderer named Sklaryk from Silesia. He spoke Polish with a Silesian accent. He was the worst type of murderer. He had a small head on a thin neck, a gaunt face, and a pointed nose, and his eyes were always moving. He would walk around with a loaded gun, ready to shoot, and he would do so on any occasion. He killed for pleasure, and he would boast that he was a few short of a thousand victims. Whenever he saw a Jew in the street, he would shoot. At the sight of him, a street emptied rapidly.

Meanwhile the German army was advancing eastward and southward through Kopyczynce, Grzymalow, and Skalat. At the end of July 1941, the Gestapo arrived from Tarnopol, and in August a Judenrat was set up with twelve to fifteen members, secretaries, and a Jewish militia consisting of twenty to twenty-five young people.

The Judenrat was placed in the house of Rabbi Leiter on Sobieski Street. At the head of the Judenrat stood a chairman, an *Obmann* (head man) of the *Judenältester* (Jewish elders) who was called *"Oberjude"* by the Germans. The first *Obmann* appointed by the Gestapo was Dr. Seret. Musyo Safrin was appointed the head of the Jewish Militia. The Gestapo issued many orders during that period. Failure to comply with them meant immediate execution by a firing squad.

Here were some of the orders:

—All radios and furs were to be handed over.

—No Jew was allowed to leave the city.

—No Jew was permitted to appear in public places, to go to shows, etc.

—No Jew was allowed to travel by train.

—No Jew was permitted outside at night.

—No gatherings were to be held; everyone was to register with the Judenrat.

—All Jewish residents of the Trembowla area had to live in Trembowla.

—The move into the city had to take place within twenty-four hours.

The Gestapo ordered the Judenrat to recruit 35 to 45 people for forced labor in a labor camp. Negotiations began. Everyone was trying to save his relatives. There were scuffles and scandals at the Judenrat until the first group left by the appointed date. They were guarded by the Judenrat and the Jewish militia.

The residents of Trembowla worked in three labor camps: Kamienka, Halowoczek, and Burki Wielki, near Skalat. Once a week the Judenrat sent a wagon to the camp with parcels of food and clothing from the prisoners' families. Occasionally, it proved possible to ransom a prisoner or exchange him. These deals took place throughout the period.

A new currency and new postal stamps were introduced. But the farmers preferred dollars and the Germans preferred dollars and gold. These precious items gradually ran out. Cash was scarce and supplies dwindled. At that stage Jews still lived in their apartments. Life was full of tension and fear. There was no quiet, day or night. There were rumors all the time of robberies and murders. Occasionally, Jews secretly came to us from the neighboring towns, and then the term "Action" became known. But no one wished to believe it. Such a thing was impossible—it just couldn't happen; it was a lie. But the people coming to us said that they saw it with their own eyes.

They themselves had barely escaped, and only after wandering at night along out-of-the-way roads did they go to Trembowla.

There were no schools — at least not for Jewish children. The children became quiet, submissive, and sad. They, too, sensed that things were bad — very bad.

Transports such as these passed through Trembowla from Kopyczynce, Czortkow, and Tluste. We saw them with our own eyes. We heard the terrible screams and cries from the railway cars on the way to Belzec. The First "Action" lasted approximately until three in the afternoon, and only after the cars packed with Jews departed, did the Jews who had gone to hiding places or to the forests begin to return. Smoke rising from home ovens signaled those in hiding that they could return. Immediately after the "Action" the size of the Ghetto was reduced.

Now it ran along Sobieski Street from Itzi Briller's house to Kaplowka. The area of the synagogues was now outside the Ghetto and the Torah scrolls were moved into the reduced area and placed in private homes. Some of the Torah scrolls, religious books, and synagogue furniture were stolen by farmers.

From this point onwards prayer services were conducted stealthily, in private homes and with few participants.

During the first few weeks after the "Action," rumors spread that some of the deportees had written that they were alive and working. But no one saw such a letter. This was surely German deceit. No one returned except the amputee Leopold Gelles, who appeared two weeks later. "Sometime during the journey," he recounted, "I was lifted through the small window of the car. I moved the barbed wire, threw my wooden leg out and jumped head first. This time I succeeded." It was as though he had realized in advance that the next time he would not succeed.

The situation in the shrunken Ghetto continued as before, but now there were frequent visits from the Tarnopol Gestapo. There were house searches resulting in more victims of violence. During one such search my cousin's husband, the dentist Perlman from Strusow, jumped through the window and began running. At that moment the Gestapo man shot and killed him. There were other such cases.

Fear gripped the residents of the Ghetto. The appearance of a German was enough to create panic.

An atmosphere of depression and despair set in. Aggressiveness, fistfights, and scandalous behavior became common. Periodically there was an alarm about an impending "Action." Sleepless nights were spent listening to every murmur. On several occasions I went with others to Pokrowka. In winter, in the snow, we covered ourselves with white sheets for camouflage. People ceased to be human beings. Fear, sleepless nights, the need for continual alertness, and the general tension engendered animalistic actions throughout. We learned to detect among others the sound of an approaching vehicle and the barking of dogs.

A special chapter in Ghetto life resulted from incessant Gestapo demands for a variety of things which had to be supplied quickly. Non-compliance would be met with severe punishment: the execution of twenty people and the deportation of the entire Judenrat to a labor camp. They referred to this *Beschaffung* (grasping) as "procurement." Once we had to hand over three kilograms of gold in twenty-four hours, another time three sets of silver and dishes for twenty-four people, and on a third occasion a piano, furniture for a bedroom, three gold cigarette cases and a crate of wine. There were collections of all kinds. The Judenrat would purchase the necessary items outside the ghetto with funds raised in the Ghetto.

The outbreak of a typhus epidemic was a severe blow. A hospital for the Ghetto was set up in a former prison. Doctor Bomze and Doctor Kolin directed hospital activities. Lysol was smeared on doors, windows and floors. The odors of disinfectants spread throughout the Ghetto because everyone wanted to live. No one wanted to die. During that period there were twelve to fifteen funerals a day. Nathaniel Melzer performed the Mitzvah of attending to the dead with praiseworthy efficiency and dedication.

Time passed. November and December 1942 were behind us and the year of 1943 was beginning. By this point we knew that the Germans had suffered a major defeat and had sustained heavy losses near Stalingrad. We read in the papers that the Germans were "disengaging themselves from the enemy." There was a feeling that the Germans could not avoid an eventual collapse and that redemption was drawing near. We had only to be on our guard to do what we could to stay alive without despairing or submitting.

And day and night we debated, discussed, and analyzed every bit of information, every newspaper article, and every rumor. The Poles listened to the B.B.C. broadcasts from London and told their Jewish acquaintances the latest good news. Our problem was how to stay alive until the moment we were longing for. The life instinct invented new forms of living and surviving. We built camouflaged bunkers of a very sophisticated kind. We built hiding places in houses and in courtyards. Every group worked furtively and covertly. Some bunkers were constructed so well that the human eye could not detect them. We also took into consideration that the Germans used dogs in searching for their victims.

We knew that after the first "Action" a second and third would follow, as had been the case in other towns. So we made preparations. Everyone thought of himself. Selfishness became common — only families were united.

After Dr. Seret and Max Steinig, who were the first to serve as *Obmann* (in the Ghetto), Mr. Goldstein was appointed to the position. He had come to Trembowla from Mikulnice before the war and opened a beer distributorship in Fisher's warehouses near the station.

The Obmann, Judenrat members, and Jewish Militiamen were periodically replaced. Their main task at this stage was to bribe every Gestapo man and to exchange the inmates of labor camps. (It is worth noting that aside from the gendarmerie and the Ukrainian Militia there was also *Kripo*, the criminal police, which consisted of two people who came to Trembowla from somewhere else and who were generally considered harmless.)

In the summer of 1942 there was a camp of French prisoners of war in Trembowla who were given the task of dismantling and destroying the Jewish cemetery. Every morning they marched off to work under guard, and in the evening they would return to their barracks. A few months later the camp was liquidated and the prisoners were transferred. It became known that the prisoners rebelled and did not want to do the work. Several of them escaped.

At night shots were heard, as if a battle was taking place. There were casualties, including a Polish woman who was a member of the Sartani family and who lived close to the Jewish cemetery. It was said that several Poles were also involved and that a number of gendarmes had been sent to the front. After this incident a group of fifty to sixty Jews was organized to complete the work of liquidating the Jewish cemetery and by the end of 1942 not a single tombstone was in place. The Gentiles, e.g., the teacher Gottwald who lived in the vicinity of the cemetery, began to grow vegetables where there once had been a Jewish cemetery, and the entire area turned into a vegetable garden.

In the Ghetto, life continued in fear and in anticipation of a miracle.

There were no births in the Ghetto, although there were several miscarriages. Women did not have their periods and they did not become pregnant. There were several cases of diabetics who were cured; the level of sugar in their bodies did not rise despite the fact that they did not keep a special diet or take any medicine. These physiological changes took place because of our living in hunger and fear — because of the events affecting us and because of our constant struggle for survival.

In the spring of 1943, the Second "Action" was undertaken. A day before, there spread a rumor that the *Baudienst* (building or engineering unit) was digging pits near the bridge for the trains at Plebanowka — at a distance of three kilometers from town. But even this time some people refused to believe that danger was near, and they even insulted the foreboders.

On Wednesday of that week, April 7, 1943, a convoy of trucks filled with Gestapo people, *Shupo* and S.D. men arrived from Tarnopol. From the town square between the Ukrainian Church and the Jewish Community offices the force proceeded, one half to the Old City and the other via Chrzanowska Street and Planty to the Ghetto. The Ghetto was surrounded. Jews who were caught were led to the field on the Planty. Many bunkers were discovered, and a good number of the people hiding in them surrendered out of despair. Twelve to thirteen hundred residents of the ghetto who were assembled at Planty were ordered to take off their upper garments.

The people were lined up in rows and marched through the streets of the city. It was already noon when the column of these condemned people, surrounded on all sides by murderers in uniform, advanced step by step towards their deaths — the death of martyrs. Among those marching was an old Christian and his sister. He was holding a big cross in his hand. His father and possibly his grandfather had converted to Christianity before the First World War.

The Second "Action" was now over and the Ghetto was again reduced in size by order of the Gestapo. Few houses remained in the Ghetto, since only 500 to 750 Jews were left.

Everyone now knew that the end was in sight. We knew that the Third "Action" was fast approaching and that it would be the last.

But the Judenrat and the Jewish Militia collapsed, as a result of which everyone came to think only about saving his own life. There was utter chaos.

Relations between Ukrainians and Poles worsened, and each side attacked the other. At night fires raged on Polish and Ukrainian farms. There were many casualties on both sides.

The Germans knew that the Ukrainians were organizing. There

was a Ukrainian Nationalist movement, the *Banderovtsi* (Bandera gangs). They were the ones raiding Polish villages, murdering, burning and destroying Polish property. Far from the main roads, bands organized self-rule of sorts. They set up an administration, schools, and hospitals.

The German army was already in retreat. Every battle ended in the deaths of thousands of Germans. The Russians went from victory to victory, and the Germans were forced to retreat from Stalingrad, the Caucasus and Leningrad after suffering heavy losses and losing entire army corps and all their equipment. In the west a second front was imminent; there was talk of an Allied landing in France, and the Germans began to construct the Atlantic wall.

After the Second "Action" a group of young people slipped out of town and headed in the direction of Lwow and Stanislawow. Only a few members of this group survived.

On June 3, 1943, the third "Action" took place. Between 100 and 200 Jews were led to Plebanowka and murdered there near the railway bridge. About forty to fifty people survived this "Action" and dispersed into the forests and the countryside. Dr. Bomza, Dr. Kolin, and Dr. Kelber were recruited by the *Banderovtsi* and taken away on wagons with their families. They didn't return. I also know of doctors and pharmacists from other cities who were recruited by the *Banderovtsi* and who worked alongside them in Wolyn. Only two of the doctors and one pharmacist returned after the war.

After the Third "Action" the Trembowla area was declared *Judenrein,* and from that moment onwards Jews were placed beyond the pale of the law. In other words a Gentile could torture or kill a Jew with impunity. If that weren't sufficient, the Germans offered a reward for anyone who disclosed the hiding place of a Jew and threatened with the death penalty anyone harboring a Jew. At that stage Rabbi Eliezer Leiter who had been hiding with a farmer in Scianki was killed.

The Jews hiding in the forests and fields were being killed, one by one (including Joseph, the son of Judah Drimmer), if not by the Germans then by farmers craving loot. Six to ten of the people hiding in the forests miraculously survived and twenty to thirty people were saved by farmers who hid them.

In July 1943, General Kovpak's partisan army passed through Trembowla. It was an irregular military force, wearing different uniforms — Russian, German, and civilian dress. They marched from east to west on foot and rode on horses and in wagons. They were armed with many types of weapons. It was said that Jewish partisans joined forces with them and were grudgingly accepted. It is difficult to ascertain the truth. We know that Kovpak's men fought the Germans stubbornly and that very few managed to reach the Carpathian foothills. In our region they passed through Iwanowka, Chatki, Zalawia, and Podhajczyki on their way west to the Carpathian foothills. Trembowla was then without a master. The Germans and the Ukrainian Militia fled to Tarnopol and they returned only a week later. This was an important event for those in hiding, for the farmers would react with excitement upon hearing the good news. The conduct of the Gentiles who hid Jews depended on the political and military situation.

As the front and the Red Army drew near, there was a marked improvement in the state of the Jews who were trying to hold out. But there were ups and downs. This situation lasted nine difficult months, but each hour brought our deliverance closer.

At dawn on March 22, 1944, Red Army units entered Trembowla.

I have tried to describe these events as accurately as possible, without adding or omitting anything. Thirty-five years have passed since these events took place and it is very difficult to describe everything and to write about people I lived with who are no longer alive.

Jews had been through difficult periods—the Cossack Massacres, the Polish uprisings, the First World War. But after each of these calamities there were survivors who continued Jewish life in Poland. After the Nazi Holocaust nothing is left of Jewish life on Polish soil. The German murderers were not satisfied with just killing people— they completely destroyed all Jewish cultural treasures. They demolished synagogues and cemeteries and they burned religious books and manuscripts—everything that had some connection with Judaism.

Was an uprising or rebellion possible without weapons and young people who knew how to use them? It was impossible to acquire a single gun, despite the many efforts of Bomba Einleger, Abraham Greenberg and this writer. Our connections with the Poles yielded no results. There was one case where Fridka Leviter literally spat in the face of a Gestapo agent and called him a criminal and murderer. Leopold Gelles, who saved himself after the First "Action," saw a Ukrainian militiaman beating his sister as she marched to Plebanowka during the Second "Action." He grabbed his wooden leg and beat the militiaman until he fell down bleeding. And Dr. Seret, at the edge of the trench in Plebanowka, proclaimed, as he was holding someone else's child, that the Germans would lose the war (that they had already lost it), and that everyone of them would be hanged for his crimes. The rattle of the machine gun cut short his proclamation.

13

Notes of an Engineer on the Holocaust in Trembowla

Gustaw Engel

Gustaw Engel, an engineer, had property in Tarnopol, and when the Soviets arrived, he was forced to move to Trembowla where he lived through the Nazi occupation. On scraps of paper he secretly made a record of the suffering that he and the Jews of Trembowla endured, as the events took place:

In the second half of the month of September, 1941, the Jews of Budzanow, Janow, and Strusow were ordered to move to Trembowla. The Jewish population of Trembowla thus grew from 1,500 people to 5,000. The order was carried out within three days. In the course of the move, the Jews of the other towns were forced to leave most of their belongings in their homes. The sight of wagons loaded with bundles and these uprooted men, women, and children roused sad thoughts in the minds of the local people.

The Judenrat housed the new residents in Jewish institutions such as synagogues, schools, etc.

On October 28, 1941, the *Sonderdienst* announced the establishment of the Ghetto which included part of Stryzelecka Street, Podzamcza, and Pokrowka (two side streets). The Judenrat's housing committee then placed the new people in private homes—several families to a room.

The First "Action"

On the third day after the Ghetto had been set up we learned of the arrival at the train station of a freight train with ten cars. The news spread quickly, and people began to scatter in search of hiding places. Early the next morning the Ghetto was surrounded by units of the S.D., the S.S., and the Ukrainian Militia. The members of the Judenrat were asked to serve as guides in the search for those in hiding.

In return, they and their families were to be spared.

The hunt for victims and the assembling of those found were accompanied by the non-stop din of gunfire. During the day the people who had been rounded up were brought to the town square and forced to sit for many hours without moving and wait until they were brought to the train station, where they were loaded onto the railroad cars. The members of the Judenrat and Jewish militia who tried to follow orders and help the henchmen were rewarded with the release of their wives but not of their children. There was a case of a Jewish militia-man's wife who was permitted to go free. When she heard the desperate call of her four-year-old son: "Mommy, you're leaving me," she returned to him, and then, the husband and father joined the transport, as well.

In the course of the "Action" groups of ruffians went from house to house, searching for people in hiding. They looked everywhere, removing hidden food and throwing it outside, turning furniture upside down and breaking it. Those they caught were dragged to the assembly point.

The "Action" lasted until four in the morning. It was marked by the crying of children and the shouting of adults.

When they returned from their hiding places, the survivors found their apartments emptied of whatever was valuable; the windows were smashed. In the apartment of this writer the large suitcase serving as a wardrobe was missing. A witness said that the murderer Miller saw it and snapped out angrily: "What the Jews still have!" And he took it for himself.

A summary of the "Action": 1,360 deportees and more than twenty dead, a third of the Jewish population in the Ghetto. During the "Action" the Judenrat was compelled to give the murderers food, drinks, and cigarettes. As a result of the "Action" the Ghetto was reduced in size, and the vicinity of Podzamcza was placed outside its confines. In these conditions it was necessary to make use of all available buildings for housing and use multiple-decker beds. From this point on, eight families were forced to live in an apartment of a single room and a kitchen, twenty-eight people in all. Nevertheless, in the apartment where this writer lived, brotherhood and peace prevailed. But this was not true of all the apartments.

Epidemics in the Ghetto

When winter came, epidemics of typhoid fever broke out in the

Ghetto. Prisoners released from the labor camps in return for bribes brought the disease back with them. The sick returnees died a short time later after infecting their relatives with typhus. The Judenrat set aside two quarantine chambers for forty patients in order to prevent the spread of the disease. The dead were buried at the edge of the Jewish cemetery, which had been destroyed the previous autumn. The area had been plowed up and the tombstones which had been removed, were now being used to pave courtyards and squares. The war being waged against the epidemics was the responsibility of a single doctor. After the district doctor visited the quarantine chambers, an order was issued to close off the Ghetto. No one was permitted to leave or enter it. At either end of the Ghetto signs in German and Ukrainian were posted — Typhus — and members of the *Ordnungsdienst* (Jewish Militia) were placed on guard. Only people working outside the Ghetto were given passes.

Abductions for the Camp in Tarnopol

Some Jews tried to evade the abductions by means of forged Aryan papers. Most of them fell into the hands of the Germans who were lurking in every corner. Others were turned in to the Germans or the Ukrainian Militia by their Aryan acquaintances who met them by chance.

An abduction operation was conducted one night in January 1942 for a new camp in Tarnopol, and with the help of the local *Ordnungsdienst* more than fifty men were taken into custody. At the head of this gang of snatchers stood the infamous Rockita together with the *Obmann* of the Tarnopol Judenrat, Greenfeld. Several of the captives were ransomed by their wives for three to four thousand zlotys per person.

The "Action" in April 1943

Our hiding place was three meters beneath the surface of the courtyard. For that reason we stopped running away to the forest. There was quiet during this period — until the sixth of April. That night we were awakened by the noise of automobiles, which stopped at the end of the street. Everyone rushed off to the apartment with the bunker and ten minutes later everyone was inside. There were forty of us. News about the course of the "Action" reached us as it was happening. We learned that those caught were being sent to

Plebanowka where, in a level area near the forest, they were murdered and buried in a common grave that had been prepared in advance. Only later did we learn that the rumor about the activity of the *Baudienst* (construction corps) was true. The military construction corps unit had been busy, the previous day, preparing large pits at Plebanowka. Until then we thought that the "Actions" in the guise of "resettlement" would be effected by means of rail transport. We had not yet heard about mass executions of the Jewish population on the spot because of a lack of trains.

That day, group after group of those seized were led in rows of six to the edge of the pits and machine gun fire was immediately aimed at them from a distance of several paces. All the victims had been forced to remove their clothes and their shoes. Several men pounced on the murderers with their fists, and they were killed at once. And the women burst into shouts and jeers, calling the murderers mad dogs who would come to a bitter end.

The "work" lasted until late in the evening. The task of filling in the pits, which were packed with human bodies, was given to the Jewish Militia. While working, they heard moans coming from inside the pits.

The Liquidation of the Ghetto

The month of May 1943 passed uneventfully. The mortality rate of the Ghetto residents reached 60 percent. Aside from the deportation to Belzec and the slaughter at Plebanowka, abductions to the labor camps and contagious diseases took a heavy toll of the Ghetto's population. Altogether there were at that time about 1900 people in the Ghetto.

Early in the morning on the third of June we were surprised by the sound of automobile motors at the edge of the district. That day most of the members of the Judenrat and the Jewish Militia perished, including the *Obmann* and the head of the Jewish Militia.

At that time all the Jewish communities in the Tarnopol region were liquidated, except for camp Rockite, and, along with them, all forced labor camps were destroyed, supposedly because of the partisans, who raided the camps and, after killing the guards, released the prisoners. Those liberated scattered and some of them joined their liberators.

On the second day of November we learned of a manhunt for survivors hiding in the forests.

At the beginning of March 1944, we learned of the entry of Red Army units into Tarnopol. The Germans launched a counterattack and the Russians withdrew. Afterwards, Red Army reinforcements arrived.

The battles lasted until March 25, 1944.

14

THE STORY OF
ADOLF DAVID HÜTLER
AND HIS BROTHER JACOB

S. Brinstein

THE FAMILY NAME "HITLER" existed long before the Nazi madman came to power in Germany. In the 1930s the Hitler family of Trembowla changed the spelling of their name to "Hütler," although the pronunciation of both names sounded exactly the same.

Both Adolf and Jack had a butcher shop, working together with their father. It was located in the old part of the small town of Trembowla. There was a third brother, Moses. The mother (Ethel) was the only female in the house. Her life wasn't an easy one, as she had no help for her duties in their busy household.

Life between World War I and World War II continued to flow more or less normally. There were lean and fat (if one can call them that) years. In general, it was hard work and not an easy life.

In the 1930's, the older brother, Jack, got married, and moved to another town — Czortkow. Four members of the family remained in Trembowla.

After the ascent to power of Adolf Hitler in Germany, the name Adolf suddenly became popular in Trembowla. "What are you doing here?" Gentile friends started to kid him. "Over there you could have a good job, and be a big shot," they continued to joke. So long as the Nazi "Führer" minded his own business in Berlin, foolish jokes didn't matter.

With the outbreak of World War II, the situation changed. The fateful year of 1941 was not far away. Adolf David Hütler, the small butcher in Trembowla, didn't have to go to Berlin to meet his "friend" carrying the same name. Berlin came to him.

On a Saturday, July 5, 1941, Adolf was standing on the main street (leading to Tarnopol) in the new part of town, waiting to meet the Nazi army, already on their way to Trembowla. There was a large crowd of Gentiles on the streets, waiting for the marching Nazi parade.

A Gentile friend, standing near Adolf, asked him: "What are you doing here? They'll kill you, don't you know?" Adolf got the message. He understood that it would be safer to stay home. He left the waiting crowd, being a little sorry to miss the moment of the Nazi takeover of Trembowla. The Soviet soldiers were long gone. There had been no struggle. The peaceful town was taken without a shot.

Being a good butcher by profession, Adolf got a job selling meat to the Germans and local Gentiles — not to the Jews. According to the Nazis, the Jews weren't human, so they did not need to eat. He continued to work for the Germans (in the Ukrainian *Sojuz*, or Union) for one year, being paid a weekly (or monthly) salary like the other Gentile workers.

The older brother, Jack, was living with his family in Czortkow. They had two children — a girl and a boy. A few weeks later, right after the Nazi takeover of the town, Jack was sent, with a group of other Jews, to the Slavelabor Camp: Kamionki 1. His family was still home. The Judenrat was ordered by the Nazis to deliver slaves.

Adolf continued to work at the same job. One nice day a Jewish messenger from the Judenrat (Sperling) came. "Adolf, come with me," he said. They went to Rosia's house (a Jewish owner). Gestapo Commander Miller had his temporary office there.

The Ukrainian *Sojuz* had notified the Trembowla *Landeskommisar* Weber, complaining that a worker they needed had been taken away. Weber arrived a little later. Knowing him well from the butcher shop where he worked, he asked: "You, what are you doing here? Come with me." They went into Miller's room. Weber explained: "We need this man; he works for us."

Adolf David Hütler was released. He continued to work at the same job. One day he was ordered to visit the German police. "What's your name?" he was asked. "Why?" "A Gentile lady mentioned it," he was told. "Yes, my name is Adolf Hütler." One Nazi officer looked at the other. "What, a Jew is carrying the name of our Führer?" That's impossible, they were thinking. "You're working in the *Sojuz*?" He was told to go home. The next day the Ukrainian police told him to go to Tarnopol to change his name. A Jew cannot have the name of the German leader of the Third Reich. He never went. He understood that he would never return alive.

A few weeks later, the Judenrat sent a man for Adolf again. He was taken from the shop. This time the *Landeskommissar* refused to intervene. "If his own people took him, what do they want from me?" Weber replied. "Now," he said, "I cannot do anything." The Judenrat received an order from the SS (or Gestapo), to deliver slaves to the labor camp. What could they do?

In July, 1942, Adolf was taken, with a group of others, to the Slave Labor Camp Kamionki. He wasn't even given a chance to say goodbye to his parents and brother. He never saw them again.

Later, in Kamionki, Podvolochysk region, he was notified that his mother died from hunger. His father and brother (according to a Gentile eyewitness) were shot in front of their house in 1943.

Both brothers met in Kamionki 1 Labor camp. After a while, Adolf was taken to a smaller camp, Kamionki 2. With little food, a small piece of bread, watery soup, scarcity of water, brutal beatings by some Jewish foremen and others made life in the camp intolerable. The cold and the heat were an additional plague. Many were starving and exhausted. Many others were shot for being useless, or for any violation of the rules, or for attempting to escape.

What work were Jewish slaves doing in Kamionki? They were forced to split large stones into small pieces. A stone quarry was in the area. The Germans were building roads to take them deeper and faster into Russia. They were marching eastward. Germans and Ukrainian Nationalists guarded the camps. Some of the guards were exceptionally brutal, some others not. One of the German guards told them: "The Russians will travel on these roads, and not the Germans." His prophecy was correct.

Sometime in 1943, Adolf fell sick with typhus. His toes froze from the bitter, icy weather. They were infected and rotten. Having lost weight, he was barely able to walk. He was already a walking skeleton.

One nice day, during a lineup outside, the German camp boss (or his deputy) noticed him. "Who is this; can he work?" The German pulled out his pistol, putting it to the side of Adolf's head. A Jewish foreman (from Czortkow), speaking perfect German, interceded, explaining that Adolf was a good worker who got sick temporarily. Adolf pleaded for his life: "Please, don't shoot, please." The German put back his pistol and left. The Jewish foreman helped to save his life.

Did the Jewish camp inmates know the extent of the extermination in other areas? Many of them knew. Periodically, the German and the Ukrainian Nationalist newspapers reported which areas were already *Judenfrei*. The extermination wave continued eastward.

Did the victims know about the situation on the front lines? Information streamed in from different sources. The more defeats the Nazi army suffered on the Eastern front, the less hope remained.

With each blow the Fascist Wehrmacht received, the extermination was speeded up. They had little hope of seeing the day of Liberation. The *Judenrein* order continued to swallow more and more helpless victims.

During the middle of 1943, the tragic situation was clear to all. The inmates started to count the days. Months and weeks were only a distant past.

Passing by a group of working inmates, a Polish man stopped for a few seconds and said: "You stupid Jews. What are you waiting for? Why are you not running? They'll kill you today or tomorrow." The slaves listened. They understood. Anti-Nazi partisans were already roaming the forests in the area. They didn't move. Where would they go, and what would they do without weapons?

The inmates from Kamionki 2 were transferred to Kamionki 1. They marched eight to ten kilometers. Some, not able to keep up, were shot on the way. The victims knew the end was near. They didn't move. To them, the situation seemed hopeless. Jack Gluck (from Budzanow) said to Adolf: "Where will I go? All my family is dead. If the Germans don't catch me, the Ukrainians will."

The night before the camp was destroyed by the Nazis, Adolf and Jack decided it was now or never. They managed to cut a hole in the fence. It was July 1943. The grass in the field was tall. The forest wasn't far away. There was a chance.

In the dark, through the fields into the woods. Rain or shine, hungry or thirsty, there was no walking through the fields during the day. The danger of being caught was lurking everywhere.

The slave labor camp, Kamionki 1, was destroyed by the Nazis on July 9, 1943. Gasoline was poured on the barracks and set afire. All those trying to escape were shot by waiting machine guns.

Some managed to run away a night or two before. The remaining victims, around 1,500, perished in the flames.

After two days underway, they met a young Gentile lady from Trembowla. She recognized them both. "Where are you going?" she asked. Back to Trembowla. "There are no more Jews there. They'll kill you." They continued to walk. The last and only hope was to reach the outskirts of Trembowla and hide, with the help of good Gentiles they knew in the area.

After four or five days without food and water, they reached their destination. During the darkness of the night, they crossed the bridge dividing the two parts of the town. The danger of being caught by the German or Ukrainian police wasn't overlooked.

Early in the morning they knocked on the door of a house known to both. A lady, Stefa Szmigelska, came out. "Oh, what are you doing here? Where are you coming from? Did anybody see you?" Both were asked to come inside. Finally, a little safety and a warm meal.

A small cellar hole, together with a goat inside, was too crowded for three. It was cold and wet, and too dangerous. After five or six weeks together, Adolf decided to find another place to hide.

Luckily, the Gentile family Friedel (of Austrian extraction), agreed to help him. In return, he promised to leave them the house after the war. A barn full of straw and hay served as a hiding place. He received warm meals regularly every day. During the winter months he had no clothes. They had been torn into pieces. He was wrapped in rags, almost naked.

From time to time, one brother tried to see the other. Once they were caught by a Ukrainian (Kowalski), who was known for his brutality. "Bring me a knife," he ordered his wife. She came outside. "Jesus Maria, what do you want from them. They have already lost their mother, father and brother. Let them go." Adolf turned to the wife: "Pani Kowalski, please help us." The Ukrainian dropped the knife. "Get lost, and don't tell anybody you were in my hands."

Jack had it much worse. The lady at whose place he was hiding, was very poor. She (and her old mother) didn't have enough food for themselves. He had to steal and beg some food from others. Dogs, cats, and rats could envy them both. They weren't Jewish. They were safe and secure.

The German Nazis and Ukrainian Nationalists often staged hunting parties. In the surrounding forests they enjoyed hunting rabbits and Jews. There were groups of Jews hiding in deep underground bunkers. Most of these were caught and shot.

For Adolf and Jack, the hiding nightmare lasted nine long months. Jack spent much of his free time killing lice and fleas. Finally, on March 22, 1944, Trembowla was liberated by the Red Army. The Ukrainian police were the last to leave the town. They knew that retribution was near. They also knew why they were on the run.

Jack was the first to return to their house. Adolf David Hütler was second. He had no clothes, so he had to wait another day.

The house was almost empty. The Gentile tenants left the premises a day or two before. They knew that the two butcher boys were alive and would return. The walls were decorated with holy pictures. Their mother, father, and brother were no more.

Thirst for revenge was on Jack's mind. The Ukrainian Nationalist police were gone. He did not give up. He remembered well the sleepless nights in the dark cellar with the goat.

The only warm sweater he had, which he had worn for quite a long time, was loaded with an army of fat lice. He lit the stove, putting more wood inside. When the stove got red-hot, Jack took off the woolen sweater. Turning to Adolf, he said: "Now I'm going to take revenge; today I will pay them back." He threw the sweater inside the stove. He was delighted hearing each knock coming from the burning parasites. "I have been waiting for nine months for this day." Jack concluded.

The next day both decided to visit the marketplace (Bazaar), called "Planta," the gathering place of the rounded-up Jews during the "Actions." Adolf noticed something was missing. The huge sign in the Ukrainian language, hanging before the Bazaar entrance: "Entrance Is Forbidden for Dogs and Jews," was not there. Gone also was the wall-poster in the German and Ukrainian languages; "Jews are disease carriers. No sale of prescriptions to Jews," hanging inside the former Jewish (Herman's) Pharmacy.

It was time for Jack to visit Czortkow. In 1941, he had left a large family there. With a heavy heart he boarded the train. There was still a ray of hope.

The place where his clay house had been standing was flat. All the family of fourteen, including his wife and two children, were gone. The gray house in which they used to live had shared the same fate. It was also gone.

Some of the victims found their tragic end in the Belzec gas chamber. Other victims were shot in the Czortkow Forest. Young children were thrown from balconies into the streets.

Jack died in the United States about eight years ago, at the age of 78.

Adolf is alive and well. He has two children, a son and a daughter, and two lovely grandsons. Adolf Hütler, the small-town butcher, managed to outlast the Führer of the "Thousand Year Reich."

More of the Story of Adolf David Hütler

During my lengthy conversations with Adolf David H., I did try to find out as much as possible about events during the Nazi occupation. Here are a few additional stories he still remembers:

"There were some Gentile scoundrels who tried to derive a

personal profit from the hounded unfortunate Jewish victims. They went into the death-dealing 'business.'

"A resident of Trembowla outskirts, Stryletsky (or Stylecki), Ukrainian nationality, lured 81 Jews to their death by promising to hide them (from the Nazis) for money and valuables.

"After a short period of time, they were liquidated, one-by-one, leaving behind whatever they brought with them. The liquidation method was brutal: Kill them yourself, or deliver the victims to the German or Ukrainian police. The combination of both methods was probably used. One young Jewish boy, David (Dudzio) Pfeffer, now residing in the U.S.A., was left alive, just in case an alibi will be needed later.

"I had found out about this tragic story," Adolf continued, "from Gentiles, right after the liberation, 1944.

In his memoirs, I. Goldfliess, also a Holocaust survivor, mentions Stylecki's name as a go-between. . . and helpful to some Jews. But at the same time he concedes (independently) that he heard some other stories about him, which he was not able to verify.

"The other Ukrainian, M. Shtyk, Jr., also a resident of another Trembowla outskirt, killed 13 Jews 'only.' The reason for his killing sprees was bestial Jew-hatred, not for personal profit," Adolf explained.

"How did you find out about this?" I asked Adolf again. He said, "I was no witness to these grisly events, but I did not invent those stories. After the liberation, some Gentiles started to talk more openly. The German Nazis and the Ukrainian Nationalist police were gone. All those things I do remember like yesterday."

Here is another interesting story Adolf H. remembers: "Before the Nazi Army entered the town Trembowla, a group of Jews (some from a nearby village) decided to run eastward. As I have found out later, they managed to reach Kiev, the capital of the Ukraine SSR.

"There was no train waiting for them at the railroad station there. They were disappointed. A Soviet railroad-man explained that the evacuation-trains are going and coming, advising them to wait.

"Hours passed and no train was visible. They started to lose patience. They changed their mind and decided to return 'home'. . . . From time-to-time, they hitched a ride, but mostly they kept walking for miles.

"During the return journey they were attacked by Ukrainian Nationalist thugs, and brutally beaten with chains and iron bars. Some barely managed to reach the town alive.

"You were already so far away, safe from the Germans, why did you return?" Adolf H. asked them. They said, "We made a terrible mistake. We regret it."

Their decision to return home was a fatal mistake, as it turned out later. It was too late to try again. Their fate was sealed. Very few managed to escape the deadly Nazi claws.

The hour was late. Our conversation neared its end. We parted with the words: *"Auf wiedersehen,"* stay well.

The following is a copy of a letter Jacob Hütler wrote to his cousin, Israel, in Soviet Central Asia. The letter is in Polish.

December 26, 1944
Chortkow

Dear Cousin Israel:

You are asking, who remains alive? I can tell you the good news that my brother, Adolf, is alive. Our relative, Josef, with his wife and son, are alive in Budzanow. A few distant relatives from my wife's side, are also alive. All the other relatives are dead.

My mother died (from hunger) on Yom Kippur, the Atonement Day, in 1942, just a few days before the first Nazi 'Action' in Trembowla. My father, my brother, Moses, and your mother, were deported to Belzec (Extermination Camp).* At that time a few hundred Jews were rounded up, transported by railroad, and all of them were burned there.

Two Nazi 'Actions' took place in Trembowla. They (the Jews) were killed in the Plebanowka pits. My wife, the two young children (a girl and a boy), and the rest of the family (around 14 people), were all deported from Chortkow to Belzec with the first 'Action,' where they were murdered.

In Trembowla, around 40 Jews remained alive. In Chortkow, around 100. In Tarnopol, there are around 200 Jews left.

I (and Adolf), were in Kamionki (slave-labor) Camp over 20 months. On July 6, 1943, we smelled that an 'Action' was planned in the camp. We managed to cut a hole in the fence, and escaped during that night.

On July 7, 1943 (or a few days later), at 3:00 a.m., the Camp was surrounded by the Nazis and set in flames, in which nearly

---

*Accounts differ. According to eyewitnesses, Henryka Stachowiak, née-Friedel, Jacob's father and brother were shot by the Nazis in front of their own house. Another Gentile witness allegedly saw the brother (Moses) hanging, head down, for a few days. The reason for the special barbaric treatment was his name — Hütler.

all inmates perished.* Very few managed to escape. We ran away back to Trembowla outskirts, where we found a hiding place for 9 long months, till March 22, 1944, when the Red Army liberated us.

Of our relative, Munio, nothing is known. He was in Russia. I am in Chortkow, and am O.K. David (Adolf) was taken to Russia. We don't have each others' address, therefore we don't correspond.

Our house in Trembowla is still there. The house of my wife's family was completely flattened. We have nothing else left, except that we remained alive, which is good.

David (Adolf) was hidden 7½ months in one place, covered with a sack only, because he was naked. I had it even worse. I was forced to beg for a piece of bread from Gentiles at night.

In the beginning we were both caught by a known Gentile (Kowalsky), who tried to deliver us to the German (or Ukrainian) Police. With tears in our eyes, begging for our lives, we were able finally to change his mind. We were released. Similar deadly incidents happened quite a few times. The threat to be caught and shot was hanging over our heads constantly.

When we will meet in the future, I will tell you the whole story. I am waiting for the moment when we can see each other. In the meantime, stay well. Regards and best wishes from your cousin, Jacob. My address in Chortkow is...Markus Nusembaum is alive.

(Translated by S. Brinstein)

*According to Mr. S. Halpern, a Holocaust survivor, 14,000–15,000 Jews perished in the Nazi slave-labor camps: Kamionki 1, Kamionki 2, and nearby camps.

15

THE AGONY OF A PEOPLE

Moshe Briller

In my reflections, I remember the little town of Trembowla, Tarnopol region, situated in the southeastern part of old, prewar Poland, in a corner, bordering on Rumania in the south, in the east on the Soviet Union, and which now belongs to the Ukrainian SSR.

Physically it somehow, even if only remotely, resembled the view I face now in the Catskills. It was a beautiful town. A part of Podolia, not far from Tarnopol and Lvov, it was one of the most picturesque towns on the road from Lvov to the prewar border of the Soviet Union. It was nestled in a valley. It spread on both sides of the small river that ran through its midst. It was surrounded by mountains and hills and if one ascended one of the hills and happened to look down from the famous Zamek (castle) or the Pokrovka (a mountain), a magnificently beautiful view spread under one's feet; roads winding among the fields of the outlying villages; and running through the midst of the town to a river that shone with brilliant reflections from the sunglare, or at night from the moon, traversing over the town. Houses stood along the whole length of the town, some proudly standing along the roads, others hidden under the protective presence of the high hills and among the numerous orchards that grew in great abundance around the town.

It was a nice town. We Jews lived there for long centuries. Generations followed generations. Children grew, married, and bore new generations. Life was poor. The Christians were our neighbors; we lived among them, right in their midst. Life was difficult. It was a constant struggle to keep alive, a struggle for a bare piece of bread. In general, we got along well with our neighbors, the Christians. It was a peaceful co-existence, or rather, to be more precise, we were tolerated. But Pogroms happened often — periodically — bloody Pogroms, in accordance with the prevailing policy. After all, a Jew was a proverbial scapegoat — a "Wandering Jew." It was a convenient policy to blame the Jews for all the misfortunes: for financial difficulties, for the grinding poverty of the populace, for the oppression by the authorities and the nobility, for miseries brought on by the constant wars and even for plagues and illnesses.

Jews suffered and accepted everything submissively. What could they do; what other choice did they have? It was the time between the two world wars. Europe was transformed by the Versailles Treaty. The old empires of Europe were crumbling. A host of new, small counties were emerging as independent states. Self-rule was the new fashion. Democratic order was to be introduced, the rights of all minorities to be respected, civil rights to be granted to all. But it was easier said than done. Frictions between the new small countries broke out almost immediately after a peace treaty was signed. The sword became preferred to negotiations, national chauvinism replaced good sense and friendly neighborly relations. Jews almost universally throughout Europe became the butt of national frustrations.

Poland was no exception. The old animosity towards the eternal scapegoat flared up with renewed force. Forgotten immediately were the Pole's own sufferings after their country was partitioned between the three neighboring powers — Russia, Prussia and Austria. All lamentations, all complaints became drowned in the outcries of new nationalistic feelings. Their own difficulties, their poverty, lack of jobs, and the quiet dissatisfaction of the masses only gave new fuel and strength to boisterous displays of great power, self-praise, and military parades. All minorities, but especially the Jews, became subjected to new outbreaks of violence, outright murder, economic persecutions, and to discrimination of all possible kinds.

The children lived in their own imaginary castles, unconscious of any other life. Of course, they were not immune from suffering. Often they were beaten by the neighbors' children, often they were reminded that they were only "dirty Jews," inferiors among the others, their "betters." Christian children chased them away from participating in their games, and at school, they had to work hard to succeed in getting satisfactory marks. But they learned early. They formed their own circles, their own groups. They played and danced, they sang and read books, and when holidays came, enjoyed it to the utmost. Even when food in the house was scarce, when scarcities became common and buying a new dress, a new pair of shoes, became an almost impossible dream, they did not despair. Youth does not cry over such things, especially when they know little about other possibilities. They were happy, or seemed to be happy, even if not always content.

It became difficult to be a Jew. Jobs were few and almost beyond the dream of ordinary poor Jews. The young lived a life of hopelessness. Some, especially those among the wealthier, could still hope that with family financial help and connections, and sometimes a little luck, they would be able to eventually establish themselves. To the vast majority, this would remain a futile dream. The new policy of the government followed the slogans of the anti-Jewish official boycott. In accordance with the new propaganda urgings, Poles were advised not to patronize Jewish merchants. "Buy from your own" was the cry. Such conditions forced the Jews to look for new outlets. Many tried to emigrate to other countries; few succeeded. All borders to other countries were tightly shut.

In Europe, the general atmosphere at that time was gloomy beyond description. Threatening, dark clouds kept gathering overhead. A new monster appeared on the horizon in the form of Nazism. A madman under the name of Adolf Hitler assumed power in Germany and, by swallowing up one small country after another, threatened to turn Europe into one large concentration camp. The Jews suffered the most. Hitler quite openly announced his intention to exterminate all the Jews. No one at that time took his words seriously, for such things seemed inconceivable. The Germans, one of the most cultured and civilized nations in Europe, could not perpetrate such a thing. This was genocide. The Jews, least of all, believed in it. Even when thousands upon thousands of their brethren were arrested without the slightest provocation, beaten, mutilated, tortured, their property confiscated, their Synagogues destroyed, burned down or leveled to the ground, and even when people kept disappearing in the confines of the terrible, inhuman concentration camps, crematoriums, death camps, the outright shootings, hangings and all the other forms of death, the Jews did not believe that human beings could do such things.

They were to learn anew what it meant to be a Jew. They were to go through the most horrendous experiences in the tragic history of their nation. The Second World War brought with it hitherto unimagined woes.

Six million were to die.

Are there words or expressions that could adequately describe the sufferings of a people, condemned to an untimely death by the "master race" of the twentieth century?

Can anyone describe the anguish of a mother who is forced to witness the deliberately slow death (one after another) of all of her family?

Or the anguish of the child whose mother is shot in front of it?

Or the forcibly suppressed tears of a mother whose child is torn to pieces by a pious and devoted Gestapo officer?

Or an old man who, pronouncing for the last time his "Sh'ma Yisroel," (Hear oh Israel) is shot in the back of his neck?

Or the multitudes of people who, having been promised resettlement, have been loaded into unsanitary cattle wagons, without food or medicines, driven on their long way to camps and then simply and cruelly gassed to death?

These were the famous extermination camps — the Auschwitzes and Treblinkas, to mention just two, the death factories, the inventions of modern technology.

Or the groups of "luckier" prisoners who, having been selected to clean up the mess after a new batch of bodies, had been burned to ashes in the crematorium?

Or the prisoners whom the jailers subjected to the most painful and degrading medical experimentations?

Six million! Can anyone really comprehend the enormity of the crime?

Six million Jews, plus millions of other nationals, on whose ashes Hitler and his thugs intended to build their "Thousand Year Reich," a "New Order" in Europe.

It is beyond human comprehension, but it happened nonetheless.

It happened in the heart of Europe, and wherever the Nazis put down their stamp of new inhumanity. It happened in every occupied city, town, and village on the European continent. It happened in Trembowla, the peaceful, sleepy, little town in the Eastern part of Poland; in a town rich in all kinds of fruit orchards, rich in natural beauty and possessing a river that cuts through its midst, dividing it into an old and new city. It happened there, too.

This was a calamity.

Photo

Documents

From The Ukraine

Trembowla, Tarnopol region, Ukr. SSR. A view of the town of Trembowla before World War II.

Former L. Shertzer house, location of Ukrainian Nationalist Police during the Nazi occupation, 1988.

Before World War II, Trembowla Jews celebrate new Torah. Rabbi E. Leiter is holding Torah under cover. Courtesy: Sol Selzer, U.S.A.

Excavated Jewish bodies, Tarnopol region, 1944–45. Courtesy: Tarnopol Museum Archive.

Monument dedicated to the Trembowla Jewish victims of German Nazism (and their collaborators) during World War II, 1986.

David Salomon Gans with a sack of bread. "Now you'll take a ride straight to heaven . . ." Trembowla, Ukr.SSR.

From the depths . . . Salomea Luft and her husband, David.

A Nazi officer and a Nationalist collaborator on the same platform. Tarnopol: June 1941.

Coadjutor (successor) and assistant to Metropolitan Sheptytsky, Joseph Slipij, from the first days of occupation faithfully served the Nazis. The Cardinal respectfully greets Hans Frank (1942), the Nazi Gauleiter.

A pile of human bodies and a pile of wood . . . the Red Army reveals Nazi attempts to erase the traces of their heinous crimes.
Courtesy: Tarnopol Museum Archive.

Monument dedicated to 22 Jewish victims murdered by the Germans, July 4, 1941.
Courtesy Tarnopol Museum Archive.

The Friedel family (Righteous Gentiles). They saved the life of a Jewish man, Adolf David Hütler, during the Nazi occupation, 1943–44.

Adolf David Hütler, a Holocaust survivor, meeting Mrs. S. Shmigielska in Tarnopol—1986. She saved the life of his brother, Jacob, and also his own life during their first weeks in hiding.

Metropolitan A. Sheptytsky of the Greek Catholic Church with his Ukrainian Nationalist assistants. The Metropolitan wears a swastika badge on his coat. Courtesy: Soviet Archives, Ukrainian SSR

This photo was found on the premises of the SD force in Stanislav. In it, local residents identified the Kindrativ cousins — Olexa and Mikhailo. The man in the second row on the right side is Yaroslav Fischer, formerly a resident of Nadvirna, the killer of Jews who eventually found sanctuary in the American city of Cleveland.

Ukrainian Nationalists took part in this massacre of Jews in Drohobych, Western Ukraine, 1942. Courtesy: Soviet State Archive, Ukr. SSR

Excavated human bodies, Tarnopol region. This photo depicts a Soviet Military-Medical Commission investigating Nazi crimes, 1944–45. Courtesy: Tarnopol Museum Archive

Volodymyr Kubijovych, Ukrainian Nationalist collaborator, authored the "Encyclopedia of the Ukraine" after the war. This photo shows him sharing a platform with Military Governor O. Wechter on the occasion of the formation of the Ukrainian-manned SS Division "Galizien."

Ukrainian Nationalists took part in this shooting of Jews in Boryslav, Western Ukraine, 1942.
Courtesy: Soviet State Archives.

This chilling photo speaks for itself. A Jewish family is flanked on the left by German soldiers and on the right by Ukrainian Nationalist collaborators (wearing white armbands). The family is being taken into the woods in the vicinity of the town of Krementzin in the Tarnopol region in 1942.

This map of the Tarnopol region dates from the late 1920's–early 1930's.

Part Three

PERSONAL

TESTIMONIES

AND EYEWITNESSES

December 1943 (New Year's Eve)
"In the evening, platoon leader Sobko of the Ukrainian Self-Defense Legion announced to his men that a shooting of Jews was to be held in the schoolyard at night. He called for volunteers. . . . On their return several hours later, [Kolesnik and Kurkash] were intoxicated and showing every mark of extreme agitation. . . . Kolesnik told the Legionnaires that the Germans had motored in about 300 Jews. They were forced to strip naked, driven to the edge of the trenches dug beforehand, and shot there. Kolesnik, for one, killed them by pistol shots to the back of the head."

From eyewitness accounts of massacres in the village of Pidhaitsi, Lutsk District, Volyn Region
(Valery Styrkul, *We Accuse,* Kiev: 1984)

16

I Shall Not Die, for I Shall Live

Esther Goldstein née Greenberg

During the occupation and afterwards I thought that I would be able to write a book about my experiences. Today, thirty-five years later, I can no longer concentrate in order to describe the suffering I went through. What happened then is unbelievable and indescribable. Only someone who personally experienced the Holocaust will understand. No detailed description of what occurred there is possible. I shall only try to describe some incidents and situations of the inhuman life in the Ghetto.

It began on the second day after the Germans arrived. We were standing on line for bread near Werber's house together with many women. The Germans removed us roughly from the line. We were certain that we were being led to our execution. We were assigned different tasks and kept there till that night. At home, no one knew what had happened to us.

Every day they took us from our homes to go to work for them. This was done until the Judenrat was established. It was responsible, thereafter, for supplying a number of workers every day. The women were sent to do a variety of tasks and the men were taken for hard work.

I worked hard at these different tasks. The hardest work was at an estate in Semenow, where I operated a threshing machine at a very rapid pace. We were beaten while working. We were forced to return home late at night by way of the Monastery, frightened and hungry.

The Gentiles were given the right to select Jews for various jobs, and they shamelessly took advantage of it, selecting former friends and acquaintances. I remember that Dr. Zelermayer and two other Jews had to take a ton of coal down to the cellar of Dr. Zaplitny, a former colleague of Dr. Zelermayer. A former classmate of my brother Milo took him to the village of Boriczowka to bury a dead horse. He hadn't told him in advance where he was being taken and for what purpose. When my brother returned home that night we were overjoyed because we feared that we might not see him again.

We were subjected to scorn and humiliation by people who had just recently been our friends and neighbors.

Our situation became desperate when we were transferred to the Ghetto. There were thirty to forty of us in every apartment. We knew what the purpose of the transfer was. We had heard about what had happened in the nearby towns and cities. The transfer was effected by means of rented wagons, in which the old people, the sick, and small children rode. The rest of the people trailed along behind the wagons and carried bundles on their shoulders. The first "Action" took place several days after the transfer. Many Jews were loaded onto freight cars and taken to an unknown destination. The Judenrat immediately paid two Poles to find out where they were being sent. There were rumors that they were being taken to Belzec.

Because of the terrible crowding and the filth, a typhus epidemic broke out. Dozens of people died daily, primarily from want of medicine and lack of proper treatment. One of the victims was my brother Milo. He had been ransomed from the camp with much effort. He came home with a high fever, suffering from typhus. The only one who attended to burial preparations was Nathaniel Melzer.

The following two "Actions" were carried out at Plebanowka. The graves had been prepared in advance. In those spring days when Christian women went with their children to church services dressed in white, Jewish mothers marched with their children to open graves.

Not everyone was fortunate enough to die at once. The following day one German boasted that he could no longer bear the moans of the wounded, so he shot them out of mercy.

After the third "Action" the city was declared *Judenrein*.

It was Friday afternoon. They shot at any Jew remaining in the Ghetto. Whoever had managed to secure a hiding place earlier left the Ghetto in time. Having no way out, the rest of the residents were doomed.

I went out of the house to see what was happening in the Ghetto. I did not get a chance to return to my parents. There was shooting a short distance from where I was standing. Many fell while running. I too ran; I thought that I was still in the Ghetto. I growled like a dog out of fear. In order to take cover from the shooting, I climbed into a dovecote with feet injured from the barbed wire. From voices of people speaking near me, I understood that I was outside the Ghetto in the house of one Koszcylniak. I heard him say to his sons that they should remove the clothes from the dead. From that remark I understood his attitude to what was happening.

The shooting stopped, and I heard only the footsteps of the guards on duty. Before dawn I decided to leave my hiding place. I went through the window, and the members of the household were not awakened by me. Outside I saw dead people in their underwear around the house.

For lack of an alternative, I sought safety in a most dangerous place. I hid there for thirteen weeks, without food and in perpetual fear. I ate dirty chicken feed. No one saw or heard me. Once every two or three days I went out at night for a breath of air. I was thin as a skeleton. I weighed perhaps 30 kilograms. My teeth were loose. I was suffering from cold and hunger. I in no way resembled a human being.

I don't know where my strength to live in these conditions came from. I wanted to live to see the downfall of our cruel enemies who wanted to conquer the world by killing women and children.

After remaining there for thirteen weeks I was forced to leave my hiding place. I wandered from place to place and begged for a night's lodging. Even people who had once displayed affection toward me demanded that I leave immediately.

When the first snow fell, I did not have a roof over my head. I was hungry, shivering with cold — a skeleton in rags. At first glance one could tell that I was a Jewess.

Finally, I arrived at the home of a farm wife in Krowinka, who had been a customer in our store and who had known me since my childhood. She became frightened upon seeing me and thought me a corpse. She took me in with great fear, but she didn't have the heart to send me away. At night she moved me to the loft above the stable. I had to promise her that in case I were discovered I would say that I got there without the knowledge of the farm wife. For that reason she didn't even give me anything to cover myself with. In the meantime the cold intensified. Suffering from hunger — once a day I received a very small portion of food — and from cold, I suddenly felt stabbing pains in my side and a high fever. I did not reveal this to the farm wife, and I prayed to God that I would fall asleep and not wake up again. This seemed to be the best solution to my distress. I greatly feared being led away and executed.

The farm wife, who was Polish, was panic-stricken. The barking of the dog terrified her. One day, concerned that I might freeze to death, she told me to leave her house. So I suggested the following solution to her. If I were to freeze to death, she should place my body in a sack — after all, I didn't weigh more than 39 kilograms — and throw it into the nearby river in the evening. That way no one would know or care where I came from. My suggestion calmed her down, and I was able to stay with her until the end of the Nazi occupation.

All our relatives perished in the second "Action," the Selzer, Ginsberg, and Strasberg families in a mass grave at Plebanowka. My dear parents, my sister and my uncle (my father's brother) were killed three days after the town was declared *Judenrein,* in an open grave near the barracks.

My uncle, Joseph Selzer, his wife, and their three sons were killed six weeks before the arrival of the Red Army in the village of Wigdorowka. One of the neighbors disclosed the location of their bunker to the Germans.

I was the only survivor of my entire family. My ordeal deeply affected me psychologically and ruined my health. I fell ill with typhus and pneumonia. Dr. Hindes, who was with us afterwards, was amazed that I recovered.

After the war I decided that I would establish a bond only with a man who had lived through the same events and the same experiences which I had lived through, a man with precise knowledge of the conditions and circumstances of those days which would be a subject for us to recollect until the end of time.

17

I Weep for My Child

Sarah Frankel (Shenhaut)

Wʜᴇɴ ᴛʜᴇ "Aᴄᴛɪᴏɴs" ʙᴇɢᴀɴ in the nearby towns, I began to wander from place to place with a baby who was not yet a year and a half. I held him in my arms. At first I stayed with him in the Wolica fields for ten days. Afterwards I began to travel illegally from town to town to places where "Actions" had already taken place, even though these trips were forbidden. I was in Mikulince, Kopyczynce, and Chorostkow.

After weeks of wandering I decided to return to Trembowla. Our apartment was being occupied by people from other towns, but that did not matter, because several days later the Ghetto was set up, and immediately afterwards the first "Action" took place on November 5, 1942. During this "Action" my mother, my baby and I hid in a small room behind Sanitela's bakery. The door was concealed by a pile of boards from the bakery. Unfortunately, those who prepared the camouflage did not remain alive. They were my Uncle Haliczer and my father-in-law. We sat there for 24 hours. Beta Weiss knew about the hiding place and thanks to her we were set free.

When the second "Action" began, I wanted to escape with the child to the forest, but it was already too late. There was shooting, and I returned to Winiarski's house, which we were living in. It was near the tax office. We went down to a shelter designated for us, together with my sister-in-law Malka and her children. The adults went into another shelter which was discovered. All the people hiding there were taken to Plebanowka and exterminated. Among them were my mother and the other members of my family.

During the third "Action" I was living illegally in Brief's apartment on Podzamcza Street. At night I escaped with my son, who was then two years old, into the woods near the fortress, without water or a slice of bread. I cannot begin to describe my suffering at the sight of my son's great distress. He could not fast.

Towards evening I decided to return to the house of the teacher, Mr. Reisberg, where I had been living. I had no alternative, and I no longer had the strength to endure. On my way through Podzamcza Street I heard Christian children calling me. Mrs. Sela, don't go into the Ghetto; they are still shooting there. Taking heed of this warning, I decided not to return to the Ghetto. Using side streets, I reached Chrzanowska Street and walked along it until I reached Wolica, where I went to the house of a farm wife with whom I was acquainted. There we were fed, and we went to sleep in the barn. The next day, which was Friday, I went back to the Ghetto with my boy. We didn't find a soul there. In the street lay the body of Mrs. Schechter, Lonka's mother. There wasn't a single child in the courtyard. Only my boy wandered about and pointed out the body to all passers-by, "Here is Grandma Schechter whom the Germans killed."

A few hours later, I learned that Trembowla had been declared *Judenrein*. I decided to go to Kopyczynce. I asked my uncle Bernklau to obtain a wagon for me, but the Ukrainian militiamen said to the wagon driver: "Let her go on her knees."

I wanted to return to the Ghetto to pick up a few changes of clothing for my boy. When I was near Dr. Stern's house, I suddenly heard shots, so I returned to Podzamcza. From there I crossed the Gniezna River, near Brodink's mill, to the new city. Walking along out-of-the-way streets I reached Wolica. As I was walking I heard the sound of footsteps behind me. I was afraid to turn around. I discovered that it was a Jew named Glazer from Budzannow who was following me because he saw that I knew the way. In Wolica, the barn where I had already spent several nights with my child was locked and there was a dog chained outside. But we found a small opening and went inside. Early in the morning the farm wife came in and told us to leave because she was frightened.

We went out to the field and she promised to bring the boy a slice of bread. But she didn't bring it, and after waiting several hours, we left. I held the child in my arms and headed for Kopyczynce; I got there Sunday just before morning. I had an uncle there. After washing the boy, I put him to bed, and suddenly panic set in; an "Action" had begun.

In my uncle's house there were two good shelters, and when the "Action" began many outsiders squeezed into them. In this "Action" my son was taken from me. After all the suffering he had endured as a Jew, a neighbor of my uncle killed him.

The child was tired after all he had just been through, after the "Action" in Trembowla on Thursday, and the flight to Kopyczynce. While we were sitting in the bunker, the boy twice said: "Mommy, I want to go home." After he said that the second time a small torch was shined in my face, and the child was taken from me. And then it happened.

I began to shout. They wanted to kill me, but my uncle saved me.

My uncle and my family, along with several acquaintances, made a bunker in the forest. We hid there, and the farmers provided us with food at a fair price. After doing this for three weeks, they stopped providing us with food, and the villagers attacked us and fired rifle shots. We negotiated with them, but could no longer stay in the bunker, and we returned to town. We entered a house full of blood. The men began to build a shelter. When they finished building it, an "Action" took place in which my uncle and cousin were killed. The Ukrainian militia discovered us in the evening, but we managed to buy them off.

At night we left the shelter and went to a farmer whom we knew, but he did not consent to let us stay with him.

We went to a farm at which a number of Jewish survivors were staying and worked there for several weeks, until the place was declared *Judenrein*. The last members of my family were killed then.

I wasn't at the farm when the "Action" took place. I was with farmers outside the village where I worked as an artisan. In the meantime many people came in great haste from the farm. Then a woman took me to a field where I was saved in a ditch covered with leaves. Several days later I wandered near the farm, and from there I went with several people to the forest. We built a shelter once again, and when we were detected by a resident of the area, we fled at night. In the last bunker in the fields of Kopyczynce, several local farmers noticed us, and then a group of five people left us (a family of four and their friend) with the intentions of hiding with farmers in the area, but they did not succeed and were killed in the forest.

I was left with two people and without any money. One of the men was an invalid; he was a good man and said that he would not leave me. We returned to our previous bunker.

We did not even have a chance to get settled when a member of the village Ukrainian militia and a murderer from the village appeared. They were looking for Jews. They had seen our tracks, and the murderer fired one shot inside the bunker. Then the gun jammed. The straw did not catch on fire as a result of the first shot.

They wanted us to suffocate from the smoke. They pretended to be moving away, but we saw their feet standing in one spot.

After that I spent one week with the wife of a farmer for whom I worked as an artisan. Then I went somewhere else, where I sat near a cow to warm up (it was winter, and there was snow outside).

From there I returned to the last bunker, and during the two weeks, before the arrival of the Red Army, I stayed with Polish farmers in a settlement near Kopyczynce.

18

THIS IS HOW I WAS SAVED

Shenya Bomza

TREMBOWLA WAS ONE OF MY favorite towns. I spent my happy childhood years there and my best years before the war. Today, Trembowla is a place that I hate. I lived through the inferno of Hitler's occupation there, I lost the closest members of my family in the town, and I lost my dearest girl friend and many other friends and acquaintances there.

The inferno began when the Germans invaded in 1941. The first to commit acts of crime were the Ukrainian Nationalists. They assembled Jews from far and wide, from Wolyn and Podolia and made them march and sing "The Ukraine Is Not Yet Lost" (modeled after the Polish anthem). Whoever could not march in an orderly procession was shot on the spot.

People were seized in the streets, led to the barracks, and there they were ordered to slaughter each other. Among the victims was Rotenberg, my husband's brother-in-law. The only one to survive was one of the Blumenkranz brothers who escaped naked and managed to reach our home. He provided us with details.

Afterwards the Germans, headed by someone named Gaukler, took charge of the town. This German Gaukler began visiting Jewish homes and confiscating the best things that he found.

The Jews were ordered to set up a council with twelve members. The first appointees were: Dr. Stern, head of the community; and the other council members: Dr. Seret, Dr. Safrin, Dr. Zalmen Einleger and they co-opted Steinig, Dr. Zelermayer, Judah Leisner, Nathan Bomza and Schwartz. The entire composition of the council was imposed on us. Everyone hid because the Germans threatened, in case their demands weren't met, to hang every member of the council. This wasn't an idle threat; it was known that in Lwow nearly all the council members had been hanged.

People thought that everything would settle down. People were still living in their apartments, but in 1942 the tragedy began. There were transports to the camps. One was permitted to send packages. The rich people were able to buy their way out, and the poor suffered.

In November all the Jews of the neighboring towns and villages and those of Trembowla as well were ordered to move into the Ghetto.

The same day, early in the morning, the first "Action" took place. Crowds of people were assembled and sent to Belzec to die in the furnaces. After the "Action" the Ghetto was reduced in size.

My husband and Nettie's (née Ginsberg) husband left the Jewish council, and people of dubious character replaced them. Disorder set in.

We were saved because we hid with a farmer's wife. During the winter there were no "Actions," but men were sent to camps.

Living conditions were very difficult. Twenty people were placed in a single room. This led to a typhus epidemic. Many people died.

On April 7, the second "Action" took us by surprise. In our house there were forty people. We had a bunker which held out until 6:00. At that hour I went out with my son for water, and we noticed Germans approaching. Local gendarmes and Ukrainians came with them. In the meantime, a quarrel had broken out in the bunker. There was shouting and the Germans heard them. I did not manage to reenter the bunker, so I hid with the boy in a bed, covering myself with quilts. The Germans searched until they found the shelter, and they took everyone away. Only my boy and I were left, along with Chanusia Ginsberg, née Horowitz, and her girl. They, too, were in the bunker, but Chanusia handed something to a German. Also saved were my husband and Silber who had hidden behind a counter. My father perished, but my mother managed to flee.

On the third of June the third and last "Action" took place. My family and I were by then outside the Ghetto, but my mother perished with everyone in the second bunker. All those who remained alive after the third "Action" were later killed in the forests or wherever they were found hiding because Trembowla was declared *Judenrein* after the third "Action." That meant that anyone could kill a Jew whenever he was discovered. Some hidden by Christians were saved, but most of them were exploited by their "saviors" and afterwards handed over to the Germans or killed by Gentile neighbors themselves.

19

TERRIBLE EXPERIENCES

Henya Selzer née Herbst

Many years have passed, but the events we lived through have been etched deeply into our consciousness. I lived beyond the pale of humanity with little children in the open air. We lived on slices of bread charitably given to us by farmers. We were in mortal danger every moment. That we survived was a miracle, an act of divine intervention perhaps for the sake of the children.

Samuel Herbst and His Friend

We spent much time wandering at night in search of shelter. The residents of Boryczowka came to see us in order to look at the girl with their own eyes. "She is so white; look how pretty she is. What does she eat?" They called me "the Jewess of the fields."

Once—it was late fall—Korcinski came to me with his sister and said: "I have come to get from you the address of Samuel, your husband's brother, in order to describe to him the last days of you and your daughter." I answered him: "First, I don't have my brother-in-law's address and second, I hope to write to him myself." "But that is impossible," he went on. "Winter is approaching, the rains have started to come down, it is impossible to live out of doors like this. I wish you luck, but you won't make it." I remember those words well.

We sat in the field for a long time and towards evening we moved closer to the village. A farm wife lived there, and from time to time she would bring us something to eat. A short while later she let us come into her barn. I will never forget that night with a roof over our heads. It was pouring, and we were in the barn, starving for bread.

Some time later the Gestapo was informed that Jews were hiding in the barn. They came and searched every nook and cranny, but they did not enter our hiding place. This was one of the miracles which happened to us.

After the liberation we went back to the apartment. I could not stand and I could not walk. For three months I had been able only to sit. I was stooping like an old woman. It was cold, and water in bottles was frozen.

Just before morning we came to Korcinski's house. I knocked on the door. His sister opened it. When she saw us she took one frightened step back. "You are still alive?" she called out. "Don't be angry," I said, "but as you see I am still alive." "Of course not," she said, "please come in."

And now several comments on life in the Ghetto.

In the Second "Action" I lost my whole family. The Germans took my older brother several days after they arrived. We didn't know what happened to him. Several days later we were informed that he was a water carrier for the Germans, and that he had asked them for bread. Without deliberating, I took a loaf of bread with me, and, carrying the girl in my arms, I went to the Gestapo. I asked permission to give the bread to my brother. They shouted at me and said they didn't have anyone named Herbst. People outside said I was fortunate that they let me leave.

At one point, only my sister-in-law and I remained. It was June 1943. We spent a whole night building a shelter. Toward morning we wanted to rest, but in the meantime, the Germans had surrounded us. I went into the old shelter, and my father handed me my girl. I didn't see him after that. He departed from this life, as did my sister-in-law. There were many victims, among them Raysel Brecher, née Leviter. Only a pool of blood remained of her husband, Samuel Brecher, which his brother, the lawyer, tearfully pointed to. In the same shelter several people survived: Dr. Kolin and his wife, the lawyer Brecher, Chaim Kolin, Mariendorf, and others. But when I returned home afterwards, I didn't find a single one of them.

20

How I Lived Through the Holocaust

Isaac Kehana

I WAS NINE WHEN THE WAR between Poland and Germany broke out. Shortly thereafter the Russians took over eastern Poland, and we found ourselves under Russian rule. In 1941 the Germans attacked the Russians and within thirteen days the Germans arrived in our town of Janow.

After the Russians fled and before the Germans came, the Ukrainian Nationalists seized power and their rule lasted two weeks. It was very cruel. They killed Jews in cold blood and in a very primitive manner (with axes).

As soon as the Germans arrived they set up the Jewish Council (the Judenrat). The Germans imposed "contributions" (indemnities) in return for which they promised not to transfer us to Trembowla. They demanded money, gold, and furs. The contribution was not a one-time matter. We were prepared to give away everything we had, as long as we did not have to move to Trembowla because we knew what awaited us there.

In the summer of 1942 the fateful hour arrived—the move to Trembowla. We could take with us only items for personal use. We moved to Trembowla in wagons belonging to Gentiles, for a fee, of course. Some walked. On the way, Gentiles lay in waiting for the Jews. They attacked them, stealing what little they had, and beat them brutally. After undergoing many hardships, we arrived in Trembowla. There was already a Jewish Council—a Judenrat—there. They began "to provide us with housing." Whoever had money received a room. Generally speaking, four families lived in one room. We arranged triple-decker beds for ourselves. We washed only rarely. We suffered from pediculosis (infestation with lice); it was inescapable. And we also suffered from malnutrition. Still, ours was a life of luxury compared with that of the poor people, who slept outside without a roof over their heads and had no means of survival.

In the First "Action," the poor Jews were the first to be taken by train to the slaughter at Belzec Extermination Camp.

During the First "Action," we lived in Podzamcza on a hill at whose foot flowed the Gniezna River in Trembowla.

To our good fortune we lived with people who knew how to make "bunkers." We dug, in a room, a bunker with a spacious tunnel and an opening for air. To camouflage it, we built a huge alcove over the opening. We went below through a panel. The work was done entirely at night through the joint efforts of all of us, men and women alike. In the bunker itself it was very hot and humid, and air was lacking.

We had to keep still so that the Germans wouldn't discover us. A two-year-old girl whose crying might have given us away was sacrificed — she was strangled to death by her mother; and so we were saved.

After the Second "Action," the Ghetto was reduced in size, and we moved to a house near Kaplowka that had belonged to a Gentile woman who was relocated together with all the other non-Jews. The house had three rooms, and seven families lived in it (including the family of Rabbi Baruch Dlugacz). We built a bunker beneath the beds. During the Third "Action" we built an additional bunker within the first bunker, and the people were divided between the two bunkers. The first bunker was discovered by the Germans. The people hiding there were forced to go outside. Only my little brother and I remained inside. My mother hid outside with the help of a Jewish policeman named Schlesinger.

In the last "Actions" many people were killed at Plebanowka. In the beginning of June 1943, Trembowla was declared *Judenrein* and the Ghetto was liquidated. Only miraculously did we manage to escape and reach the forests. On March 22, 1944, the Russians liberated us.

21

THE HORRORS OF THE THIRD "ACTION"

Regina Diner

BETWEEN THE THIRD AND FIFTH of June 1943, the process of destroying Trembowla's Ghetto reached its terrible climax. In these three days the most frightful horrors were perpetrated. Trembowla became *Judenrein*.

At that time we, a group of twenty women and twelve men, gathered the corpses of the dead. With our own eyes we saw women and children being thrown alive into the pit. Some of them had been shot but not killed. A Ukrainian woman and her brother opened one pit from which terrible screams could be heard. They took four children out of the pit who managed to live for four hours. They also took out a girl of about seventeen from the pit. Her name was Sonia Altstadt, and she was from Budzanow. She told us what had happened in the pit in which she lay for six or eight hours: People went out of their minds. They tore off pieces of flesh and some gouged out each other's eyes. They ate the flesh they tore out. She herself was horribly mangled. This girl lived for another four days.

After that our group, which numbered about forty by that time, was transferred to Tarnopol. There a "selection" was made. The weak ones were shot to death, but the strong ones were taken to work. At first they were put into the prison. They had to take away people who had been killed, apparently hanged by the Ukrainian police. From there a group of 430 people were transferred, in June 1943, to Janowska Street in Lwow. There we were witnesses to a horrifying scene. They took the son of Mrs. Ochsenberg who came from Gryzyalow, tied his feet to two cars and tore him in half in front of his mother and in front of us.

22

THE MUNICIPAL HOSPITAL IN TREMBOWLA DURING THE NAZI OCCUPATION

Dr. Natalia Weiselberg

A WEEK AFTER THE GERMANS ARRIVED, all former members of the hospital staff were summoned to work. The director of the hospital, Dr. Dunecki, handed me the keys to the laboratory and promised us, my husband and me, suitable conditions for work — food and living quarters — which delighted us.

Jewish doctors were not engaged, in accordance with a directive which the director of the hospital received from the authorities.

After the Second "Action" Dr. Dunecki suggested to us that we hide, if necessary, in a corner of the laboratory especially prepared for such an eventuality.

In 1943 a typhus epidemic broke out in the Ghetto. It was caused by the terrible overcrowding, the hunger, and also by infected people returning from the labor camps. The families with means were able to ransom their relatives who became ill with typhus in the camps and were thus in danger of being shot by the camp authorities. The ransom was effected by a "contact," a member of the Judenrat. These ransomed prisoners didn't last long after their return from the camps, and a short while later they were dead.

Near the hospital a department for patients with contagious diseases was set up, a sort of quarantine room. We, the laboratory workers, would receive blood samples from both the hospital patients and those in the quarantine room for tests.

In charge of the tests was Dr. Szkwaruk, a Ukrainian who ordered us to prepare a weekly report indicating the test results. One day a Judenrat member (A.) came to us with tears in his eyes and begged us not to make public the existence of more than one or two cases of typhus in the Ghetto. He explained his request by describing a conversation he had had with a Gestapo man in Tarnopol. The latter made it clear to him that in case a typhus epidemic broke out in the

Trembowla Ghetto, an "Action aimed at sick people" would be undertaken in which all the residents of the Ghetto would be executed.

Upon hearing of this peril, we decided to make only a few cases of typhus public although there were actually a great many cases.

Several weeks later, Dr. Szkwaruk appeared in the laboratory in an extremely angry mood. He slammed doors and shouted that he was being given falsified reports because on his daily rounds in the quarantine room he found hundreds of typhus victims.

I replied to him that we took the responsibility for the test results upon ourselves and that the illnesses were influenza, skin diseases, etc., but not typhus. "And if there will be an inspection?" asked Dr. Szkwaruk. "You may send our tests to a different laboratory for verification," I replied, for lack of anything else to say. This was a dangerous game on our part. If Dr. Szkwaruk had actually sent a sample of one patient to be tested elsewhere, we would have been doomed.

As I sat near my microscope I expected death to come every day. This was the period during which the Ghetto was being liquidated. No "Action aimed at sick people" took place in Trembowla.

Unfortunately our falsified diagnoses did not save the residents of the Ghetto from the final liquidation. But if there is one person who fell ill with typhus in the Ghetto and was saved thanks to these reports, that is my reward.

The number of deaths in the Ghetto was very large. There were days when we didn't manage to bury the dead, and hundreds of bodies remained in apartments together with the living.

23

ONE DAY IN A BUNKER
(A PAGE OUT OF A DIARY)

M. G.

Thursday, June 3, 1943

THE WATCH BEGAN AT 2:30. At 3:30 a loud noise of motors woke us up, and at Podzamcza the guard, G.K., charged in shouting that four cars full of Germans had entered the district. Everyone burst out with a cry of despair: "Action," and all of us went down in haste to the shelter in our underwear (some people, the more stable ones, took their clothes with them). Several people from the next house pushed their way into our bunker, causing us great anxiety because there wasn't enough room even for the residents of our own house.

The Germans were already in the courtyard, but to our good fortune we had all managed to enter and close the bunker. And now the terrible torment began because of a lack of space and air. Upon hearing approaching footsteps we held our breath, and when the first shelter, which was just ahead of ours, was discovered, a deathly silence set in, with only an occasional sigh and the mumbling of a prayer.

At approximately 9:00 we no longer had air to breathe, and we felt that we were choking. The suffering of the children was particularly difficult. So we risked detection by opening the entrance to the first shelter. Everyone eagerly inhaled some air. But only for a little while because we heard German voices overhead, and it was necessary to close the entrance. This occurred repeatedly throughout the day. Nerves were frayed. Everyone reproached the person next to him for making noise. Mothers with small wailing children were pushed out, and they, understandably, refused to leave. There was a highly charged atmosphere in the bunker. Some people were prepared to exchange blows for a drop of water and a slice of bread. To all this one must add the impossibility of reaching the bathroom, which was installed near the entrance. Everyone relieved himself where he sat, and the terrible odors destroyed what little air was left. It is impossible for one who has never been in such a situation to understand it, and the most talented writer could not succeed in describing it.

Towards evening part of the earth in the corridor in front of our shelter caved in, and to our good fortune it was impossible to see our hiding place from above.

We sat this way until 7:00 in the evening. Suddenly we stopped breathing when we heard footsteps above and knocking at the entrance to our shelter. A cry of despair and horror burst forth from us: "We are doomed." The children began to cry; the old people began to sigh. The Germans discovered our bunker, and we began to hear shouts of *"Heraus!"* The ones sitting near the entrance went out, not to breathe fresh air, but to die. Several of us, including my parents and I, decided not to go out voluntarily. We even moved the beams so that the earth would cover the secondary passageway. And then we heard a mad scream: "Come out, we've been saved! The 'Action' is already over. The gendarmes released us." We were convinced that this was a trick, and we continued to sit, holding our breath and waiting for what was to come. A few minutes later Mr. M. came down and verified what we had heard before. It turned out that the *Volksdeutsche* from the barracks discovered our hiding place and wanted to lead us to Plebanowka. And then, upon seeing this, the Jewish Militiaman Z. Melzer got up and ran out to the gendarmerie. He rushed the Hauptmann and Mr. N. over, and they managed to take care of everything.

In view of what had just occurred, my parents went out, but I continued sitting where I was. Only when the Militiaman Z. Melzer came down to me and swore that everything was true and that one could now go out did I leave that hell like someone drunk. For a little while I was about to faint, but I finally calmed down and thanked God for the miracle that he had performed for me.

24

MEETING HOLOCAUST SURVIVORS

S. Brinstein

Conversations with the Leichtner Family

FROM A BALCONY SEAT in the Jewish Theater on Second Avenue in New York, I looked down with my binoculars. During the twenty minute pause, I was watching the audience moving back and forth, leaving their seats and coming back.

Through the binoculars I could see the faces much better, so I kept looking for a familiar face among the crowd.

Suddenly, I cried out loudly to my wife: "I found them, there, in the fourth row, two women and two men." I recognized them all.

When the show was over, I went downstairs, waiting near the exit door. The two couples came closer to the spot where I was standing. Not waiting for them to recognize me, I said: "You are Joseph Leichtner, and this is your wife Regina, and you are Jack Ellman and your wife Cily." They were astounded, but after a few minutes all four recognized me too. This was our first meeting since 1941. The last time we met was in Trembowla, Tarnopol region, in the springtime of 1941. In a small town, everyone knows everyone.

Both couples were Holocaust survivors, residing in Brooklyn, New York. During periodical meetings of the Trembowla Society, I had a chance to meet them (and other friends) more often in the 1980's.

A few years ago, I made a special trip to visit both families in their private homes. There is a ten minute walk between the two houses. First, I went to the Leichtner family. The following is the content of our brief conversation about events during the Nazi occupation in Tarnopol region:

"You didn't run eastward during the war; how did you manage to survive the Nazi rule?" I asked Mr. Leichtner.

"You want to know how we survived?"

"I am here, so I would like to know how it was," I replied.

Concentrating, friend Joseph went back to his painful memories:

"When Nazi Germany attacked the Soviet Union, in June 1941, I was mobilized into the Soviet Army. For training and other purposes, we were taken deeper inside the Ukraine. It did not take long, and the entire army (around 50,0000) found itself surrounded by the Nazi Wehrmacht. Considering the situation probably hopeless, the isolated command surrendered.

"Wanting to communicate with the war prisoners, a German officer asked: 'Who speaks German?' I lifted my hand up. The order was to step forward. 'My name is Josef Lichter,' I said. 'O.K., you'll be the interpreter,' the German officer replied. So I had a new job. For the moment, I thought it was not bad, but how about later. What if somebody in the army should denounce me and tell them that I am Jewish? Then it would be all over. It was too risky a business to stay. The first chance I got, I left the army and took a train going to Trembowla. The train conductor knew me well, so he agreed to find a safe place for me. Having reached Trembowla, I joined my family.

"Seeing that the situation under the Nazi occupation was getting worse, especially for the Jewish people, the family decided to leave the town, and move into a village and hide with Gentiles we knew to be good people.

"There we had to dig a deep underground bunker. During a raid of the Ukrainian and German police, we had to run for cover. My father was among us. When the search outside was over, we dared to leave the covered bunker. My father was the first victim of the sudden raid. He suffocated inside the bottom of the bunker. It was a tragedy that touched all of us deeply. With the help of our Gentile friends, we managed to hide from the German Nazis and the Ukrainian Nationalist collaborators.

"On March 22, 1944, the town of Trembowla was liberated by the Soviet Army. We were free again as humans. The Nazis and the Ukrainian Nationalist collaborators retreated in disorder. This spared damage or possible destruction of the town.

"From a lively Jewish community in 1940, the town of Trembowla was left *Judenrein*. Only a handful managed to survive the Nazi bloody occupation. We were among those who were able to walk the streets of Trembowla again. Most of the town's Jewish community found its end in the pits of the mountain village — Plebanowka."

This was the end of our conversation about events during the Nazi "New Order" in Tarnopol region. Those were the tragic extermination years of 1941 to 1944.

Conversation with the Ellman Family

After a tasty meal with the Leichtner family, which Mrs. Regina (Stern) had prepared, the time came to say thank you, and *auf wiedersehen.* Together with my friend Josef, we went to the Ellman family's house. It was a nice ten minute walk.

The reception was also a friendly one. What an exceptional feeling it was to once again be together with Trembowla friends after so many years of separation.

I was eager to find out how this couple survived the Nazi Holocaust. Due to Jack's advanced age, his wife Cily, was not too enthusiastic about refreshing the old, bitter memories of the past. Her reluctance was understandable. Having no intention of giving up, I asked only for a brief description of events during the Nazi era.

Jack Ellman: "I could tell you a long grisly story, but the time isn't appropriate now. Before the Ghetto was created, I, and many others, were forced to work in the Jewish cemetery."

"What did you have to do there?" I asked.

"You don't know? We had to pull out the tombstones that were in the Jewish Cemetery and split them into small pieces. The Germans were building roads to be able to move Eastward faster. Working in the cemetery were also French war prisoners, doing the same job we were doing. They were stationed in the Military Barracks. I don't know if they survived the war or not.

"Seeing many other Nazi brutalities, we decided to run away from Trembowla. In some of the surrounding villages we had some Gentile friends. After a long conversation, they consented to help us. So, thanks to our good friends, we managed to avoid the bloody Nazi claws.

"On March 22, 1944, if my memory is correct, the Soviet Army liberated Trembowla. After a long terrible nightmare, we were finally able to walk the streets again. Gone were the German Nazis and the Ukrainian Nationalist collaborators.

"How sad and empty Trembowla looked. The town was almost *Judenrein,* free of Jews. Only a small group remained alive. Most of our people found their end in the pits of Plebanowka, and in the extermination camp—Belzec."

Conversation with Mrs. Ruth Ryles

Before World War II, Mrs. Ryles resided in the village of Janow, near Trembowla, Tarnopol region. From time to time, she used to visit the town, her friends, and the library. She remembers all those years very well.

A few years ago, I had a chance to meet Mrs. Ryles in Newark, New Jersey, U.S.A. Our conversation was mostly about events during the Nazi occupation in the Tarnopol region. Here is, in brief, her personal story:

"Janow was a small town (some called it a village), located near Trembowla. Up until the war, life was peaceful and normal. The trouble started when the Nazi Army occupied the area. Some of the Jewish residents were later rounded up, and transported to the Trembowla Ghetto. Some others went into hiding.

"We were a group of fourteen people, hiding in an isolated house in the forest. It belonged to a Gentile family who knew all of us very well. They agreed to help us. The house wasn't bad, but not safe enough in case of real danger. We had no other choice, but to dig a deep, well-masked (camouflaged) underground bunker. A long, narrow air-passage, reaching far outside, had to be built. In case the bunker had to be completely covered, this lifeline would save us from being suffocated.

"In the attic, high up, we had to cut a small opening, in order to be able to observe the narrow road leading toward the house in which we were hiding. From this lookout, we could see who was coming or going. We decided to keep a constant watch—just in case.

"From Gentile friends, we were able to find out that the German Nazis and Ukrainian Nationalists were hunting Jews everywhere. A watchful eye was constantly near the look-out hole. We had to be vigilant.

"One nice day the alarm came to hide inside the underground bunker. The lady of the house covered the entrance with straw, and barrels containing potatoes, and other stuff on top. It wall all done quickly. The young son helped his mother to finish the camouflage.

"A group of German Nazis and Ukrainian policemen started to search all over. '*Sind hier Juden versteckt?*' (Are there Jews hiding?), they asked. The lady told them that there were no Jews there, and that they could look around. The Ukrainian police smelled something fishy. They didn't believe the lady's assurance. The eleven-year-old boy (the son) was told to face the wall, with his hands up. The order came:

'Talk now, where are the Jews? If you don't you will be killed on the spot.' A shot rang out over the boy's head. He kept silent. Facing death, he didn't budge.

"We heard the shot inside the bunker. All of us understood the gravity of the situation. A young child started to cry. The child's mother realized fully the mortal danger to the fourteen people inside the bunker if the child did not stop crying. In order to save the group from falling into the bloody hands of the Nazis, the young mother suffocated her own child with her bare hands. Not a whisper was heard. A deadly silence engulfed the bunker.

"An innocent child was the victim of the Nazi hunt. It was sacrificed in order to save the others. There were many other ordeals we went through during the Fascist occupation.

"Thanks to our Gentile friends, all fourteen survivors were able to see the end of the Nazi rule. The Red Army liberated the area on March 22, 1944. We were free again, able to walk the streets as humans. However, most of our relatives and friends and all the others did not live to see the day the sun shone again. This is the story of our survival in brief. Around forty years have passed since, but our memories and our wounds are still fresh. All this one can never forget."

After our conversation in the restaurant, we had to part. A few years later I was able to visit the spot (in Janow) in the Ukrraine SSR, where fourteen Jews were able to save their lives during World War II.

Conversation with Mr. Salo Silber

When the Nazi Army marched into Trembowla, Tarnopol region, on July 5, 1941, Mr. Salo Silber was in his early teens. Being very young at the time, it is understandable that he does not remember many events during the Nazi occupation.

"How did you manage to escape from the Nazis and save your life?," I asked. Here is his own brief description of how it happened:

"We were already in the Ghetto. During the last "Action" in 1943, we were all driven out of the Ghetto. The old, the sick, and the youngsters all were forced to ride on the waiting horse-wagons. All the others were ordered to walk.

"German and Ukrainian policemen were keeping guard. Passing the bridge, dividing the two parts of the town, we came near the Ukrainian church, located in the city center. At the same time we passed the church, a large crowd of worshipers came out from inside the church into the streets.

"Knowing well that our destination was Plebanowka, and what was awaiting us there, I decided to jump from the horse-wagon. In order not to get caught, I sneaked into the crowd moving in the opposite direction. Luckily, I was not apprehended.

"At that time, my father was still alive. He managed to evade the roundup, hiding outside the house.

"One of the Ukrainian policemen notified my father that he saw me jump down from the wagon near the church and that I was alive, and he didn't tell anybody about it. My father was very scared initially. The decision to jump at the right moment saved me from the pit waiting for us in Plebanowka. This is, in brief, how I survived the Holocaust."

To my question "And what next?" Mr. Silber replied: "That's another chapter that I prefer to leave for later." It was still around ten months to the time of liberation. The fear of being caught was lurking in every corner.

For reasons not completely clear to me, Mr. Silber declined to participate, refusing to mail the ready manuscript. Despite my detailed explanation, he did not change his decision. I have considered it my duty to report survivors' stories, anything pertaining directly to the Holocaust tragedy. Any documentary evidence, Archive documents, eyewitness accounts, etc., that shed more light on historical events, is of the utmost importance.

Mr. Silber's story is a unique one. He is one of the few who managed to escape the already waiting mass grave. His entire family: parents, uncles, aunts, cousins, etc., weren't that lucky. All of them perished during the Nazi occupation. One uncle, Icie Schechter, is mentioned in the "Eyewitness Account" of I. Malinowski, who was present during the bloody massacre in Plebanowka.

This writer knows and remembers Mr. Silber's family and relatives very well.

Conversation with Sol Selzer

I do remember Sol long before World War II. Early in the 1930's he emigrated to South America. During the late 1930's, Sol visited his family in Trembowla. He was one of the lucky ones, being able to leave Europe before World War II.

"You weren't there during the Nazi occupation, but can you tell me how many of your family perished in Trembowla during the war," I asked.

"Yes, why not," Sol replied. "There were fourteen in our family. With the exception of my late sister-in-law (older brother's wife) and her child, all of them perished in Trembowla. Most of them, as I found out later, were shot in front of the house. That's all.

"My wife died here years ago. My daughter and grandchildren reside in another state. So, as you can see, I'm alone now."

As an amateur photographer, Sol Selzer deserves full credit for the preservation of the many negatives and pictures reproduced in this book. He is in his eighties; still active; and what remains is to wish him many more years to come.

Conversation with the Halpern Brothers

Both brothers, Aaron and Sam, resided before World War II in the village of Ivanivka, near the town of Trembowla, Tarnopol region. From time to time, they, and their father, used to visit the nearby town.

During the Nazi occupation of this area, I think it was in the year 1942 (if my memory is correct), both brothers were taken to the Nazi Slave Labor Camp Kamionki 1, Podvolochysk region.

The Jewish slaves were used in the camp to build roads, to make it easier for the Nazi war-machine to advance eastward, deeper into Soviet Russia. Life in the Labor Camp was hard, with little food and water. The German and Ukrainian Nationalist guards were devoted servants of the Third Reich, making sure that the slaves kept working hard and nobody escaped alive.

The Halpern brothers continued to labor, like all the other human slaves, until the year 1943. After Stalingrad, and the increase of partisan activity in the area, the German Nazis started to feel insecure. They were retreating in many areas. Many camp inmates were waiting for miracles that never came.

It was midsummer, 1943. The mood started to get tense. Rumors started to circulated about the imminent destruction of the camp, together with the inmates. Thanks to reliable information, it was possible to establish the intended date of destruction. There was little time left. The hour of decision was nearing. To remain in the labor camp meant certain death.

Both brothers decided to take a chance. There was nothing to lose. During the dark of the night, Sam was the first to escape. In order not to be discovered by local residents or the German and

Ukrainian police, it was dangerous to walk during the day. The night was for walking. The days were for resting in the fields—rain or shine.

"Where did you go?" I asked.

"After four or five days," Sam replied, "I managed finally to sneak back to the same village I came from—Ivanivka. There was a Gentile Polish family I knew and trusted. My intuition was correct. The Gentile lady (Fam. Gorniak) opened the door. The house was my hiding place for the next nine months, until the area was liberated (March 23, 1944) by the Soviet Army."

"And how did your brother Aaron make it?" I asked.

"He did the same thing—just one day later. Not even knowing at the time where I was, my brother came to the same house, the same family. The house door was opened and we were together again," Sam joyously explained. The hiding wasn't without danger. It took nine long months of waiting, hoping and waiting. . .until the sweet hour of liberation arrived.

This is the abbreviated story of two Holocaust survivors—the Halpern brothers. Both have happy families, residing in New Jersey, managing a successful construction business. They consider it their duty to make donations to the needy—here and in Israel.

For the writer of these lines it was a pleasure to meet with, and talk to, the Halpern Brothers—Holocaust survivors. Their stories, like many others, are unique. Not all those who managed to temporarily escape made it; during the long wait for liberation, many fell again into the executioners' hands.

According to the eyewitness accounts, the Slave Labor Camp, Kamionki 1, was locked, with the inmates inside. It was set in flames with gasoline. Those trying to escape through the windows were gunned down. That was the tragic end of more than 1,000 Jewish victims of the Nazis. We honor their memory.

25

Eyewitness Accounts

L.S. Roth, G.I. Leheta, An-Thon, Meir Selzer, H. Stachowiak, I. Malinowski

I Call It The Dark Period

At that time I was ten years old, but many Nazi atrocities and horrors of war are still engraved in my memory. I do remember the exact date, July 2, 1941, when the city Berezhany (Brzezany), Tarnopol Region, was bombarded by the German Luftwaffe for the first time. On July the fifth, the city was bombarded again. The lethal load fell mostly on the Jewish quarter, turning many buildings into ruins.

The city cinema was also destroyed the same day. On Thursday at dawn, the streets of the city were already crowded with Hitlerites.

Retreating isolated groups of Red Army soldiers tried to evade the onrushing Nazis. Some managed to escape eastward and rejoin their units. Those who didn't manage to flee, fell into the hands of the Nazis and the Ukrainian Nationalists, being massacred on the spot. The Tarnopol street was flooded with human blood. It was called Black Thursday.

A great misfortune fell upon the Jewish population. The day was Sunday. From the very early morning the air in the city was laden with uncertainty.

The quiet didn't last long. Ukrainian Nationalist thugs crowded the streets here and there. In the Ukrainian Church the dean served the sermon "In the Name of the Führer." A lot was prattled about the "Independent Ukraine." The church colors were taken outdoors.

The same day in the afternoon, groups of Ukrainian Nationalists at once formed their police, the so-called "Hundred Group." The bloody Pogrom started. They attacked the quarter where Jews lived. With iron bars and sticks the Jews were cruelly bludgeoned to death — all those who didn't manage to escape.

The German Nazi cutthroats did their devil job more efficiently. They finished their victims at once, on the spot. Among the dead was my grandfather: Isaak Goldgaberg. Right thereafter German Fascists and Ukrainian Nationalists shot around twenty Jews at the City Cemetery.

In the meantime, on the "initiative" of the Hitlerites, the Judenrat (Jewish Council) was formed. Its duty was, among others, to gather contributions from each family. It was like a donation for some days of comparatively peaceful life.

The quiet didn't last long. Most of the men from the Jewish community were rounded up, lined up in rows near the Old Fortress. The more physically strong were separated, loaded on lorries and transported to the prison, where many Soviet activists were kept. All of them faced the same tragic end.

The violence of the Hitlerites and the OUN (Organization of Ukrainian Nationalists) almost never stopped for a day. Each time the murderers used different methods. Jewish people were told that they would be resettled to other towns where they would work. Instead, they were taken to the Lityatin Forest where they were shot. Others were transported to slave labor camps in Czernyi, Kamiany; Velikiy Hlubochek, and elsewhere. Conditions in the camps served only one purpose—to work them to death. Those who dared to disobey the orders were shot at once.

As is known, atrocities against Jews (and non-Jews) were committed not only by the German Nazis. The Ukrainian Nationalist Police already had its hands dripping with human blood. The Chief of the Police was a Ukrainian Nationalist named Snylyk. He behaved toward innocent people no less brutally than his Nazi masters. His great fun was to beat and torture elderly people and children, rob families of their possessions, or kill a Jew in the Ghetto. Eliminating Jews was a profitable business. As Ukrainian Police Chief, he had no problem in seizing the possessions, including gold, belonging to his innocent victims. Nothing stopped him from making a "quick buck." He seldom hesitated in killing.

Ivankevich, another member of the Ukrainian Police, didn't differ much from his chief in bestiality. He too considered amassing fortunes belonging to murdered victims. The bloody path of Snylyk and Ivankevich wasn't much different from Hubert—the Nazi chief of the Berezhany SS. Their path is marked with the blood of the innocent.

The SS man Hubert, an "Aryan," proved to be a butcher and murderer, who had been accumulating "property" over the bodies of robbed and then executed Jews. He wasn't alone in this bloody business. He and his father-in-law, Folkdeutsch Shimlet, a Pole by nationality, stationed with the Polish Army in Berezhany before, knew well how to enrich themselves.

German Fascists and Ukrainian Nationalist henchmen left an imprint in my memory as inhuman robbers, traitors and murderers. I call that period of my life a dark one because I had witnessed the ruin and destruction of hundreds of people. I was within a hairbreadth of death myself. It's a wonder that I managed to survive the Holocaust. On June 18, 1943, I did escape the Jewish Ghetto and managed to hide in the nearby vicinity.

After my escape there were only Jewish Policemen, and some women and children left in the Ghetto. They were all shot thereafter by the Nazis and the Ukrainian Nationalists.

I was lucky...and lucky were also people of many other nationalities who had gone through the bloody Nazi occupation, when finally, the Red Army liberated Berezhany, Tarnopol, and many other cities and towns.

Now, together with all the Soviet people, I do enjoy peaceful skies and peace on earth. It is the greatest happiness a man can ever experience.

L. S. Roth
Tarnopol, Ukrainian SSR
(Translated by Halyna V.)

I Couldn't Act in Another Way

A considerable number of Jewish families resided in Berezhany before the Nazi occupation. Their houses were side by side with those of Ukrainian and Polish families.

With the arrival of the German Nazis, almost everything changed. The Fascists incited wild hatred against Jews. It didn't take long before the Jewish Ghetto was created by order of the Nazis. Anti-Jewish "Actions" began.

In this dirty, human-hunting job, the first helping hand of the German Nazis were Ukrainian Nationalist policemen and also Jewish policemen.

The wealthy Jews, merchants, and intelligentsia happened to be the first to suffer. The further down, the worse. Many Jewish women and children were shot. No words can describe all the horrors. And misfortune befell not only the Jewish community. Many Ukrainians and Poles were transported to Germany to perform hard jobs. Jewish people were exterminated daily.

Life under the Nazi occupation was terrible. But despite the suffering and many dangers all around, there were people who didn't lose their human nature.

Like many other residents of Berezhany, I suffered greatly, watching how Ukrainian and Polish people were transported in freight trains to Germany, and how Jews were brutally beaten and later executed.

During the Nazi Occupation I came across a young Jewish boy, V. Seidenbaum, in the ruins of the city center. He was in despair and intended to go to the Ghetto where his parents were. I realized the danger he would face and suggested that he stay with me for some time. Having supplied the boy with my son's birth certificate, I took him to my relatives residing in Kotiv. With this step, the boy's life was saved.

At approximately the same time, I was hiding two other young Jews. I only took money from them to buy the food they needed. I couldn't behave in any other way toward people facing death, despite

I also brought food to Doctor Falek, who was hiding with his two children in the Rurish Forest. I also helped David Kwertal and his son Beyo, and the Jewish porter's son, whose name I don't remember. I acted according to my conscience. I considered that all this should be done in such a way that no profit would be derived from the misery of others. I knew that if anybody denounced me to the Ukrainian Police or the German Gestapo, I would have been killed together with the Jews. But I couldn't act in any other way. I did what I could in order to help people in need.

V. Seidenbaum, who now works in the mines in the City of Marganets, visits me from time to time. I speak to him as if he were my native son. I'm happy that my conscience is clear. I consider conscience to be the greatest human treasure. I long for only one thing: Let every person in the world care dearly that his own conscience be clear. Let him, or her, treat it as the most sacred thing. Then happiness for all will come to our planet Earth.

G. I. Leheta
Tarnopol, Ukr. SSR
(Translated by Halyna V.)

Over the Dark Precipice

The year was 1941. Newly formed Ukrainian Nationalist "liberators" appeared in the town of Zbarazh, Tarnopol region. Their aim was to form a so-called "Ukrainian Army." Meetings were held and passionate speeches were made. Ukrainian Uniate priests were also quite active. One of the propaganda speakers was a "patriotic" Ukrainian Nationalist: Lyubomir Kuzyk.

Present among the listeners were also the family Savchak and son. The younger Savchak expressed a desire to serve in the ranks of the newly formed "Ukrainian Police." He was appointed as a platoon leader.

From the very first days of the formation of the Ukrainian "Auxiliary" Police, the German Nazis used it to arrest Soviet activists, and persecute Zbarazh residents.

In comparison with the other Ukrainian Police, Savchak was treated in a special privileged way. It was the beginning of the bloody path of treason. He personally appointed the policemen and their duty details. He did not hesitate to escort Soviet citizens under arrest from the prison to the Gestapo. He imagined himself as a representative of the "New Order." He admired his new police uniform, feeling like a "Superman."

The date was October 2, 1941. Several lorries full of Nazi Gestapo men, and Ukrainian Auxiliary Policemen, left the city Tarnopol for Berezhany. During the "Action" they rounded up civilians—Jewish people.

Trying hard to curry favor with the German Gestapo, Savchak did his best. He hurried up the subject policemen, made sure that everybody was put on the waiting lorry, and escorted the victims to the place of execution near the Village of Riy.

The same day, another group of detained Soviet citizens was taken away from the Berezhany police building to another destination, where they were shot. And, once again, Savchak showed himself as a real bloody sadist.

With the drunken smile of a killer, he tore the clothes off the victims, watching the people crying, pleading for mercy before the execution. It was a grisly scene.

After the extermination of the innocent Jewish victims, Savchak, together with the Gestapo officers, went to the restaurant to have some more drinks.

In addition to the crimes described above, Savchak and his

Ukrainian Nationalist comrades in arms took part in many other inhuman crimes.

One day, early in the morning, the German Gestapo and the Ukrainian Nationalist "Auxiliary" Police, arrived on trucks at the courtyard of the Tarnopol prison.

After barbaric torture, the arrested victims were loaded on the open trucks. Those who couldn't walk anymore were dragged on the ground. And, again, Savchak revealed his bestial nature. SS Chief Muller (and his cohorts: Reibel, Lamberg, and Herman) admired Savchak's devotion to the Third Reich.

In July, 1943, Savchak enlisted in the Ukrainian SS Division *Galizien*, as a machine gunner, swearing allegiance to the Führer and Fascist Germany.

After the defeat of the mentioned *Galizien* SS Division, on the battlefield near Brody, Savchak fled to his parents, residing in the Village of Blajhiv, Sambir region, Lvov District.

He tried to mask his true identity, acquiring, for money, a false "diploma" of higher education. With the false diploma he managed to get a job as a teacher in one of the schools.

In August of 1944, trying to evade the call of duty into the Soviet Army, fearing also of being unmasked, Savchak changed the date of his birth and the name of his father, plus his own name.

With a changed social origin, he got married and became an "honest" citizen. He told his wife and son that he was an "orphan" and originated from a family of teachers. He claimed that his parents perished during the Nazi occupation.

The truth was that his parents were alive, residing at that time in the village of Blajhiv, Sambir Region, and later on in Lvov. He called his father uncle, and his mother, aunt.

But his luck started to run out. The bodies of State Security, with the help of rank and file Soviet citizens, managed to tear off his false mask and expose his real face.

Savchak's countrymen from the village of Zarubintsy, Pidvolochysk Region, where he was born, and those from the village of Shelpaky, where he grew up, were very much surprised to find out that their beautiful village had been growing a future Nazi henchman and bloody killer. Nobody could know how much evil he would bring to his own people, to his country, and to people of other nationalities.

Savchak's bloody path of treason came into the open. He wanted the court to believe his crocodile tears, his sincere repentance. But all his attempts to whitewash himself were in vain. Nothing helped. New, and now undeniable facts drove the Nationalist renegade into a corner. The living eyewitnesses exposed the "patriotic" traitor.

In what a cynical way, with what a stony cold heart, Savchak narrated to the judges, one of his bloody "Actions":

"Yes, we brought the victims to the pits. The German Gestapo fired at their necks." He tried to convince the Court that he was forced to join the Ukrainian Volunteer Division of the Waffen-SS. He claimed that he never fired a single shot at the Soviet Army. When Savchak was reminded about the battles near Brody (where the Ukrainian Nationalist hirelings were defeated), about his active part on the enemy side, his memory came back to him at once.

It was the end of his bloody road. He was brought to justice, and received what he deserved.

But the price of victory was paved with human blood, tears, destruction, and ruins. In the Tarnopol region alone, more than 200,000 people were exterminated by the German Fascists (with the help of the Ukrainian Nationalists). Among them 180,472 civilians, 5,486 Soviet soldiers and officers — prisoners of war, 1,000 Italians, 4,000 Frenchmen and others.

More than 42,000 citizens were deported to Nazi Germany for slave labor. Thousands of people perished of starvation and diseases in concentration camps.

During almost 36 months of Nazi occupation of the Tarnopol region, the Fascists ruined nine cities, 207 villages, 211 cultural and educational institutions, 511 schools, many hospitals, more than 30 large enterprises, 529 collective farms, 38 machine stations. The total losses of the economy of Tarnopol Region amounted to nearly one billion rubles, according to the new course of the ruble.

And all this was performed with ruthless efficiency by the "superior" Aryan race, with the voluntary help of Ukrainian Nationalism — the "subhumans," Savchaks, Kuzyks, and Co., who were especially useful in the extermination of human beings. They, like their Nazi Masters, had nothing humane in their hearts. They were partners in crime and genocide with German Nazism.

An-Thon
Tarnopol, Ukr. SSR
(Translated by Halyna V.)

Report on My Sister's Death

The following was written in Polish, April 11, 1943, and was received July 26, 1968:

The 7th of April this year was a horrible day for the inhabitants of the Ghetto and to people who had a spark of human feeling left. The things that happened exceeded all that had been told, and they cannot be compared with the last local "Action." The barbarism of the past centuries is pale against the present one, which is in complete contrast to the culture of the 20th century.

People were shot in their houses, in the streets, in the gutters, in the yards, in the squares of the Ghetto and outside it. The living ones were led to the square near the market, were undressed to their underwear, their shoes removed; they were stripped of their last possessions and led outside the city to the place of their last rest. The procession of the living dead ones moved slowly while the children clung to their mothers crying loudly and with tears, and the mothers wore expressions of pain and fatigue and were moaning. And there were some (like the old Seret), quiet, upright, with uplifted head, a serious expression, looking right and left, taking leave with a nod of their heads, from friends, streets, and houses, which surely reminded them of better times, who went quietly to their place of execution.

Under the mountain of Plebanowka the white crowd was once more seen moving slowly, and soon the last act of the tragedy was heard — a "salvo" of guns.

On that rainy day, sad and cold — as if adjusted to the serious moment — the first group of about 300 people was led in the morning to the railway bridge in Plebanowka, and the second group, in the afternoon, of about 500 people was led to their common grave. And every time, instead of funeral music, the machine gun played, and they threw into the common grave those who, at that moment, stopped feeling, and those whose sufferings became stronger, and others who were spared a bullet by the cruel fates and who finished their lives under the pressure of the human mass. They didn't even cover them with earth. And for the children they didn't even waste a bullet.

At dusk the grave began to teem. A row of ghosts in human bodies began to creep out — some able to walk, others to creep and others to turn. The stronger ones reached the village, the weaker ones the railway, as if waiting for the iron dragon in order to forget in its hugs "the pleasures of life;" and the remaining listened as if to the sound of the guns, hoping that this time they would not be spared.

The next morning this weird grave on which life was ebbing out, was refilled with a few wagons of bodies and covered with a thick layer of earth.

A part of the killed ones was transported towards evening to the old cemetery, which witnessed sad scenes. One of these victims was Mania Selzer — she lived near the train ramp. She was shot in the marketplace where she remained for a few hours. The bodies were collected on a wagon, and it became clear that she was not only alive but fully conscious, and she begged the favor of the men who were burying — the militia men, whom she recognized. She kissed their hands, called them by their names, and begged them to treat her gently. She maintained that she was still strong enough, and that she could live, if she would be helped. She was thrown roughly on the wagon together with the bodies, was transported to the cemetery and left to her fate. At this particular time it could not have been otherwise because the killers were going around there and they were afraid. Finally, late in the evening, they left.

At the cemetery she asked for help from strollers who went around there but they were afraid. At last an elderly woman from Rakowica, who helped her, laid her down somehow in the company of the dead bodies, gave her water and comforted her. At night she brought her a bundle of straw to lie on for the night in the ready grave, because those who knew her forgot her and did not come to help her, which was terrible and unforgivable.

The poor wounded one had to lie in the cold night in those ghastly surroundings. Hyenas appeared, in human bodies; they took off the (remaining) clothes from the dead bodies, and from her they took her last pennies. In the morning she was taken to the Ghetto hospital. The poor girl wanted very much to live because until then she had hardly enjoyed life, and she had wonderful prospects for a splendid future: under the effect of morphine she had the illusion that she would live — but the pity of it was that she was wounded not only in the legs but in the abdomen, and her intestines were outside her body. A belated operation, gangrene, general weakness — her condition was serious. In the evening the illusion vanished. The poor thing knew that the situation was critical. Weakness increased. She felt that her strength was leaving her. She was fully conscious until the last moment. She remembered seing her parents in the marketplace and her sister, Helena, who, after she was shot in her face, had to proceed outside the city to the common grave. After the terrible sufferings in her last moments, she fell asleep under the effects of the morphine, which turned into eternal sleep.

I knew her. She was pretty and gentle, and after her death she was beautiful. The expression on her face was calm, without any trace of terrible suffering. The breeze of the wind, which stole into her room through the open window, stroked her face and hair, as if it tried to awaken her to life, but in vain.

(Translated in sorrow by her brother,
Meir Selzer)

"Actions" in Trembowla

The following is an abridged letter from Holocaust survivor Henryka Stachowiak, written from Poland where he now lives.

Szprotawa, October 30, 1981

Dear Sidney,

Have mailed a few letters to you. It is hard to remember everything after so many years. Early in September, 1942, there was a large "Action" against Jews in the town. Many tried to run, and the German Gendarmes, with the help of the Ukrainian Police, were shooting.

The Ghetto was behind the Pokrovka Mountain, at the road leading to the military barracks. Many Jews were in the Infection Hospital (typhoid). During the "Action" the same day, they were pulled out from the beds, lined up outside the building and shot. Dr. Bomze took care of the sick. He was killed later, not the same day.

In the spring of 1943, I saw Jews who were led to their death, to be shot. In the group was Weisbrod's cousin with her husband and children, terribly changed. Don't remember all the names. The other Weisbrod family emigrated to Israel.

I saw the third "Action" in the autumn of 1943. Many Jewish families were rounded up by the Germans and the Ukrainian Police. They were shot behind the barracks, near the forest. There were two large pits ready. The Jews were ordered to undress; standing naked, they were shot. The bodies were covered with soil, which kept moving. It looked like all were not completely dead. The killers left the site.

Before Christmas (1943), there was also a large "Action" against Jews. The Judenrat was obliged to keep order in the Ghetto, and see to it that nobody ran away. They carried white armbands. At the end they were also shot with the remaining Jews left in the Ghetto. The massacre took place in Plebanovka Village. Two large pits were there. Not all were dead. Some were injured only. The soil was soaked with blood; it continued to move.

Gentiles were ordered to cover the pits with additional soil, being afraid that epidemics would spread.

The family Stern was shot. The teacher Goldfliess is in Israel. He was hidden with a Polish family who saved his life.

The late Szwager told me that the Gestapo man, Szklarek, always took part in the "Actions" to liquidate the Jews. Once he ordered a little Jewish girl to lace her shoe, and, when the child bent down, he shot her.

I forget many Jewish names. The Shertzer and Mariendorf families were killed. Dr. Poleshchuk did hide Mariendorf's daughter. He married her. Later he died in Cracow of throat cancer.

The Ukrainians killed Poles and Jews, robbing their possessions. Jews who survived were saved by Polish families. There was a death penalty for hiding Jews.

Th wife of Dr. Sass was murdered. A Gentile family saved his little daughter. (Dr. Sass, with his brother, escaped to the Soviet Union.) He is working in Wroclaw, Poland.

At the end, no Jews were left to be transported to the Camps. They were all liquidated. I described what I do remember.

> Greetings —
> Henryka Stachowiak (Friedel)
> (Translated by S. Brinstein)

Scenes of the Plenovka Massacres

When the German Army captured the town of Trembowla and the surrounding region, on July 5, 1941, I was living in the Village of Plebanovka. There, I continued to work on my little farm continuously during the entire Nazi occupation, being witness to the cruel Nazi crimes committed by the Fascist "New Order." I want to tell the story and the facts which I witnessed myself. Some of the stories I did mark down in my notebook, when and what happened; some other stories will remain in my memory for the rest of my life.

Right from the beginning of the Nazi occupation the Germans declared that Ukraine would belong to the Ukrainians. Persecution of the Polish people started. Entire Polish families were exterminated by the Ukrainian Nationalists. These bloody mass pogroms were tolerated by the Germans. The Nazis themselves were interested in the spread of national enmity and hatred among the local population. The Ukrainian Nationalists asked in their wall-posters everywhere to read and believe only what they were saying.

The Ukrainians killed Polish and Jewish people. Such wall-posters I did read myself. I saw myself dead bodies of Poles and Jews, with their hands tied with rope, floating in the Seret River, in villages, Ostrovets, etc. where the dead bodies continued to swim. All this happened in the beginning of the Nazi occupation. After that, when the German army marched deeper eastward, the Nazi rulers declared Western Ukraine as part of the "General Government" of the German Reich. With this proclamation, nothing was left of the "Independent Ukraine."

In the year 1943, the Germans created the Ghetto for the Jews, starting with the Red Army Street, leading to the old barracks. The Jews from all other parts of the town were driven into the Ghetto area.

On April 7, 1943, the German Gestapo gathered over one thousand Jews, among them children, women and old people. They were driven out. One day before it happened, special detachments arrived from Tarnopol, called *Baudienst,* who dug out the pits in which the dead bodies were thrown.

About this tragedy, which I witnessed myself, I can recall the following:

In the morning, April 7, 1943, I went to work in the field. At 8:00 a.m., from the mountain top where I worked, I saw a huge group of people moving from Trembowla toward Plebanovka. Most of them were half naked, only in their underwear. As I found out later, they were undressed at the gathering places in town. I was interested to find out what kind of people they were because I couldn't comprehend that such a huge group could be driven to annihilation. I stopped working, and started to observe what was going on there. I saw the following picture:

All the people I'm talking about were brought near the waiting pits. They were ordered to undress. All were naked. On all sides were Gestapo guards, four in a group, in black gloves. Two men on each side of the pit were standing with machine guns. The third Gestapo group brought the naked (two at a time) closer to the pit, where they were shot. The bodies fell into the mass grave. Some tried to run, but were caught and shot, and thrown into the pit. This continued till noon. The job wasn't finished yet. In my notebook I did mark down that day: "Year — 1943, day — April 7, A Jewish "Action" took place on the mountain of Plebanovka. German soldiers shot and killed Jewish families, around a thousand people."

At 2 p.m., the "Action" continued. The same afternoon of April 7, 1943, my daughter, Shmigelskaya Paulyna, arrived at the field. She told me that I was ordered to travel with the horse-wagon to Tarnopol. Right then I had to show up at the Judenrat in Trembowla. I arrived at the designated place. Near the Judenrat there were already fifty horse-wagons, waiting to transport the clothing left from the naked Jews to Tarnopol. While I was standing with the others waiting, a German came out of the house, ordering three horse-wagons to separate from the waiting group. I was among the three selected drivers to transport people to Plebanovka. Four women were ordered to ride on my wagon.

One German accompanied them. On the other two wagons were ten on each. On the way, before reaching Plebanovka, one woman started to beg the German to let her go. The German told her to run. She jumped from the wagon and started to run. With the shot from a pistol, the German killed her on the spot. Another woman jumped down. She was shot in the head. The third and the fourth women were murdered in the same way.

Leaving the dead bodies where they fell, we continued our journey toward the pits. At a near distance, I stopped the horse-wagon. At the same time a young Jew stepped down from the other wagon. The same German, traveling with me, killed him with four shots. The young man wasn't completely dead. A second German came closer, killing him with the fifth bullet. I was ordered to bring his body closer to be thrown into the pits. Two Judenrat policemen carried the body to the wagon. I brought it approximately 10 meters from the open grave. The two policemen took him down, throwing the body into the pit. The German traveling with me was a sergeant, whose family name was Sklaryk, and who committed those crimes before my eyes. The others I didn't know. After the dead body of the Jew was thrown into the mass grave, I turned to a German officer standing nearby, asking if I could go nearer the pit to take a look at the dead. The drunk German permitted me to come closer, where I saw a grisly picture:

The pit was full of human bodies. Many were not yet completely dead. Many were lifting their heads, moving their hands. Others were moaning. Some were crying. There were also old people, women and children. A group of Germans started to cover the pit with sand. The sand was sinking down. The covered bodies were moving like a wave. The blood from the murdered people was running in all directions. At the same time, shots were ringing, killing those buried alive. It was a terrible sight. The hair on my forehead stiffened. I stood around 10 to 15 minutes, and, almost unconscious, left the pit. I went to the same German who permitted me to take a look, asking if that was all?

The German replied, "No. This isn't the end. Today, only one thousand were killed. There are still many Jews left alive."

Among the dead, I personally saw people I knew well, residents of Trembowla: Schechtera Icka, two Ginsburg brothers, I don't remember their first names, Strassberg Ycek, Brenrowu, don't remember the first name, and many others.

Signed: Ivan Malinowski
(Translated by B. Sabrin)

Summary of Nine Additional Eyewitnesses' Accounts of the Plebanovka Massacres

Among the archives are nine more accounts. The testimonies of eight are signed. The ninth has three "X" marks — the illiterate person.

All of the eyewitnesses describe the bloody Plebanovka massacres in a similar way as Ivan Malinowski in his account above. All witnesses remember the year — 1943. Some don't remember the month, and most don't remember the day or days of the massacre.

Most mention the *Baudienst* that arrived a day before to dig out the pits. All know about the existence of the Ghetto — that most were victims in their underwear only, undressed completely later. Mentioned are the figures of 600 and 1,000 people killed in the "Actions" in Plebanowka.

Eyewitness Shmigelska P. L. describes the following: "When the Germans occupied Trembowla, they promised the Ukrainians an "independent" Ukraine, after the Jewish race was cleaned out. At that time the OUN started to shoot Poles and Jews. In our village the Bandera bands killed 15 Poles.

"Many of the Jews had their hands tied near the pits."

Mentioned also are attempts made by the victims to run away. Almost all were caught and shot. Another witness mentions the brutal mass murder of Polish families by Ukrainian Nationalists. Two of the witnesses mention the name of a man, Diner, a Jew who ran away.

He was caught and shot. Near the pit, a picture of a Jew was found. He was called: "Moshko." One witness remembers the name of a victim: "Helsher" (Helicher?).

Most do remember German gendarmes and Ukrainian Nationalist Police guarding the Ghetto. Witness: Penkowski (Pepkowski?), mentions the size of one pit — 5 × 5 meters. Some of the eyewitnesses saw the picking up of the victims' clothes left near the pits. Others mention Trembowla and Tarnopol where the clothing was delivered.

Eyewitnesses' Names

1. Juchnevich Paulina Ivanov
2. Wojtkovich — illiterate
3. Glywa Anton Mich
4. Szmigelska Polyna Lukj
5. Szmigelska Katarina Pawl
6. Krzewski Ignatij Filip
7. Kretowksi Stanislav Ivan
8. Kozak Stefan Grin
9. Penkowski Michal Adam

(Translated by B. Sabrin)

Part Four

AFTER

THE WAR

"Some local elements hate us for our
cooperation with Germany. We are proud of
this cooperation . . . and are sure that the
New Order created by Adolf Hitler shall reign
supreme in Europe and throughout the world
on the ruins of the degenerate ideologies."

Ukrainian Nationalist newspaper—
Ukrainski Shchodenni Visti,
July 26, 1941

26

Ukrainian Nationalism
Since World War II

I. Gartner

Accⲟrⲇing to statistical data, there are around three million Ukrainians on the North American continent. As a person who was at one time close to the events of the Holocaust in the Ukraine, I was naturally interested in learning more about the activity of Ukrainian Nationalism in the U.S. and Canada.

The Ukrainian Nationalist community in both countries seems to be a lively one. There is an array of many "patriotic" Nationalist newspapers and periodicals in the Ukrainian language. There are also a few in English, while others contain a mixture of both languages.

As before and during the war, Ukrainian Nationalist groups have claimed the right to speak in the name of the Ukrainian people, propounding a monopoly on patriotism and truth as related to the aspirations of all Ukrainians. I think there can be no doubt, in view of the documented crimes that have been committed in the name of Ukrainian "Nationalism," that theirs is a questionable claim.

The main Ukrainian Nationalist organizations are: UCCA— "Ukrainian Congress Committee of America," UACC—"Ukrainian American Coordinating Council," UCC—"Ukrainian Canadian Committee," and WCFU—"World Congress of Free Ukrainians."

The old Bandera faction of the "Organization of Ukrainian Nationalists"—OUN—maintains its world headquarters in Munich, West Germany, and its U.S. headquarters in New York City.

In the U.S., the *National Tribune* (published in New York) is the mouthpiece of the die-hard, Nationalist OUN "patriots" with European experience. Their counterpart in Canada, is called *Homin Ukrainy,* or *Ukrainian Echo.* Both are weeklies. Other publications available are: *America, Svoboda (Liberty), Ukrainian News, Ukrainian Voice, Ukrainian Weekly, Ukrapress,* and *Lemko Voice.*

After the defeat of German Fascism in Europe, and the changed post-World War II situation, Ukrainian Nationalism transformed itself into a movement of "freedom-loving" liberals and democrats, defending human rights and liberties. On the first page of the above-mentioned OUN weekly, *National Tribune,* one can read the slogan: "Freedom for Individuals — Freedom for Nations." Yesteryear's Nazi allies have become today's Jeffersonian ideologues.

In my research work on the Holocaust, I was naturally interested to find out how the Ukrainian Nationalist leadership in the U.S. and Canada interprets the events in Nazi-occupied Ukraine almost five decades later. What does Ukrainian Nationalism today have to say about the subject? Here is a typical explanation:

"The enemy of my enemies. . .was considered our friend. Nazi Germany was the enemy of Poland, and Soviet Russia. She was also against the Bolsheviks and the Jews. . .England and France helped Poland — our enemy. On the yellow-blue horizon, Germany was viewed as the most likely country to go to war against Poland and Russia, our hated enemies. War presented an opportunity to win Ukrainian Independence. So it seemed to be a natural alliance, a good opportunity, not to be missed. . . ."

Why, one might ask, should Nazi Germany agree to give the Ukrainians, the "subhuman" Slavs, an "Independent Ukraine?" To this question, the Ukrainian Nationalists have a shrewd answer:

"For German recognition to establish an independent Ukraine, the OUN, and the Ukrainian Nationalist Movement, would mobilize Ukrainian support (in the liberated Ukraine) for the Nazi Wehrmacht in case of war against Russia." The Nazi *blitz* attack against Russia generated high hopes in the Ukrainian Nationalist community.

The Nazi-Ukrainian Nationalist Alliance came into being and proceeded to give birth to its bloody offspring. The Ukrainian Nationalist "Nachtigal" and "Roland" battalions, under German command, marched together with the Nazi army, "liberating" the Ukraine. Other elements within the Ukrainian Nationalist movement provided the Germans with energetic assistance in executing their racial policies. All of this is documented history. Ukrainian Nationalism today, however, still persists in denying itself an accurate account of its own background.

Ukraine and the Ukrainians

In his book *Ukraine and Ukrainians,* Dr. Iwan Owechko, a "patriotic" Ukrainian of European origin, concedes that the World War II alliance (U.S., England, and the U.S.S.R.) fought for the "noble" cause of destroying the Fascist beast—the "Thousand Year Reich." But what were the enthusiastic expectations of the Ukrainian Nationalist patriots on the eve of the war? Dr. Owechko provides his answers.

There were three categories of Ukrainian Nationalists. The first group was politically illiterate and didn't understand the true intentions of the German "liberators." The second, "less than knowledgeable" group, met the Nazi invasion with high hopes that, with Germany's assistance, an Independent Ukraine would be established.

The third, "literate" group, was fully aware of the nature of the Nazi political state. They had read Adolf Hitler's *Mein Kampf.* They realized the Führer's intention to colonize and enslave the Ukraine. And they agreed with the Nazi attitude toward "impure" races, and held the same view towards the disparate ethnic groups of their homeland. If they could assist in ridding their beloved Ukraine of its human blemishes, then surely it would become evident to the Germans that the Ukrainians were worthy partners and allies for future struggles. If one examines the pre-war history of the Ukrainian Nationalist movement, it is apparent that its adherents did indeed have much in common with the Nazi mentality.

The bloody anti-Jewish Pogroms during the Khmelnytsky era (1648–1657) in the Ukraine are not forgotten. "Jewish merchants," Dr. Owechko explains, "were selling weapons to Ukraine's enemy, the Poles.... Profiteering adventures perpetrated by Jews... led occasionally to anti-Jewish Pogroms."

The Petlura Nationalist Pogroms (1917–20), under the Yellow-Blue flags with the Trident, continued the tradition of anti-Semitism when some 200,000 Jews were bludgeoned to death by Ukrainian Nationalists.

From the testimony of Charles Jacobowitz, Secretary to the Belgian Consulate in Kiev and a witness to Petlura's Pogroms in 1919:

> "...In one of the rooms, a whole family, father, mother and a little girl, were lying in a pool of blood, their bodies terribly mutilated, their hands torn and cut away from the bodies by sword cuts. The faces of those martyrs were covered with wounds. Is it necessary to add that the poor little girl had been violated before she was killed?"

After the Bolshevik Revolution in 1917, the hopes of all nationalists within the Tsar's polyglot empire soared, and within the period of the Civil War against the White armies, the breakdown of national order unleashed sentiments which until then had just barely been suppressed. A participant in the struggle against the nationalist gangs of Otaman Halaka in Chernihiv region in 1922 recollects:

> "From Jewish homes, village cabins, cellars and barns one could hear desperate shrieks and pitiful shouts for help. No one was spared, neither the old nor young. Infants were smashed against walls, mothers were raped and killed. Young girls were violated and crippled. Communists were tortured with special gusto. This picture shall never fade from the memory of those that saw it."

Ukrainian Nationalists today who claim they were coerced, or, in an even further stretch of the imagination, forced to cooperate with the Nazis, against their better nature, must not only deny their behavior in World War II, but also much of their pre-war history.

Still, with very few exceptions, the Ukrainian Nationalist leadership (and their apologists) in the United States and Canada deny Nazi-Ukrainian Nationalist collaboration in Western Ukraine during the Nazi era. Documentary evidence of wrongdoing is explained away as the invention of Soviet propaganda or the KGB. They are helped by the fact that Jewish witnesses to the crimes are obviously not in abundance, most of them having been hastily buried in mass graves, and those who did survive are now becoming aged.

The leaders of the United States have contributed their share toward enhancing the self-esteem of the Ukrainian Nationalists. In the bimonthly magazine "ABN (Anti-Bolshevik Bloc of Nations) Correspondence," there is a picture of former Ukrainian Premier (during the Nazi era) Yaroslav Stetsko, posing with (former) President Ronald Reagan. When Stetsko died, on July 5, 1986, President Reagan sent a saddened condolence to his widow, in which he mentioned the "courageous struggle" the late Ukrainian Premier waged for "human rights." "Your cause is our cause. God bless you," Reagan wrote.

The same issue of the magazine features pictures of (then) Vice President George Bush, and (then) United Nations Ambassador Jeanne Kirkpatrick also posing obliviously with Stetsko.

Senator Alphonse D'Amato (D-NY) sent a particularly touching condolence message to Stetsko's widow, terming Stetsko a "towering figure" and "patriot" who "cherished freedom."

Did all those who shook hands with the Hon. Yaroslav Stetsko, the former Premier of the Nazi-controlled puppet state of the Ukraine, realize the nature and extent of his wartime actions? Did they know that the Ukrainian Nationalist movement he represented, and the Nazi state that the western allies fought to destroy, were melded together in a Fascist partnership?

Ukraine and the Ukrainian Nationalist "Patriots"

Every survivor of that evil time, whose story can still be told, must continue to come forth with testimony to the true nature of what transpired in the Ukraine during World War II. If the leaders of the "Free World" cannot see danger where it still exists, it is the survivors who must continue to educate them.

> "Ukrainian Nationalism must be prepared to employ every means in the struggle . . . not excluding mass physical extermination, even if millions of human beings, physical entities, are its victims."
>
> Ukrainian newspaper, *Meta,* April 17, 1932

27

LESSONS TO BE LEARNED

S. Brinstein

BEFORE REACHING ANY CONCLUSION, I wish to deal with past events first. Combined with the present, it will give us a more objective, clear picture, and help us to view events from the proper perspective.

Returning to the past, I would like to share with the reader a few episodes from my personal World War II experiences in Europe. They are as follows:

Being a little too slow in thinking and assessing the political-military situation at the time, I did not manage to leave Warsaw, Poland, before it was surrounded by the Nazi Wehrmacht. For 26 days and nights we had to endure the barbaric Nazi bombardment of the Polish capital. Nazi Germany, as is known, attacked Poland on September 1, 1939.

The Marshalkovska Street in Warsaw, Poland, (or whatever was left of it) was lined with eager spectators, watching the victorious Nazi Army march into the ruined capital. The parade was an impressive one; a triumph for Nazism.

It is understandable that I and a friend of mine, Herman Herlich* didn't want to miss such an historical event. We joined the crowd.

Standing in front of us were middle-aged Polish people, talking to each other from time to time. One of the ladies turned her head around as if to see whether anybody was listening, and said to the man standing near her: "You know, now the Germans will settle the score with the Jews." ("*Teraz Niemcy sie, Oblicza, z Zydami.*") The man nodded his head. It was September 29th or 30th, 1939.

---

*Herman Herlich was drafted into the Soviet Army in 1941, in Tarnopol region. Fighting against German Fascism, he fell on the battlefield on the Eastern Front. Let us honor his memory.

The Polish lady was not politically near-sighted. She saw clearly the danger awaiting the Jewish people. Was she bothered by the loss. of Poland's independence? Did she think that the Jews would be the only Nazi victims? I don't know. The fact remains that she was able to "see" the nearing catastrophe awaiting the Jewish people.

After ten days or so in Nazi-occupied Warsaw, we decided to move to the other side of the Wisla (Vistula) River to Praga. My determination to get away from the Nazis was irreversible. I said to my friend: "If you want to stay, I'll go by myself. Any other country, any other place, on bread and water to live on only, but not with the Nazis. I see no future with them."

Not being able to continue our journey eastward, we had to find a place to sleep. We knocked on the doors of a few houses, but there was no answer. We tried another house a few blocks away. Finally, an elderly lady opened the door, inviting us inside. The "apartment" consisted of one long room: living room, bedroom, and kitchen, all in one. Near the window, on a long wooden bench, where Jewish children learned their A-B-C's, an elderly, good-natured gentleman had been sitting. It was the lady's husband, a Hebrew teacher.

The reception was a friendly one. We explained our precarious situation. We had no place to stay, and the Germans were not permitting anyone to leave for the Eastward area. Rumors were circulating that the Wisla River would be the new frontier between Nazi Germany and Soviet Russia. The couple consented to our staying without hesitation. They were poor, good-natured people, ready to share misfortune with others. After a friendly conversation and hot tea and bread, we lay down on the floor, which had some straw underneath. Being overtired from walking all day, we had a good night's rest. This friendly place was our new home for about two weeks.

Our main problem was solved. We had a roof over our heads. What was needed was food. Being young, we found ways to get it. Nearby, there were water-barges (small freighters) loaded with sacks of rice, sugar, etc. It was wartime. If one could not buy it, he had to find a way to get it, one way or the other. Who would want to starve from hunger?

During those days we tried to find a way to get rid of the German Nazis. However, the situation was still fluid, not stabilized as yet.

We had information that refugees attempting to leave were turned back by the Germans. We had to wait. There was no other choice for a while. Rumors started to circulate again that the British and

French were coming here, and that the Germans would leave. We decided to take a long walk, in order to find out from the Germans what was what.

Here and there Nazi soldiers were directing street traffic. We went to one of them. There was nobody else around. A black pistol was hanging down on a chain from the soldier's belt. I don't remember if the sign, *"Gott Mit Uns"* ("God with us") was on his belt buckle. We tried to find out about the new frontier. He wasn't sure where it was. Suddenly, as if from nowhere, we were surrounded by a group of Polish people, also eager to find out what was new.

The German soldier didn't like to be encircled by strangers, especially with no other Germans present. In plain German he ordered the group to disperse. They did not understand the language. They didn't move. Asking me to translate, he repeated the order. I translated it into Polish. They kept standing there. A few of the group pointed their fingers at us, shouting: *"Jude, Jude"* ("Jew, Jew"). The soldier didn't care about that. Lifting his gun, he repeated again: "Tell them to get lost, or I'll shoot." They understood the message (and the word *"Jude"*). They dispersed in different directions. Also, we understood the intentions behind their description of us correctly.

It started to get dangerous to walk in the streets. The Germans began to catch people to clean up the rubble in the street. Some didn't return. My friend was lucky to come back home twice. We stayed at home most of the time. I was not interested in seeing Nazi faces.

One nice afternoon, the elderly teacher asked us to sit down at the long table. From his bookshelf on the wall, he took down a flat leather-bound large Hebrew book. I don't know if it was a "Gemarah," "Talmud," or some other book. Turning page after page continuously, he finally stopped. We both understood that he probably found what he was looking for.

Making a gesture with his right hand, he asked us to pay attention and to listen carefully. Looking straight into our faces, he said: "I want to talk to both of you." We replied that we were ready to listen to what he had to say. Moving the book a little closer he started:

"What I am about to tell you is interesting and important. You are still young, and you have a chance to make it. When you manage to get out of here, try to get far away, very far. We are too old for such journeys. Where and how far can we go? It is for the young.

"True, Poland lost, and the Germans won. But the war isn't over. It's just started. Dark, threatening clouds will cover the sky. The war will continue." With whom? I asked. Taking a deep breath, this time interpreting from the book (from Hebrew into Yiddish) an historical event, he made himself clear:

"Amalek will attack Melech Juvon."* Not being able to understand the meaning of it, we asked for an interpretation. "Amalek-Hitler, will attack Melech Juvon (the King of the East) — Russia." When? I asked. Interpreting directly from Hebrew, he replied slowly: "Thousand Nine Hundred Forty One." .

His prophecy wasn't over. He continued: "The horizon (sky) will get very dark, so dark that it will look like Amalek-Hitler is winning the war. He will achieve victory after victory on all fronts. He will penetrate deep into Melech Juvon — Russia. Very many people will die, but after much bloodshed, the situation will change, the sky will clear, and the King of the East — Soviet Russia, will win the war. They will win, despite the fact that they do not believe in religion. After the victory over Amalek-Hitler, there will be peace in the world for many years."

It took me many years to comprehend fully the wisdom and extraordinary vision of the Jewish Hebrew teacher I never met again. He was an innocent victim, like many others, of German Fascism. Honor his memory.

Our stay with the Jewish teacher and his lovely spouse neared its end. One nice morning, around the third week of October 1939, we noticed a new German (and Polish) poster on the wall on a nearby street. We were interested in its contents.

The Germans gave permission to all those who wanted to leave Warsaw and its vicinity. This was due to overcrowding and a shortage of food in the capital. Most of the food stores were destroyed (or emptied) during the war. The Germans were simply afraid of epidemics. They were eager for the people to move to the countryside.

For us, this was good news. We were waiting for just such an opportunity. Now we could continue our journey eastward. The next morning we thanked the teacher and his wife (I think they had no children) for everything they had done for us. We said goodbye to them — forever.

---

*The Amalekites were a nomadic, war-like tribe in the Sinai Peninsula. Their existence dates back, according to the Bible, to Abraham's time (Gen.14:7). They were enemies of Israel. Israel's persecutor's were dubbed Amalek. They were also in existence about 1,000 B.C.E., at the time of King Saul. They disappeared from historical view after their destruction by King Hezekiah (1 Chronicles 4:39.43). "Melech Juvon" (in Hebrew) means: "King of the East."

We continued marching again, passing towns and villages. There were quite a few obstacles to overcome, until we managed to reach the new frontier area. The more eastward we continued, the less visible German soldiers became. How wonderful it was to know that the days were near when no Nazi soldiers would be around. I didn't miss them at all. Both of us were eager to get away from them. There was nothing good to be expected from German Fascism — especially for the Jews. And all this we understood very well. We weren't blind to the reality existing at the time. This kept us going, walking hundreds of miles.

Finally we were nearing the new frontier, Bug River.

We were very exhausted from the long march, with little food and water. I cannot even remember the name of the last small village on the German side. After a resting pause, we continued walking. From a distant house, on the left side of the street, a German soldier appeared. He was running toward us, ordering us to stop and wait until he returned. He had no weapon, and the tone of his voice was not menacing. We did not read any bad intentions in his eyes. A few other German soldiers were visible from a distance near the house. They didn't come close. We were not at all afraid. We just waited.

After about four to six minutes, the German soldier returned, still not armed. In his hands he carried two round breads, and two large cans of meat. He knew that we were refugees running eastward. Before handing it over, he said to us: "Yes, I understand. You are being very smart. Go as far as you can, far away. There is nothing good you can expect here. I wish you luck, and hope you will make it. Take this with you, you'll need..." He waved his hand, and we thanked him for the food. This was an unexpected surprise for us. This, from a German soldier. During those years we already knew that there were Germans and German Nazis. And Nazis are not only German. Fascism is international.

There was still quite a distance to the new frontier. Tired or not, we continued to walk. The German loaf of bread and the can of meat tasted good, especially after many days of walking.

The weather was nice, and no German soldiers were visible anymore; we had left the last German outpost behind. Late in the evening we reached the River Bug.

Again, tired and exhausted from the long march, we looked for a place to stay overnight. Nearby, a farmer's house was visible. Wonderful. After knocking on the door, it was opened by a young Polish lady. "Come in, sit down, make yourself comfortable. You must surely be thirsty and hungry. I'll prepare something for you."

We washed ourselves, and kept wondering about the friendly reception. It didn't take long before a hot meal was on the table. The soup (made from dairy products) was delicious. It was a delicacy. The lady knew quite well what our destination was, and who we were.

"If you had come yesterday, you could have gone with the Russians. They went back over the river. They were very friendly, nice people. Last night there were people like you sleeping here. There were others before. They come and go. There's a small boat ferrying people across the river. You will pay something and tomorrow you'll make it. You must be very tired. Lie down over there."

The "bed" on the floor with straw underneath was already waiting for us. We didn't need any sleeping tablets. We were safe and secure. No Nazis around.

After a good breakfast the next day, we thanked our hostess for the friendly reception and help. There was still a nice walk to the river.

The boat owner was quite busy, crossing the fast, shallow river back and forth. We paid a small amount of Polish money, and in about seven to ten minutes, we were on the other side of the new frontier.

A friendly Soviet soldier (most likely from Central Asia) greeted us in accented Russian. "Come, come to us, you'll be all right." Understanding what he said, we shook hands and thanked him for the welcome. From there it was still a long walk and ride to our final destination — Tarnopol region.

There were many others who did the same thing, managing to escape from the claws of the Nazis. According to reliable data, around 250,000 (or more) Jews succeeded in finding a safe haven in the USSR. The Soviet borders were wide open. Only in a few places were they turned back. Few border-guards were visible along the wide frontier.

I do understand that yesterdays cannot be brought back, and that the dead cannot be resurrected. However, the question still arises: Why did only a small minority understand what should be done in time of danger, and the great majority of the Jewish people did not? Some will say they didn't know about Auschwitz, Treblinka, Belzec, etc., at that time. The minority didn't know about it either.

Looking back, we can now understand the situation much better. There is no doubt that during the 1930's the Jewish establishment in Poland (and in many other countries) did not stand up to the test of time. There were few exceptions. Hitler's *Mein Kampf,* the Nuremberg Racist Laws, the *Kristallnacht,* and the *"Sieg Heil"* weren't enough food for thought. Six long years of Nazi rule until the war (1933-1939) weren't enough to wake up the Jewish leadership from its lethargy. When it came to the question of survival, Jewish survival, the Jewish people were almost leaderless. How else can one explain it? Frontiers were wide open, no quotas, no visas were needed, and a majority of Jews preferred not to move away from the Nazi onslaught. Were there any reasons for it?

As the saying goes, nothing happens without a reason. There were other contributing factors. A decade or so ago, I came across an article in a European publication which dealt with a similar question. Up until now, I was not able to verify its authenticity. But I am still intrigued by its contents.

The year was 1934, it was somewhere in Europe. I don't remember the name of the city. Chaim Nachman Bialik, a famous Jewish writer and poet, made a speech. According to the source, he said, among other things:

"We, the Jewish people, have to be vigilant. The situation is serious." Pointing his finger, he continued: "The threat to the Jewish people is coming from the East." And all this at a time when the Nazi SS boots were already marching on the streets of Berlin, hollering *"Sieg Heil."* If this story is true (and there are reasons to believe it, because there were many others sharing his mistaken, unjustified fear), there is little wonder why the majority of the Jewish Nazi victims were paralyzed and frightened to move eastward. Was there any other direction to move to? There was not. My reasoning is simple. If a quarter of a million could make it, why not 2.5 million? Even many more, especially the younger generation, could have escaped in time, had they been told to run for their lives. The deadly Fascist menace was not explained to the Jewish people of Poland and other European countries. Six years of Nazi rule, 1933-1939, was not enough to understand what was underway. It is a sad chapter in Jewish history.

The ignorance of many Jews about the Nazi threat was appalling. Before our group left the town of Trembowla, Tarnopol region, (July 1, 1941), J. Einleger, the father of Josef Einleger, came to say goodbye to his son (and to us). These were his parting words:

"Run away, 50-100 miles from here, where you will not be known as Jewish. I do remember the Germans from World War I. They were good people. They did not do anything bad to the civilian population." We were lucky that we did not listen to his wrong advice. His son saved his life and now resides in Israel (died in 1987).

After World War II, I had a chance to meet some Holocaust

survivors. As a student of international affairs, I naturally was interested in finding out about events during the Nazi occupation in Poland and the Ukraine.

What did you think, I asked, after the Nazi army marched into the town? Weren't you survivors afraid that bad times were coming for the Jews? The answers were almost identical: "Sure we were afraid. We didn't know what would happen. We said to each other and to ourselves: What will happen to all the others (Jews) will happen to us. What else can we do? So, it happened. It was a tragedy. You know about it."

These and other similar answers, coming from Holocaust survivors, confirmed fully the failure of the prewar Jewish leadership in Europe (and not only in Europe) to stand up to the crucial test of time. There was almost nobody to sound the alarm, to explain, and to lead. There was no Moses, and no miracles in Nazi-occupied Europe in the 1940's. Had the Soviet Union not held out, if the Red Army had collapsed in 1941, there can be little doubt that the "Final Solution" would have been an accomplished fact and there would have been no Israel either. The Eichmanns and Demjanjuks would still be performing their jobs. After the Jews and the Gypsies, the Slav people (the Ukrainian Nationalists included) would still have been going up in smoke ("straight to heaven") through the chimneys of Auschwitz, Treblinka, Majdanek, Mauthausen, Belzec, and all the rest. The Nazi bible *Mein Kampf* and other Nazi publications and speeches, made this clear long before the war.

The conclusion that can be drawn from this lesson is a clear one. The prewar Jewish leadership in Europe (and overseas) lacked the vision of the Polish lady watching the Nazi victory parade, the Jewish Hebrew teacher in (Praga) Warsaw, and the German soldier near the new frontier, the River Bug. If one likes it or not, this is the naked truth. The past cannot be changed, it is true. But it should serve as a lesson for the future.

The Jewish people have an obligation to the past. It is the duty of the Jewish people to remind the world about World War II events, and the Holocaust tragedy. It was the Second World War that made this tragedy possible.

Human history has no comparison to World War II. The price of victory was a bloody one. Over fifty million people lost their lives. Among them were six million Jews in Europe, twenty million people in the Soviet Union ("only" three Austrias or six Israels), and millions of people in other countries of the world, including Americans. It should be remembered that an obligation to the past does not exclude a responsibility to the future.

Now let us turn to the present. How does the world situation look in the 1980s, almost five decades later? Is history repeating itself? Not in exactly the same way.

Dark, dangerous clouds are gathering on the horizon again. This time the threat is a triple one: nuclear, conventional and chemical warfare. The production of nuclear, conventional and chemical weapons in different parts of the world is continuing. The stockpiling of deadly instruments of war, plus medical supplies, is already going on in many strategic locations the world over — including Israel.

Does the clear vision and prophecy of the Jewish Hebrew teacher (almost five decades ago) apply to the present world situation again? There is no doubt about it. In the nuclear age, the threat of annihilation is a universal one. All will share the same fate. Nuclear missiles and bombs will make no distinction between whites and blacks, Jews and Gentiles, capitalists and communists. It will ultimately crush all civilization. What the Nazis did in the concentration camps is now designed for the peoples of the entire world.

AFTERWORD

The Committee

THE ACCUSATIONS AGAINST Ukrainian Nationalism in general, the OUN-UPA (and other Nationalist groups) in particular, are based on archival documentary material; eyewitness accounts; survivors' stories; and, other reliable evidence. Pictures and documents speak for themselves.

Members of the committee, responsible for the contents of this book, have tried to illuminate historical events in Western Ukraine during the Nazi era. Future historians will undoubtedly try to give a more complete picture of events in Nazi-occupied Ukraine.

Not even one member of the committee is an adherent to the view of "collective guilt" and "collective innocence." There is no such thing as "German anti-Semitism," "Russian anti-Semitism," "Ukrainian, Polish and American anti-Semitism." Racism may be more or less widespread, but this is no reason to blame everyone for it, when specific criminal groups exist.

Former OUN-UPA leaders (and others), active in Western Ukraine during the Nazi era, are now eulogized by their followers, ideological comrades, and apologists in the U.S. and Canada.

Without any feeling of shame, they are portrayed as "great ideologues" of Ukrainian Nationalism "great strategists" of the past "liberation struggle," and "heroes" raised in the "Christian spirit," for "God and Ukraine." As sons of priests, they naturally had . . . a deep, strong faith in God. How the Ukrainian Nationalist "patriots" behaved, and what they did during World War II, is now well known to the reader of this book.

The naked fact remains that the U.S.-born and Canadian-born Ukrainian Nationalist leadership didn't find the courage (almost five decades later) to come out with the truth, to disassociate themselves from the old "heroes," and the Nationalist "patriots" of the past. The old policy remains: No remorse, no regret, and don't admit anything.

In this book, the accusations are directed against the Ukrainian Nationalist movement in Western Ukraine during World War II. The enormity of the crimes are unparalleled. It's a crime of genocide.

Genocide, as is known, is defined as attempting to exterminate in whole or in substantial part, an ethnic, national, racial or religious group, through murder.

It will be no exaggeration to say that hundreds of thousands of Ukrainian Nationalists were partners in crime with German Nazism, committing war crimes, crimes against humanity, crimes of collaboration, leading to the "Final Solution" — to Genocide.

The fact that there were also Lithuanian, Latvian, Estonian, Polish, Russian, French, Dutch, Jewish, and other Nazi collaborators, doesn't lessen the guilt and responsibility of the Ukrainian Nationalists. No Nationalist movement (or group) can blame others for its own crimes.

Were it not for the complicity and close collaboration of Ukrainian Nationalism with German Nazism, there can be no doubt that millions of people (Jews and non-Jews) would have been saved. Without the help of Ukrainian Nationalist "patriots," the Nazi killing machine could not have accomplished what it did.

This is precisely the reason why Ukrainian Nationalist (and other) Nazi collaborators deserve another Nuremberg.

The Crimes of Stalin

The participating authors recently had a chance to review the final proofs of *Alliance for Murder* before its publication. During the meeting one author voiced criticism about the lack of material in the book which would illuminate events during the Stalin era in the USSR.

The critical observation made by the author was taken into consideration. After a unanimous agreement, the majority decided to state the following:

I. The responsible authors of this book had a limited objective. Their task was to shed more light on the tragic, bloody events, mainly in Western Ukraine, during the Nazi occupation. Of utmost importance was the documentation of the available material, which was the most difficult part of the job.

II. The participants had no authorization, and therefore no right to alter the content of any material contributed by other authors.

III. Monstrous crimes perpetrated by the Stalin regime, against many nationalities in the USSR, were already known years before the Second World War. This is an historical fact and an open secret.

IV. None of the authors had documentary and/or archival evidence in hand revealing Stalinist crimes, or access to such.

V. Among the millions of victims, Ukrainians were *no* exception. Stalinism's victims were also: Russians, Poles, Jews, and many other nationalities. The list is quite a long one.

VI. All of this is *another* tragic chapter in human history. Two separate monstrous crimes don't eliminate the guilt of either. Both are fully responsible for their deeds. The Nazi Holocaust is unique in history. It should *not* be mixed up with other inhuman crimes on the same level.

There is good reason to assume that the extent of Stalin's crimes will be investigated, documented and published in the USSR. This is a job for Soviet historians, and a field of endeavor recently made possible by Gorbachev's initiatives.

VII. Inclusion (or exclusion) of any additional material revealing Stalinist crimes and brutality in this book, will *not* eliminate or lessen the guilt of German Nazism and their bloody henchmen and voluntary collaborators of all shades. The documented evidence presented in this book can *not* be disproved. It is *undeniable.*

VIII. All attempts by International Neo-Nazism (including the U.S. variety) to detach German Nazism from the Third Reich atrocities, and to deny the Holocaust, are bound to fail. Facts remain facts, forever.

Likewise, Ukrainian Nationalist attempts to detach Ukrainian Nationalist complicity and partnership in genocide with German Fascism during World War II are in vain.

German Nazism, in the first place, and Ukrainian Nationalism in the second, are both guilty of committing heinous crimes against humanity. For the deaths of millions of innocents, Jews and Gentiles, we can only strive today to remember. And we can learn.

For the Committee:
B. Sabrin

APPENDIX A:
FROM THE
SOVIET STATE ARCHIVES
UKR.SSR

TO THE CHIEF OF 1st Commissariat UKR. POLICE
in LVOV

On the day — 17.8.42, near the str. . . . I fired six bullets during the action . . .
Weapons were used because the Jews were running away.

Lvov, 17.8.42

Olyjniak Mychajlo
I K U P
in Lvov

AN USSEREN FÜHRER.

Dem allgemeinen Willen der Ukrainer entspre-
chend, wurde heute die Unabhängigkeit und Vereinigung
von sämtlichen ukrainischen Gebieten verkündet.

Die sehnsuchtsvollen Wünsche von vielen Gesch
lechtern haben sich erfüllt. Dein Kampf hat sich mit Er-
folgen bekränzt. Das gesamte Ukrainische Volk hat sich
zum weiteren Kampf um die volle Freiheit der Ukraine
unter Deinen Fahnen eingefunden.

Wir glühen heute vor Wonne, beseelt von einer
Idee, und einigen uns im Gedanken mit unseren Volksgenos-
sen der gesamten Welt.

Eilen wir nach der ukrainischen Hauptstadt -
dem goldkuppeligen Kyjiw ! In diesen grossen Augenblick
senden wir Dir, unerschütterlicher Held der Nationalen
Revolution ,unsere innigsten Wünsche.Wir sind überzeugt,
dass Dein Vorhaben und das sehnsüchtige Begehren des
gesamten ukrainischen Volkes bezüglich der Wiederherste-
llung eines mächtigen Ukrainischen Staates sich ver-
wirklichen wird.

HEIL DER UKRAINE !

Telegram sent to Adolf Hitler by the Nationalist rally held on June 30, 1941.

To our Führer.

According to the will of the Ukrainians, the Independence and
Unification of all Ukrainian territories is proclaimed today.

The longing wishes of the many sexes have been fulfilled. Your struggle
was crowned with success. The Ukrainian Nation is prepared for the
continued struggle to achieve complete freedom for the Ukraine under your
banners.

We are glowing today with happiness, inspired by the spirit of an idea,
and are uniting in thinking with our Volks-comrades of the entire world.

We are rushing to the Ukrainian capital — the golden dome Kiev. In
this great moment we are sending you, unshattered Hero of National
Revolution, our sincere wishes. We are convinced, that your intentions,
and the longing cravings of the entire Ukrainian Nation, regarding re-
establishment of a mighty Ukrainian State, will be realized.

Heil the Ukraine

5 Комісаріят
Української Поліції у Львові   Львів,дня 21.8.1942.
Ч:..2820/42...............
Відносно: Звіт в жид.акції дня 20.8.42.
Основа: приказ К-ди У.П.

                    до
              Команди Української Поліції
                        у Львові

     Голошу,що жидівська акція на терені 5 Комісаріяту у
почалася о год.13 дня 20.8.42.та продовжалася до год.21.
Участь в акції брали 24 поліцистів 5.К.У.П.та 30 поліцист
із Шу-що в Тарнополя.
     Разом допроваджено до збірного пункту 525 жидів,
утікаючих,та ставлячих опір вбито--------- 14
                       ранено---------   6   "
     Ужито зброю та ужито набоїв:Цудик........4
                            Венгльовський4
                            Крявіцький...2
                            Токаренко....5
                            Леськів......2
                            Чуманський...7
                            Ільчишин.....2
                            Бахмун.......2
                            Панас........2

     разом ужито револьверових набоїв,.......40 штук
Підкупства за звільнення аголосили:
  Борух Роман.....685 зол. одержав у формі хабара
  обмін Оленський-оден золотий годинник
  Ігхак-Тадей......800 зол. і оден киш-ніклевий годинник
  Панас Володимир 700 зол.
  Керобух Іван.....100 зол. і одна золота обручка
  _____
      разом ....1785 зол.
     з чого 1485 зол. і золотий годинник та золоту обручку
приняв в збірнім пункті -/здано йому на категоричне домага
керівник акції із Шу-по ппор.Леман,а 300 зол.і оден ніклеви
годинник "Цима" пересилається до дальшої розпорядимости.

     Прилоги:- 5 звітів-
               300 зол. і 1 годинник
                                    Керівник Комісаріяту

5th Commissariat   Lviv, Aug. 21, 1942
Ukrainian Police of Lviv
Document #2820/42

Pertaining to: Report of Jewish action 8/20/42
Basis: Orders of Command of Ukr. Police.

To Command of Ukrainian Police in Lviv.

     Reporting, that the Jewish action on the territory of the 5th
Commissariat Ukr. Police began at 1 o'clock on 8/20/42 and continued until
9 o'clock in the evening. Participants in the action included 24 police of the

5th Commissariat Ukr. Pol. and 30 members of the German Police from Ternopil.

A total of 525 Jews were delivered to the location of detention. During an attempt to escape, 14 Jews were killed and 6 were injured.

The use of firearms was recorded as follows:

Pudky 4
Venhlowsky 4
Krevitsky 9
Tokarenko 5
Leshkiv 7
Shumanski 7
Ilehyshyn 2
Kalymun 2
Danas 9

Using a total of listed shells — 49

Bribes offered for freedom were reported as follows:
Roman Borukh — 683 Gold coins received as a bribe.
Olenski — 1 gold watch.
Tadej Hizniak — 300 Gold coins and 1 nickel plated pocket watch.
Volodimir Panas — 700 Gold coins.

III Commissariat   Lvov, 8/21/42
Ukrainian Police
In Lvov
Nr. 2809/42

Re: Report Jewish Action, 8.20.42
Reason: Order K-Dy U.P.

To: Ukrainian Police in Lvov

Declare that Jewish Action on 5th Commiss. Ukrainian Police started at 13:00, PM, 8.20.42, and continued till 21:00 PM. Twenty-four policemen from 5th Commiss. Ukr. Police, and 30 policemen from Shu-Po from Tarnopol.

Together they delivered to the gathering point 525 Jews. Those trying to run away, and others resisting, were shot. Killed — 14, injured — 6. Nine policemen (names given) used pistols. Bullets fired — 49 pieces.

A total of bribes — money: 1785 Zl., plus one gold watch and gold ring was taken. On the categorical request of the Shu-Po leader, Leman, 1483 Zl., and one gold watch, and gold ring were handed over. 300 Zl. and one nickel "Cima" watch is sent for further consideration.

Enclosure: 5 Reports

300 Zl. and one watch.   Commissariat Chief
                                              (signature)

```
 5 Комісаріят
 .Поліції у Львові          Львів,дня 14 серпня 194: .

                --S__B__I__T__

   в перебігу жид.акції протягом дня 14 серпня 1942 р.

       Голошу,що протягом 14.8.1942 р. з терену 5 Комісаріяту
  ір.Поліції доставлено до вбірного пункту 2128 жидів,убито
  ітікаючих жидів 12,пострілено 7 жидів.
       Поліцисти 5 Комісаріяту У.П.:
  Леськів Микола вужив револьверових набоїв 6 штук ┐ разом
  Калимун Іван  "        "        "    4  "        │ вужито
  Борух Роман   "        "        "    3  "        │ 14
  Юртин Михайло "        "        "    I  ".       │ набоїв
                                                   └────────
       Гроші і всякі речі давані поліцистам у формі хабарів
  редавали поліцисти на місци КерівниковІ Н.С.КК- за винятком
  ліц.Леськова Миколи,котрий прийшов останній з акції та вложив
  депозит-хабар в Комісаріяті -250 зол./двіста пятьдесят золотих/
  і одeн кишенковий годинник/бeз марки/.
       Опорожнено 37 жидівських мешкань,з котрих Ключі предло-
  жено в Комісаріяті.

                        Керівник Комісаріяту
                        Н. П.
```

Fifth Commissariat   Lviv, August 14, 1942
of the Ukrainian Police
in the City of Lviv

REPORT

On the Jewish action carried out on August 14, 1942

I report herewith that on August 14, 1942, 2,128 Jews were delivered from the 5th UP Commissariat area to the assembly point. 12 Jews were killed in an attempt of escape, 7 Jews wounded.

The following policemen from the 5th UPC resorted to firearms:

Mykola Leskiv fired 6 shots from his revolver

Ivan Kalimun 4

Roman Borukh 3

Mikhailo Yurtin 1

Total of shots fired: 14.

Money and other valuables given to the policemen as bribes were immediately delivered by the latter to the squad leader N.S. KK. Except for Mykola Leskiv who was the last to return after the action. He, upon checking on the Commissariat, handed over 250 zloti, as well as one wrist watch bearing no trade mark.

Jews were evicted from 37 apartments. The keys were delivered to the Commissariat.

Chief of the Commissariat

(signature)

5 Комісаріят
Українськоі Поліціі у Львові   Львів, дня 15 серпня 1942 р.
Ч: ...2783/42...........
відносно: звіт з жид.акціі з дня 15.8.1942 р.
Основа: Приказ К-ди У.П.

                         до
          Команди Украінськоі Поліціі
                       у Львові

      Голошу, що з терену 5 Комісаріяту У.П. в часі жидівськоі
акціі допроваджено до збірного пункту 1660 жидів.
      Узили зброю за втікаючими жидами:
      1/ Журда Григорій -6-набоів
      2/ Думанський Пилип -6- "
      3/ Леськів Микола   -5- "
      4/ Стахів Тимко ____-2-_"_____
      разом зужито набоів 19 штук

      В часі акціі убито 8 жидів і 4 пострілено.
      Грошт та інші вартісні річи як також ключі від жидів-
ських помешкань передано в збірнім пункті Керівникові
акціі.
      Прилоги:-/-
                         Керівник Комісаріяту
                         Й. Г. Драбан

The Fifth Commissariat
of the Ukrainian Police in Lviv City
No. 2783/42   Lviv City,
                                               August 15, 1942

REPORT on the Jewish Action
Carried Out August 15, 1942
Grounds: The Ukrainian Police Team Order

To the Ukrainian Police Team in the city of Lviv

I report herewith that during the Jewish action, 1,660 Jews were delivered to the assembly point from the Fifth Commissariat of the Ukrainian Police area.

The following policemen fired shots at the Jews trying to escape:

Furda Hrihoriy . . . . 6 shots
Shumansky Pilip 6
Leskiv Mykola 5
Stakhiv Timko 2
Total of shots fired: 19

During the action, 8 Jews were killed and 4 Jews wounded. Money and other valuables, as well as the keys from the Jewish apartments were delivered and handed to the officer in charge of the action at the assembly point.

No enclosures.

Chief of the UP Commissariat

(signature)

---

5 Комісаріят
Української Поліції у Львові   Львів,дня 22 серпня 1942
Ч:......28 26/42......
Відносно: звіт від.акції з дня 21.8.42.
Основа: приказ К-ди У.П.

до
Команди Української Поліції
у Львові

Голошу,що протягом дня 21.8.1942.в території 5 К.У.П. допроваджено до збірного пункту 805 жидів.
Зужили револьверові набої:

1/ Біктович Михайло вистрілив набоїв I штук
2/ Жеребух Андрій " " I "
3/ Кривіцкий Лев " " 2 "
4/ Петрушевський Лев " " 2 "
5/ Калимун Іван " " 2 "
6/ Борух Роман " " 4 "
7/ Штьо " " 4 "
8/ Леськів Микола " " 4 "
9/ Ставів Тимко " " 6 "

разом зужито набоїв . . . 26 штук
Убито 12 жидів а ранено 5-.

Гроші в сумі 1095 зол. одержані від жидів у формі хабарів за поквітованням здано/на категоричне домагання/ ш четареві Лу-шо Леманові,котрі задучую.

Прилоги:-2-
Кертвдик Комісаріту

The Fifth Commissariat
of the Ukrainian Police
in the city of Lviv
No. 2826/42

Report on the Jewish action
carried out on August 21, 1942
Grounds: order from the Ukrainian
Police Force

Lviv City
August 22, 1942

To the Chief of Ukrainian
Police in the city of Lviv

I herewith report that on August 21, 1942, 805 Jews were delivered to the assembly point from the Fifth Ukrainian Police Commissariat area.

Revolver shots fired:

Viytovich Mikhailo	1 (shot)
Zherebukh Andriy	1
Krivitsky Lev	2
Petrushevsky Lev	2
Kalimun Ivan	2
Borukh Roman	4
Fityo	4
Leskiv Mykola	4
Stakhiv Timko	6

12 Jews killed, 3 Jews wounded. A total of 1,095 zloti were taken from the Jews as bribes and at the demand of the officer Lemanov are enclosed herewith.

Enclosures — 2.

Chief of the Commissariat
(signature)

---

5 Commissariat   Lviv, June 25, 1942
Ukrainian Police in Lviv.
Document #2090/42.

Pertaining to: Jewish action.

Basis: Instructions C.U.P. (Commissariat Ukrainian Police) 6/24/1942

To:
Command Ukrainin Police in Lviv.

In accord with the instructions of the command of Ukr. police of 6/24/1942, at 11 o'clock at the start of 6/24/1942 at 13:50 o'clock an anti-Jewish action was started, which was concluded this same day at 23:30 o'clock.

In agreement with a German elder, the Jews were herded into the yard of the NSKK. In accordance with the instructions of the command of the U.P. (Ukr. Police) in relation to the closing of residences, all this was completed before the start of the action. All the keys, money and other articles were left in the headquarters of the NSKK. Among others, there were 4 gold watches and one large gold chain.

About 900 Jews were brought to the camp. The following took part in the action: 20 police from the 5 Commissariat as leaders of the watches, 25 police from the 5 Commissariat as leaders of the watches, 25 police candidates from the Police School, 30 Shutzmen of the Nskk, 13 from the Sonderdienst. At 22:30 14 police from the 4 Commissariat arrived.

During the night 3 police from the 5 Commissariat U.P. were released to the 1 Commissariat. The district was divided into 12 watch points. Watch points listed and being presented to Command of U.P. (Ukr. Police) in Lviv. Enclosure: (1)

(signature)
Head of Commissariat.

IУ. Комісаріят   Львів, дня 22.8.1942.
ьаїнськоï Поліціï
м. Львова
Ч.п. 2505 /42

До
Команди Украïнськоï Поліціï м. Львова
у Л ь в о в і

Відносно: звіт із жидівськоï акціï в дні 21.8.42

     Голошу, що в дні 21.8.42 відставлено до ляґру при вул. Яківській 312 жидів. Випадків ужиття зброï 4, при чім вистріляно 13 набоïв. Застрілених німецькою Поліцією 9 жидів.
     Намагання підкупства були, після чого відмано Поліціï Охорони 3 золоті заріжки, 1 шнур перлів і 6650 зол. в готівці.

Керівник Комісаріяту:

(signature)
От. Сухомил Украïнськоï Поліціï

IV Commissariat Ukrainian Police   Lviv, August 8, 1942
City of Lviv.
Document #2505/42

To:
Command of Ukrainian Police in Lviv.

Pertaining to: Report of Jewish Action 8/21/42.

I report that on August 21, 1942 there were 312 Jews delivered to the Yanivsky Camp. There were 4 instances of use of firearms, using 13 cartridges. 9 Jews were killed by the German Police.

There were attempts at bribes. Later these articles were turned over to the Security Police. They included 3 gold chains, 1 string of pearls and 6650 gold coins.

Head of Commissariat
(signature)
Olesh Sokolyshyn
Officer, Ukrainian Police

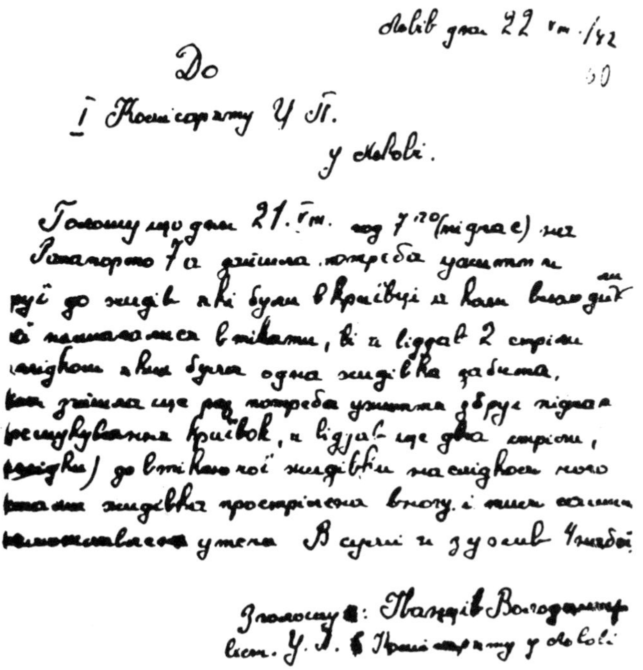

[handwritten document in Ukrainian]

To: Lviv, 8/22/42
1 Commissariat UP
(Ukrainian Police) in Lviv.

I report that on 8/21 at 7:20 during which time, at 7 Rapanopto it became necessary to use firearms against Jews who were in hiding. When they were discovered they started to flee, and as a result a Jewess was killed. Once again it was necessary to use firearms during a search of the hiding places. I fired two shots resulting in the escaping Jewess being shot in the leg and her attempted escape thwarted. In the encounter I used 4 cartridges.

Reporting: Ivanchiv, Volodimir
Lieutenant, Ukr. police.
1st Commissariat in Lviv.

I K.U.P.
in Lvov

Lvov, 17.8.42

REPORT

On the day of 16.8.42, at 15:30, I, Wistun, I.P. Sulyma Mychajlo, used up eight bullets on the str. Nr. 19, where Jews were hiding. They started to run, refusing to stop on my order, after which I fired eight shots. Two Jews were killed.

Wistun, I.P. Sulyma
Mychajlo
Lvov, 17.8.42

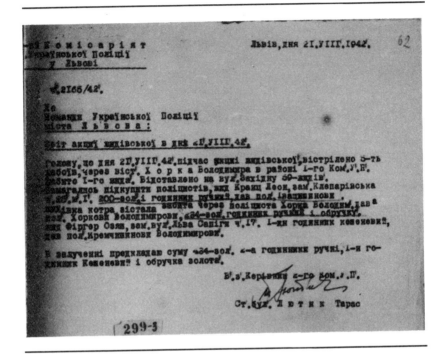

To
Command Ukrainian Police
city Lvov:
Report Jewish Action, 8-21-42

Declare that this day..., during Jewish 'action' five bullets were fired. One Jew was killed and 59 were delivered. Some tried to bribe the policemen. The Jew Kranc Leon, residing at..., gave 200 Zl. and a hand watch to the policeman. A Jewess (killed by policeman Chorka W.) gave 234 Zl., a hand watch and a ring. Jew Firger Oziash, residing at...gave one stone watch.

Enclosed: 434 Zl, 2 hand-watches, 1 stone watch and one gold ring.

(signature)
Chief 2nd Commissariat
Ukrainian Police
Lutyk   Taras

5 Комісаріят
раїнської Поліції у Львові   Львів,дня 18 серпня 1942 р.
2494/42
дносно: звіт жид.акції з дня 17.8.42.
нова: Приказ К-ди У.П.

До
Команди Української Поліції
у Львові

Голошу,що протягом дня 17.8.1942 р.вт терену 5 Комісаріяту У.П.
о збірного пункту допроваджено 1235 жидів.
Зужито револьверових набоїв:
1/Петрушевський Лев -10-штук
2/Пашко Павло   -6-   "
3/Борух Роман   -6-   "
4/Кривіцький Лев   -5-   "
5/Чурда Григорій   -5-   "
6/Забровський Григорій-2-   "
разом зужито набоїв 34 штук
Вбито одного,а пострілено 4 жидів.
Гроші та дорогоцінності ,які діставалися поліцістам у то
хабарів,віддано негайно керівникові акції цього пункту.

Прилоги:-/-

Керівник Комісаріяту
г. ч.

5th Commissariat   Lvov, 8/18/42
Ukrainian Police
in Lvov
Nr. 2794/42

Re: Report Jewish 'Action,' 8/17/42
Reason: Order Command Ukrainian Police

To Command Ukrainian Police in Lvov. Declare that during the
8-17-42, on territory of the 5th Commissariat Ukr. Police, 1235 Jews were
delivered to the gathering point. Six policemen fired a total of 34 bullets.
One was killed and 4 injured.

Money (bribes) and other expensive items were handed over to the
'action' leader of this engagement.

Enclosure: - / -

Chief of Commissariat
(signature)

Excerpt from letter by the Head of Ukrainian Nationalist Council of Volyn, Stepan Skrypnik, to Reichscommissar for Ukraine, Koch, about the Nationalists' desire to participate in management of occupied areas and cooperate with the German invaders in their war against the USSR.

September 11, 1941

Since long ago the Ukrainians have been aware of the integrity of their destination with that of the great German people, especially in the struggle for the new order. The Ukrainians are supporting the glorious German troops in their war against Bolshevism in the full conviction that Greater Germany and Ukraine share a common destiny, that the Ukrainian state can become strong only after Germany's ultimate victory and that Greater Germany will have all the backing of Ukraine in establishing the new order in Europe's east.

As Head of the Ukrainian Council of Trust which expresses the feelings of the nationalist-minded Ukrainians of Volyn, I am aware of the military requirements and war needs of Greater Germany whose victory we are trying to facilitate as best we can. We know quite well that some of the main branches of administration, particularly in the economic field, must be managed by German authorities, the Reich's government possessing the necessary plenary powers as a guarantee of Ukraine's security and territorial inviolability. We are also sure that the German administration will incorporate Ukrainian functionaries in leading positions that will never be occupied either by Poles or by Russians, and that only the German and Ukrainian languges will be used in German institutions for official written and oral communication. We are also convinced that the German authorities in Volyn will take into account the opinion of the Ukrainian Council of Trust in major economic and state matters. At the same time we firmly believe that scrupulous and methodicial formation of all other Ukrainian departments is not contradictory to the above requirements and needs of the Great German Reich, but is desirable since it will foster healthy national and social life of the Ukrainian folk and strengthen its heartfelt trust in the new order purused by Greater Germany in Europe.

Under these conditions, I can take upon myself the responsibility to my national conscience and the government of the German Reich for further successful management of the Ukrainian Council of Trust of Volyn.

(signed) Stepan Skrypnik
Head of Ukrainian Council
of Trust of Volyn

Courtesy: Ukrainian State Museum of the History of the Great Patriotic War (1941–1945), entry book 11479, file 2064, pp. 28–30.

REGIERUNG
DES GENERALGOUVERNEMENTS
HAUPTABTEILUNG INNERE VERWALTUNG
ABT. 1.
Staats-u.Kommunalverwaltung
K: 962/43 (III a - 6)

Krakau, den 29. April 1943.

An den
Herrn Metropoliten der griech.-kath. Erzdiözese Lemberg,

L e m b e r g
St. Georgsplatz.

Betr.: Unterabteilung Kirchenwesen
Hier: Überweisung von Geldmitteln für die Bedürfnisse der
griech.-kath. Kirche.

Durch die Hauptkasse der Regierung des Generalgouvernements
wird Ihnen demnächst ein Betrag von
360000.-- Zloty
zugehen. Aus dem anliegenden Schreiben bitte ich die Herkunft
und den Bestimmungszweck dieses Betrages ersehen zu wollen.
Einer Rechnungslegung über die Verwendung der überwiesenen
Summe bedarf es gegenüber meiner Dienststelle nicht.

Im Auftrage.

Photocopy of the letter describing the transfer of money from the Nazi Administration of the Generalgouvernement for the sum of 360,000 occupation zlotys to the treasury of Metropolitan Sheptytsky. "My Office does not require an account for this money" reads the document significantly.

STAFF UKRAINIAN DEFENSE POLICE
—REGIONAL SERVICE—   Staff Order Nr. 50

Personal thanks:

Expressing gratitude to policeman Kirichuk, Y.W., for stopping one Jew, 27.8.42, in his non-service hour. For this devoted act, he is rewarded with I. kg. fat, and I. kg. flour.

Sign. Kabajda
Commander Staff UOP
Soten Kabajda

APPENDIX B:
HISTORICAL RECORDS
(EXCERPTED)
AND ARCHIVE DOCUMENTS
(TRANSLATED AND ABRIDGED)

The Role of the Catholic and Orthodox Clergy
During the Nazi Occupation

The Concordat (agreement) between the Vatican and the Government of Nazi Germany was signed on July 20, 1933. It laid the foundation for cooperation with the Holy Church which in various forms lasted till the end of World War II.

On the eve of the war, the Greek Catholic Church was the advanced post of Catholicism in the East. It was a hotbed of naked Nationalism and, later on, of Fascism, under the absolute rule of Metropolitan Andrey, Alexander Roman, Count Sheptytsky. For many years he exerted a notable influence on the political situation in Western Ukraine.

The Uniate clergy, including the "Prince of the Church," Metropolitan Sheptytsky, strongly influenced the formation of the OUN's mankind-hating ideologies. Many of the OUN (Organization of Ukrainian Nationalists) leaders came from families of priests. Among them were: S. Bandera (OUN Chieftain), Y. Baranovsky, I. Hrynyokh (former Priest of Galich), S. Lenkavsky (OUN ideologist), Y. Stetsko and others.

Numerous documents have proven that Greek Catholic Prelates gave their all-out support to the Nazis. Organizations like the "Ukrainian Catholic Union," the "Catholic Action," theological schools, newspapers and journals, such as *Meta (Goal)*, *Dzvoni (The Bells)*, *Niva (Sown Fields)*, were pro-Nazi mouthpieces.

The supervisor of Andrey Sheptytsky's estates was A. Melnyk — the other OUN Chieftain. He succeeded Y. Konovalets, who was assassinated in 1938. The OUN Headquarters were stationed in Berlin.

In those years the Ukrainian Nationalist camp eagerly awaited the Nazi "liberators," who would help destroy "Godless Bolshevism" and resurrect a "Free Ukraine" under Hitler's protectorate.

The OUN adjusted its entire policy to the military aims of Nazism, maintaining close ties with the German Army Intelligence Department (the

Abwehr), allying itself with Fascism.

By the spring of 1940, two Ukrainian death battalions, "Nachtigal" and "Roland" were formed (in the occupied part of Poland), under the leadership of Abwehr Nazi officers: Herzner, Oberländer, and OUN member, Roman Shukhevych, taking the oath of "Fealty to the Führer and Great Germany," being blessed later by the Metropolitan.

Both Ukrainian churches (Orthodox and Catholic) in Western Ukraine, together with the Ukrainian Nationalists met, in 1941, the German Nazis as their "Liberators and Allies." In their sermons and church services they proclaimed "Long life to Hitler" (the "Liberator") and his glorious host, justifying later the Nazi policy of extermination of the Jews.

It was the "Nachtigal" Battalion that took part in the pogrom, the bloody massacre of the Jews in Lvov (early July, 1941), in which 7,000–10,000 Jews (and non-Jews) were murdered. Similar bloody orgies were repeated later in Tarnopol and many other cities in Western Ukraine. I. Hrynyokh was appointed as Chaplain of the "Nachtigal" battalion.

After the Nazi "Liberation" of Lvov, the "Lord's-anointed" prince of the church, Metropolitan Sheptytsky (in a wheelchair) held a "Thanksgiving Service" in honor of the "invincible" German Army and its "glorious" leader—Adolf Hitler. The Metropolitan addressed the crowd with the words: "We are overjoyed with the liberation of our land from ungodly Bolshevism. We pray to the Lord to give the victory to German arms over Bolshevism. I bless you my sons in your sacred struggle for truth in God's name. In your hands you hold the fate of your people and our future. God bless you!"

Thus did the Metropolitan "bless" Nazi hirelings from the "Nachtigal's" Death Squads for the bloody crimes they committed on the very first day of the Nazi occupation of the city of Lvov.

On the evening of June 30, 1941, the former "Prosvita" (educational) house on the Market Square, became the residence of the OUN leaders who were arriving from Cracow. Among the 'leaders' were: P. Lebed, Y. Stetsko, S. Bandera, S. Lenkavsky and others. There, in the presence of Sheptytsky's representative, J. Slipij, Chaplain Hrynyokh, and Hans Koch of the Abwehr, a farcical ceremony was staged, a so-called "Restoration of Ukrainian Statehood."

From the rostrum, Yaroslav Stetsko read the "Act on the Proclamation of the Ukrainian State." Article 3 of the "Act" stated: "The reestablished Ukrainian State shall closely cooperate with National Socialist Great Germany, which, under the leadership of her Führer, Adolf Hitler, is instituting the 'New Order' in Europe and the world at large, and is assisting the Ukrainian people to liberate themselves from occupation by Moscow."

After Stetsko, the floor was taken by I. Hrynyokh and J. Slipij, who delivered the personal salutations of the Metropolitan, Count Sheptytsky, to the "German Army Liberators" and to the "highly esteemed public."

The OUN newspaper *Surma,* not only published the Metropolitan's appeal, but also an article headed: "Let the German Army Feel That It Is a Welcome Guest in the Ukraine." Cries of joy were followed with slogans: "Long live the invincible German Army! Long live its Führer, Adolf Hitler!"

On July 5, 1941, Metropolitan Sheptytsky addressed the Uniate clergy and the parishioners with another "pastoral message":

"By the will of the Almighty and all-merciful Lord, a new epoch has opened for our Motherland. We welcome the victorious German Army with gratitude and joy for liberating us from our common enemy. At this important historical moment I call upon you fathers and brothers, to be thankful to God and loyal to his church, to obey the authorities and render energetic labor. Long life to the German Army and the Ukrainian people."

On behalf of Sheptytsky, J. Slipij welcomed the leaders of various Ukrainian Nationalist groupings, urging them to put aside their strife...in order to join forces and thereby "render much broader and effective aid to the liberating German Army." The resolution passed by the meeting read: "Representatives of the Ukrainian public in Lvov who gathered together on July 6, 1941, extend their heartfelt greetings to the victorious German troops under the leadership of the great Führer, Adolf Hitler."

The OUN murderers from the "Nachtigal" battalion were sanctified by Sheptytsky's "blessing" and trained on money expended by the Gestapo and Nazi Abwehr.

The Commanders of the battalion "Nachtigal" were: R. Shukhevych, A. Lutsky and V. Sidor. M. Lebed came to Lvov as an envoy with "special powers" from the Nazi Abwehr and OUN leaders. On July 4th, the "special powers" were transformed into bloody deeds. The mass massacre in Lvov began. Thousands of Jews and non-Jews lost their lives. Together with the "Nachtigal" battalion, the Ukrainian police of Lvov took part in the massacre.

Wholesale murder was also committed according to plan. Lists (black books) were compiled by Ukrainian Nationalists well in advance. Telephone directories were used to determine whom to eliminate. This was the job of the OUN.

Blessing the "Nachtigal" and Ukrainian Nationalist "patriots," the Uniate Priest, Ivan Sadovsky, said: "The time has come when we are fully free, with the assistance of the victorious German Army — our Liberators."

The "Nachtigal's" bloody route passed through the towns of Lvov, Zolochov, Tarnopol, Vinnitsa, etc. The "Nachtigal" and "Roland" battalions were later (1942) merged together as the Schutzmanshaft Battalion 201, under the command of Yevhen Pobihushchy, which continued its bloody orgies.

While the blood of innocent people was being spilled in Ukrainian cities, towns, and villages, the Greek Catholic Hierarchs, along with Ukrainian Nationalist leaders, held gatherings and "manifestations of gratitude and respect to the Führer, Adolf Hitler, and the German Army." Bishop J. Slipij,

Bishop J. Kostilovsky and others took part in such gatherings in which the latter cried out: "Glory to the great Führer, Adolf Hitler, the liberator and best friend of the Ukrainian people."

The OUN and the Ukrainian clergy helped to form a 'Ukrainian Police' in every district, city, town, village and region of Western Ukraine. The Schutzmans from the mentioned police took part in killing of thousands of Jews in Lvov and other cities and towns. In some localities Ukrainian police units were formed before the German Army arrived.

Here is what the Regional Commandant of the Ukrainian police, Vladymir Pituley, wrote in his report:

"During the Jewish 'Action' in Lvov, on March 25, 1942, the first (UKR.) Commissariat brought in 500 Jews, the second, 238, the third, fourth, fifth, and sixth, delivered 510, 240, 600 and 160 Jews respectively — a total of 2,248 persons."

After dispersing the "state administration" headed by Y. Stetsko, the Nazis showed their OUN hirelings that they did not only consider it impossible to recognize any form of Ukrainian statehood whatsoever but would not permit the establishment of a protectorate or an autonomous government in the Ukraine. Planning to turn the Ukraine into a colony deprived of all rights under the German Reich and, following the old Roman dictum *"Divide et impera"* (divide and rule), Hitler decided to divide up the occupied Ukrainian territory. On August 1, 1941, Governor-General Frank issued Directive No. C-441 which stated: "From 12 a.m. on August 1, 1941, according to the Führer's Decree, civil administration on the territory of Galicia which formerly belonged to Poland shall be incorporated into the administration of the Generalgouvernement and come under my control. The lands of Galicia, formerly belonging to Poland, shall in accordance with this directive become part of the Generalgouvernement.

1. The District of Galicia shall be administered by a Governor. The Governor's permanent residence is the city of Lvov.

2. I appoint the Chief of the District Dr. Lyash to the post of Governor of the District.

3. The state language of Galicia shall be the German language. The use of the Ukrainian and the Polish languages is permissible.

That was the way the colonial Nazi regime became established in Western Ukraine, a regime the Nazis planned to extend through the whole of Ukraine. With the aim of preventing the Ukrainian people from uniting together, the Hitlerites later on divided the Ukraine into several parts. They gave the Transcarpathian area to Hungary; Bukovina went to Rumania; the Rovno and Volyn areas as well as the central regions of the Ukraine were joined to form the so-called Reichskommissariat "Ukraina." The Eastern regions of the Ukrainian SSR were turned into a zone under the jurisdiction of the Military High Command; but the southern lands, including the city of Odessa, came under a newly established Rumanian occupation administration. With the aim of artificially dividing the occupied lands of Ukraine, Rosenberg issued a special directive which categorically prohibited the population from crossing the bounds by lines of one part to another. Anyone found guilty of violating the directive was sentenced to imprisonment or to be shot.

The colonial regime in the Ukraine was maintained by means of a ramified network of punitive-police organs such as the SD (security service), the Gestapo, Gendarmerie, Police, and Zonderkommandos of all types. Those forces arrested and executed, without any legal procedures, thousands upon thousands of Soviet people. From the very outset of the occupation, the Nazis set up in the Ukraine, including its western regions, a dense network of concentration camps. Such camps existed in Rovno, Lutsk, Chernovtsi, Dubno, Kremenets, Zdolbunov, Rava-Russka, Kostropol and near many other Ukrainian towns and villages.

Specially trained Nazi colonizers arrived from Germany to take over administrative posts controlling the national economy. The ephemeral hopes dreamed up by the Ukrainian Nationalists and their spiritual mentors at St. George's — i.e., hopes of receiving "statehood" from the occupiers — burst like bubbles, once and for all.

On February 3, 1943, the "Ringleader" of the OUN, Andrey Melnyk, addressed the head of the Wehrmacht's General Headquarters, Gen. Field Marshal Keitel. With Sheptytsky's blessing, he wrote the following: "We believe that the time has come to include the Ukraine in the anti-Bolshevik front. It is necessary to create an active Ukrainian Army. We hope that the issue on the formation of Ukrainian Armed Forces will find due interest and understanding."

All this activity was after the Nazi Stalingrad debacle. So, the idea of forming the Ukrainian Division Waffen-SS "Galizien" came into being. The Ukrainian Central Committee (UCC), headed by V. Kubiovych, took part in the organization of the SS-Division "Galicia." Joining the division to fight on the Eastern Front meant killing their own people — Ukrainians, Russians, Byelorussians, Jews, etc.

On Sheptytsky's instructions, more than 20 Uniate priests were attached to the "SS Division," so these people would be able to promote the "holy war" against the Soviet Union. The Uniate Catholic Church was thus a signatory to the Oath the SS Halychyna division swore to Adolf Hitler in November 1943. Those who took that oath were to "wage a struggle against the enemies of the whole world, against the Jews and the Bolsheviks."

Some Jews (for the sake of staying alive) attempted to accept the ritual of Christian baptism. The head of the Uniate Church forbade the baptism of Jews.

During the Nazi occupation Stepan Skrypnyk (Mstislav), began publishing a Nazi-like leaflet — *Volyn*. Here is what he wrote: "The day of final victory is close at hand," prophesied Skrypnyk on March 29, 1942.

"The time is near when the fanfare of the German soldier will ring out the joyous song of victory all over the world."

On May 14, 1942, the new Bishop, S. Skrypnyk, 44 years old, adopted the name of Mstislav. In a telegram to Hitler, Skrypnyk and other clergymen wrote:

"We believe that the time is not far off when, in a rejuvenated Europe built on the basis of genuine Christian morals, the bells will ring out joyously, telling the whole world about your victory" — Nastup (Prague), July 12, 1943.

The above-mentioned J. Slipij, was later Metropolitan Sheptytsky's successor. The mentioned Ivan Hrynyokh, former Chaplain of the bloody "Nachtigal" battalion, wound up as "Professor" at Saint Clement's Ukrainian Catholic University.

Source: *Swastika on Soutanes,* Klym Dmytruk,
(Kiev, 1981 — Ukr. SSR)

Holocaust Tragedy in the City of Chortkiv, Ukr.SSR.

The following original "ACT" Archive Document, consists of 19 pages, typed in Russian. It was received in 1986 in the Ukr. SSR.

Translation of the "Act" was made in 1988, in the U.S.A. The document is abridged. Some words, and signatures, are illegible.

The Archive Document describes the findings of the Extraordinary Commission in detail, the heinous crimes committed by the German Nazis and their accomplices — the Ukrainian Nationalists against the Jewish and other people, in the city of Chortkiv, and Region, Ukr. SSR.

Reproduced in this book are only the first and last pages of the original "ACT" — Archive Document. It dates back to June 21-28, 1944.

(Translated by S. Brinstein)

"ACT" ARCHIVE DOCUMENT

Date: June 21-28, 1944

Report of Soviet Special State Commission conducting investigation of crimes committed by the German Fascists on the territory of the city Chortkiv and Region, Western Ukraine, Ukr. SSR.

The Commission consists of the following persons: W. H. Druginina; S. I. Turkevich, H. I. Brytskoho, H. I. Cheverda, A. P. Prokopova, V. A. Krupko, T. S. Litvinenko, K. A. Kozachenko, P. E. Chermisonova, Mateush Shuster, Stanislava Ivanovna, Lutsyk Petro I., I. B. Shorr, M.

M. Goldberg, J. U. Bolansky, K. M. Aisenberg, S. T. Kuzmina, P. J. Chervivsky, M. G. Chursanov.

The exhumation of the victims of German Fascism in the city of Chortkiv and Region, Ukr. SSR., started June 21, 1944, and lasted till July 28, 1944. The city Chortkiv was occupied by the Nazis in July 1941, and liberated by the Red Army in March 28, 1944.

The Special Commission established the following: Mass "Actions" and shooting of Jews, Poles, Ukrainians, teachers, doctors, lawyers, intelligentsia, party-activists, old people and children, took place during the Nazi occupation. Life started to get intolerable.

The extermination of the Jews were called "Actions," which ended in mass shooting of the victims. There were three mass "Actions" in Chortkiv. The first "Action" took place in 1941.

The Nazis ordered the creation of the Jewish Ghetto, in which around 8,000 Jews were forced to reside. The conditions inside the Ghetto were terrible. The Jews were forced to wear the Star of David. Many were taken out for hard physical labor outside. It was forbidden to leave the Ghetto or bring in food, under the threat of death. The victims received a little watery soup with a piece of surrogate bread. Many died of starvation and diseases.

The second anti-Jewish "Action" took place in the year 1943. As a result of this mass massacre, not many Jews were left in the city. Some tried to hide in underground bunkers or in the forest.

Around 115 Jews were working on a farm-estate. One day they were surrounded by a group of Germans and Ukrainian (Nationalist) policemen. A real bestial pogrom was underway. Some were shot in the field, others were massacred with shovels, iron bars, sticks, etc. Many others were caught in the street, in the houses of the village. The dead and injured were loaded on horse-wagons and thrown into an empty water well.

Groups of 50 or 100 Jews were taken out of the Ghetto, (allegedly for work), outside the city where they were shot. Some individuals managed to escape from such "Actions." Among them were: Rosa Shnermlib, born in 1925, Bernknopf Josef, born in 1923, Berkovich Zoya and a few others. The German Fascist beasts threw the dead, injured and children, alive, into the pits and buried them together.

According to eyewitness accounts in the city of Chortkiv, German Nazis, and Ukrainian Nationalists, threw Jewish children down from balconies (third and fourth floors) into the streets. The dead and injured victims were later thrown into the River Seret. Those few who remained alive were hiding in underground bunkers, in the forest, with Gentiles, or with false papers.

Mass executions of Jews, Poles, Soviet Activists, etc., took place in the prison courtyard, on the former airfield, on the old and new Jewish Cemeteries, in the Black Forest, in the Villages: Yagolnitsa, Swydova,

Mylowe, Ulankovtse, Marelovka, Sosulivka, Rossoxan, in the Galileya Forest, and other places.

The special Investigative Commission ordered the opening of the pits and excavation of the bodies. The following was established:

1. 16 Pits (different sizes) were found on the former airfield, located Westward of the City Chortkiv, near a highway leading to the City Chernovtsi, Ukr. SSR.

Pit No. 1 was 3 x 2 x 1.5 meters. It contained 27 bodies. Most were naked, shot in the back of the head. Pit No. 2, 4 x 3 Meters, contained 22 bodies, in a decomposing stage, men and women. Many had their hands tied with telephone cable. Most of the victims were shot in the head. Pit No. 3, 5 x 7 x 2.5 Meters. Most of the victims wore old, torn clothing, men and women — around 40 bodies, skulls smashed, hands tied in the back. Pit No. 4, 25 bodies. Some wore military-like uniforms. Hands tied in the back.

Pit No. 5, 29 bodies, Size 6 x 5 x 1.7 Meters. Pit No. 6, 4 x 5 x 1.5 Meters. Women — 19, men — 2, children — 4. All naked. Decomposing bodies. Pit No. 7, 4 x 3 x 1.75 Meters, 15 bodies, naked, shot in back of the head. Pit No. 8, 5 x 7 x 1.75 Meters, men 9, women 19, children 8, total 36 bodies, shot in back of the head. Pit No. 9, 10 bodies. Pits No. 10, 11, 12, approximately as above. Pits: 13, 14, 15, 16 — not opened.

OLD JEWISH CEMETERY, Westward City Chortkiv: Total, 5 pits. Around 45 bodies. Shot in back of the head.

NEW JEWISH CEMETERY, Location — Eastward City Chortkiv. Pits: 3. Bodies — 450. Victims: Men, women and children. All shot.

Location: Prison courtyard. Bodies — Men. Many with documents, names, Passport numbers. Also some women. Names: Wasserman Sofia, Bronde Israel, Schecter Meyer, Shoter Mojsej, Wolyster David, Wolf Yakubovich, Abram Broder, Berkenfeld Herman, Elner, and others, all shot.

Location: Black Forest, Eastward, City Chortkiv. Two pits. Total bodies: 140 men and women. Shot with machine guns. Smashed skulls. Thrown in Water Well.

Location: Village Miliontse, Chortkiv Region. Well-hole depth: 8 M. Victims working on farm. All Jews. Men and women. Bodies — 123.

Village Yagolnitsa. Two large pits. Total bodies 950. Most shot in the head. Men, women and children.

Village Swydova, Chortkiv Region. Two pits were found, sizes: 10 x 4 x 2 Meters, and 3.5 x 1.5 x 2 Meters. They contained 18 bodies, men and women, in decomposition stage. Some completely naked, some others in underwear. According to eyewitness accounts, around 350-400 people were buried in this area.

Village Marelovka. Chortkiv Region, Ukr. SSR: Two pits were found, sizes 2 x 2.5 meters. Most were shot. Some victim's heads were smashed.

A total of 55 bodies were counted.

Village Ulashkovtse, on Farm Estate. One pit, size 15 x 15 x 1, bodies of men and women, some were shot, some others were butchered with knives and other instruments. 17 bodies exhumed. According to eyewitness accounts, around 185 people lie buried in this area.

Forest Galileya: In the dense part of the forest, in a bunker-like hideout, size 5 x 2 x 2 meters, 15 bodies were found, all women. All naked, scattered in different positions. All in decomposition stage. All were shot in back of the head, most with damaged skulls. As it looked, the underground bunker served as a hideout for the victims.

The Commission concluded that in the above mentioned places (and also other pits, not excavated yet), more than 13,000 bodies of innocent citizens of the City of Chortkiv, and Chortkiv Region, were found.

The Special Investigation Commission considers the following persons guilty of committing crimes:

1.	Hildeman	Captain, Chief Gestapo
2.	Pekman	Captain, Chief Gestapo
3.	Stefan	Captain, Chief Prison
4.	Maierhofer	Chief Prison
5.	Rozenhof (?)	Chief Prison
6.	Paal	Commander, Jewish Camp
7.	Tumanek	Commander, Jewish Camp

Gestapo Men:

1. Kelner, 2. Richter, Lt., 3. Frank, 4. Keltswich, 5. Breitschneider, 6. Hagerman, 7. Rimpler, 8. Ruks, 9. Radke, 10. Kuchman, 11. Tsich, 12. Meier, 13. Basso, 14. Eisel, 15. Martin, 16. Miller, 17. Felde, 18. Kimperg, 19. Keller, 20. Lutsel, 21. Knispel, 22. Kaminsky, 23. Ferus, 24. Grocholsky, 25. Shudert, 26. Hubert, 27. Otto, 28. Gross, 29. Urban, 30. Frynd.

Traitors of the Fatherland. —(Ukrainian Nationalists):

1. Mula Ivan, 2. Mulyk, 3. Roshko, 4. Mykechans, 5. Hushulak, 6. Starovsky, 7. Skab, 8. Skorevych, 9. Ivasiv, 10. Moroz, 11. Podlubny, 12. Gnatkivsky, 13. Slobodyan, 14. Leschinsky, 15. Kachmanyuk, 16. Krchak, 17. Melnychenko, 18. Tyll.

Commission Members:

Doctors: Shorr, Goldberg (signatures)

Citizens, City Chortkiv: Wolanski, Eisenberg.

Military: Major Justice Dept. (signature)

Lt. M/S (illegible) (signature)

Priest, Roman Catholic Church (signature)

Priest, Greek Catholic Church (signature)

W. Druzhynin, Turevich, Brytski, Cheverda, Prokopov, Krupko, Litvynenko, Evstygnewa, Kozachenko, Cheremysinov, Shuter, Lutsyk.

Head of Extraordinary State Commission:

Investigating Fascist crimes: Kuzhmin
Medical Expert, Major M/S: Chervinsky
Medical Expert, Major M/S: Chursanov
(stamp signatures)

Courtesy: Soviet State Archives. Ukr. SSR.

Translated Archive Document

Before me are two archive Nazi documents in German language (not reproduced in this book) little known in the West. For this reason, I think, that the reader will find the content of both documents interesting.

The first archive document: "Pol.202/9, directed to the local authorities in the city of Drohobych," Western Ukraine, during the Nazi occupation, states the following:

"Re: Rewards and support for non-Germans.

"From the sum of money available for such purposes, I am asking to make the following reward payments (suggested by the Gendarmerie – Zug Drohobych) to the mentioned non-German Police Commanders – Beamters:"

"200 Zloty to Police Chief...Pol. Post....
  200 Zloty to Police Chief...Pol. Post....
  300 Zloty to Police Chief...Pol. Post....
  300 Zloty to Police Chief...Pol. Post....
  300 Zloty to Police Chief...Pol. Post....
  300 Zloty to Police Chief...Pol. Post....
  300 Zloty to Police Chief...Pol. Post....

"The Police Commanders will be notified to pick up the rewards. Report briefly about the made payments." Signature, I. A.

The names of the award-recipients, and locations of the Police Posts they served, are mentioned in the Archive documents.

In addition to the paid regular salary, the Ukrainian Nationalist henchmen received periodically money (and food products) awards for their loyalty and devotion to the German Nazis. As can be seen from this archive document, the Ukrainian bloodhounds were handsomely rewarded for their service in rounding up and annihilation of undesirable Jews, Communists, Commissars, activists, anti-Nazi partisans and others.

The second archive Nazi document, dated Aug. 2, 1941, reads:

In Re: THE FALL OF MOSCOW." Directive issued by the chief of the occupied Poland.

The day the capture of the capital of Soviet Russia is announced celebrations should be held in all towns under German authority, in the course of which due tribute should be paid to the brilliant accomplishments of the German armed forces, especially in connection with the taking of Moscow. Where possible the celebrations should be held in the open air. It goes without saying that all Germans should take part in them.

Besides, it is desirable that also the Polish population take part as spectators.

The exact date of the celebration will be announced in due time.

In Cracow, the Governor-General (Hans Frank) will speak on the occasion. In the evening there will be a fireworks display on the banks of the Vistula (river) Opposite Wawel Castle.

I would ask you to begin technical preparations at once for the celebrations in your districts.

The speakers for the celebrations will be appointed by us.

It was a celebration that did not come off. It will be interesting to note in this respect that on July 3, 1941, the German land forces chief of staff, Franz Halder, made this entry in his diary: "It will be no exaggeration to say that the Russian campaign has been won in 14 days."

To wind up this brief excursion into history, it should be mentioned that there was a Victory parade in Moscow — to celebrate the Victory over Nazi Germany. The Nazi decorations originally intended for the Wehrmacht parade in Moscow, together with the battle standards of Nazi regiments and divisions, are now on display in the Historical Museum in Moscow.

Source: *"New Times," U.S.S.R.*
(Translated by I. Gartner)

ACT (Abridged)

June 1944
City: Tarnopol

The City's Commission consisted of the following members:

Supreme Soviet Delegates — Kompanec I. K., Panasenko A. D., City Delegate — Zueva I. P., Captain Gudemchuk J. A., head of health dept. — Wojtkewich M. I., City Pries — Yvantiuw A. A., Captain (Justice) — Nowikowa A. M., Major (Justice) — Kozachenko K. A., with active participation of the Deputy of the Court-Medical expert of the First Ukrainian Front — Major M/S Chervinskotto P. I., and members of the Special Government Commission — Kuzmina S. T., compiles this ACT, that in the period from June 26-29, and from July 27-29, 1944, investigations were conducted about Nazi atrocities in the city of Tarnopol and surrounding areas, where mass graves were opened. The following was established:

The German Fascist Army occupied Tarnopol on July 2, 1941. On April 15, 1944, the city was liberated by the Red Army. Nazi brutalities started right away against the civilian population. Robberies and shootings of innocent people continued. Bookkeeper Melcnev, and merchant Mester were shot because they weren't friendly enough toward the entering Nazi army.

During the first days of Nazi occupation, the Germans started to round up and shoot Soviet citizens of Jewish Nationality. Germans, with the help of local Ukrainian Nationalists, were hunting down people on the streets of Tarnopol, beating them mercilessly, and shooting many of them on the spot.

Eyewitness Glass, L. L., saw the tragic scene on the Ostrowski Street, where about 80 people were shot. On the Lvov Street number 32, around fifty people were murdered. Mittelman N. J., witnessed the latter tragedy. Eyewitness Bondarenko saw Nazi atrocities in the city of Tarnopol. She saw the daughter of Mr. Keller, who told her that she had just been just raped by a German, and that her father and two brothers had been shot. Dr. Kalyna had also been murdered for resisting a rape attempt.

German soldiers were running wild in the streets, murdering whoever fell into their hands. People were afraid to walk the streets, locking themselves up inside their houses.

Eyewitness Libergal, Y. S. was ordered during the first day of the Nazi occupation to hand over to three Gestapo men two pairs of shoes, cloth material, bed covers, and pillows. The wife was ordered to carry all this to the waiting machine. Immediately thereafter, the wife and children were shot.

According to the findings of the investigation commission, during the first days of the Nazi occupation of the city of Tarnopol, around 5,000 peaceful Soviet Citizens, among them women, children and elderly people were murdered.

During the preparations of the mass Pogroms against the Jewish people, the Nazis themselves set fire to a house, blaming the Jews for it.

Eyewitness Eisenstein, B. N. testified that on the night of June 4-5, 1941, on the Russian Street, where peaceful citizens lived, among them: Family Katz, six people; Family Eichenbaum, eight people; Family Tumish, five people, and around ten more families in the house, were locked up inside, doors and windows closed, and the house set afire. Whoever tried to escape from the burning inferno was shot by posted watchmen. Neighbors who attempted to put out the flames were met with machine gun fire. Eisenstein was among those few who managed to escape.

The first Pogrom against the Jews in Tarnopol took place on July 5, 1941. Soldiers, under the command of the SS, forced their way into the house, driving out all the males. All were driven near the house of citizen Mojky, where they were shot. The house was in the marketplace.

On July 6, 1941, the Jews were ordered to move the dead bodies to the Bonia Street. After three or four weeks, the Germans permitted the relatives of the victims to bury the dead at the cemetery. This permission was given only after the payment of 300 to 350 zlotys for each body.

This is how the "New Order" started in Tarnopol after the start of the German occupation.

After the first Pogrom, the Jewish community decided to send a delegation to the German authorities, asking them to stop the brutal treatment of the Jews.

The Jewish people were thinking that the Nazi brutalities were committed by passing army units, and that only they were responsible for the inhuman behavior toward the Jews. A delegation of about 100 men, consisting of the most educated people — doctors, lawyers, professors, teachers, etc. — went to meet with the German authorities.

The Jewish delegation was met with hostility. They were all arrested and driven to the village Petrikow, where they were shot.

After this tragedy, the German authorities decided to organize the "Judenrat." The Gestapo ordered 15 people to show up, suggesting to create the committee. All refused to take part. They were driven toward the brick Factory, on Tornovska Street, where they were buried alive.

Witness Fishman L. M. testified that among those buried alive were Doctors Ginsburg Isak, Horowitz Salomon, Weistaub Samuel, and Bereon Isak. After the bestial murder of 15 doctors, the Gestapo hoped to scare the Jewish people into submission. With the created Judenrat the Gestapo hoped to realize their plan of robbery and extermination of the Jewish population.

The Gestapo ordered Mr. Gotfried, Dir. of the Jewish School, to appear. He was told to gather 40 people among the educated in order to create the committee. He was promised that nothing would happen to him. He managed to find 40 people. After the arrival of the delegations at the Gestapo (Mickewicha Str. 10), the group refused to accept the offer. In reply, the Gestapo and the police drove the people to the Jewish cemetery, where they were brutally beaten and ordered to dig a grave. The victims were tied up with barbed wire and tortured mercilessly. Eyes were cut out, and ears and fingers were cut off. Thereafter, they were thrown into the pits and covered with earth.

Of the 40 murdered people, the Gestapo spared Gotfried and the interpreter Kapan, who were told that they would not kill them. They would die themselves. Kapan was later shot, and Gotfried was sent to the extermination camp Belzec. His fate is not known.

After the two futile attempts to create a Jewish committee, the Gestapo decided to organize such a body themselves. At the end of 1941, the German authorities organized the Judenrat.

The Gestapo gave the following orders:

1.) Exact count of the Jews in Tarnopol.

2.) During seven days, a sum of 20,000 rubles in gold is to be delivered.

In case this order is not fulfilled, a second Pogrom against the Jews will take place.

3.) All Jews were ordered to wear the Star of David.

4.) The Jewish houses shall be marked with the same sign.

5.) Mobilize all the Jews, ages 14 to 50, for hard physical labor.

The Jewish committee completed the count of the Jewish people. The figure was 20,000. The Gestapo forewarned the committee that every armband sign would cost 50 zlotys, and the price for every house sign would be 100 zlotys. All those found guilty of disobeying the order would be penalized and made to pay 500 zlotys, or be sentenced to death.

In August 1941, special orders were issued by the German authorities. Jews were forbidden to walk outside without the Star of David. It was prohibited to ride bicycles. Jews were ordered not to greet the Germans. The Jews were beaten whether or not they greeted the Germans.

On September 5, 1941, the German authorities issued an order that anyone having Jewish grandparents was to be considered Jewish. Until September 25, 1941, all Jews had to move to the Jewish Ghetto. Death was the penalty for disobeying the order. The streets: Perla, Ryga, Pola, Berka, Russka, Lvovska, etc., were designated for the Ghetto. The streets were separated by barbed wire, and guarded by the police.

From the Ghetto people were taken out in orderly columns to and from work, guarded by police. The delivery of food to the Ghetto was forbidden. The daily ration in the Ghetto was 100 to 150 grams of surrogate bread, and a watery soup. The sick in the Ghetto weren't treated. The death rate was growing. Some of the sick people were killed. With the worsening of the prevailing conditions, it often happened that 100 to 150 people died daily from starvation or sickness.

In order to soften the words "Jewish Pogrom," the Germans substituted the word "Action," which sounded nicer. To justify the extermination of the Jewish people, the Nazis declared that every Jew was a communist, an American or English capitalist, with whom the Germans were waging this war. And if a Jewish child was not now an enemy, it would be an enemy later.

On March 23, 1942, the "Action" took place in Tarnopol. Before the "Action" was carried out, the Gestapo ordered the Judenrat to select all children and the old people, to be transferred to another place. The figure given was 3,000 people. If the order was not carried out, the Gestapo would take more, and the Ghetto, with the remaining people, would be destroyed. To find a way out of this terrible situation, the Judenrat bribed the Gestapo, and the figure was reduced to 700.

During the same day, the separated victims were taken out and driven to the Janowski Forest where they were all shot. The children were not shot. They were thrown alive into the pits and covered with soil. The 40 children taken from the childrens' home were suffocated.

The second "Action" took place on August 31, 1942. At 4:00 a.m., the Ghetto was surrounded by the SS. At 6:00 a.m., the Gestapo arrived at the Ghetto and started robbing the inmates, driving out the people to the market place, where the men were separated from the women. All men were transported to the labor camp. At 8:00 a.m., empty trucks arrived. The waiting women, children, and the old were all loaded onto the trucks and transported to the Tarnopol railroad station. There the people were loaded into cattle wagons, about 100 and 200 in each car. Their destination was not known.

The third "Action" was on September 30, 1942. The fourth was on October 1942, and the fifth "Action" was on November 8th and 9th, 1942. These "Actions" were similar to the previous one.

The German Fascist occupation authorities waged a policy of extermination of Soviet citizens. In addition to this, they ordered that contributions be paid under the threat of harsh penalties. In September 1942, the Judenrat was given the order to collect from every Ghetto inmate two grams of gold, promising that no Jewish pogroms would be repeated in the future. The "penalty" contribution was collected. The Gestapo accumulated more than 30 kg of gold. The Pogroms continued.

The Gestapo exterminated not only Tarnopol citizens but also those brought from Tarnopol region, and other locations. More than 50,000 people were transported to Tarnopol from other towns and villages.

Not only peaceful Soviet civilian citizens were murdered. More than 1,000 Soviet Red Army prisoners were shot in Tarnopol.

The German Fascists also shot in Tarnopol around 40 Czechoslovaks, who tried to cross the front line into the Soviet Union, in order to save themselves.

In the village of Borki, the Gestapo brutally ⸗royed the concentration camp. The wooden barracks were soaked with kerosene and lit aflame. All inmates perished in the flames. In the same camp, people were burned alive, also on wooden piles. Around 600 people were in the camp, among the civilians there also were war prisoners.

Soviet partisans who fell into German hands were also shot. The bodies were thrown into the river Seret.

In addition to those methods of extermination of Soviet citizens, the German Fascists staged "hunting" raids, rounding up innocent victims, shooting them in the Dragunov Forest. There were around six or seven such massacres in which nearly 8,000 people perished.

At the end of 1943, the Germans liquidated the Ghetto in Tarnopol. All remaining victims were transported under strong guard to the Dragunov Forest, where they were shot. After the last "Action" and the liquidation of the Ghetto, the Nazis hung out a sign: *Judenfrei,* that is, that "the city of Tarnopol is free of Jews."

After that, any remaining Jew who fell into the hands of the Nazis, was shot on the spot, or driven to the Dragunov Forest, and shot there. The remaining Jews in the camps were all shot on July 23, 1943. Among the murdered were also the Jewish police, which was created to keep "order" in the Jewish Ghetto.

The Investigative Commission found 26 pits during the excavations. According to the figures established by the Court-Medical Experts, over 18,000 bodies of peaceful Soviet citizens were found in the mass graves.

According to the preliminary investigation report, the German Fascists shot in Tarnopol and surrounding areas over 21,000 innocent Soviet citizens, war prisoners, and Soviet Partisans. In addition to the above, around 700 people were transported by railroad to the town of Belzec. Their fate is not known.

Guilty in the extermination of peaceful Soviet citizens, war prisoners, and partisans in the city of Tarnopol, the Commission considers:

    1. General Kittel—Kommander Stronghold, City Tarnopol.

    2. General-Major Neidorf—Garrison Command, City Tarnopol.

    3. "Podpolkovnik" Henrich Heinsburg—Adjutant Garr. Cmdr.

    4. General Von-Horbun-Gestapo Command. Tarnop. Reg.

    5. Rakita—Dep. Gestapo Reg. Comm., also Commandant of the Jewish Slave-Labor Camp.

    6. Captain Struchlas—Command. Gestapo staff.

    7. Captain Welker and Herman—Gestapo Officers.

    8. Palfinger—Gestapo, Referent Jewish Questions.

    9. Dornida—Helper Command. City Tarnopol.

    10. Rain—Gestapo-Man.

    11. Sturmfuehrer Graf Von Miller—Gestapo Command. City Tarnopol.

    12. Leks Fritz—Dep. Comm. Gestapo.

    13. Gagar (Hagar)—Commandant City Tarnopol.

    14. Mysh—Prosecutor SD.

    15. Tumynik,—Dep. Comm. Jewish Camp.

    16. Chervonyj—Dep. Comm., Executions.

    17. Rieman—Reinish, Miller—Gestapo

    18. Borykovich, Olejnik—Gestapo Agents

    19. Pramor Ernst—command. War Prisoner Camp.

    20. Sklaryk, Reitord, Weipel, Gibky, Winkler, Gensprowski—Criminal Police.

    21. Spinger, Fleg Willy—Secret Police.

    22. Chechowich Wasia—Agent Secret Police (Polish).

FATHERLAND TRAITORS—POLICEMEN
(UKR. NATIONALISTS)

    1. Madarskij

    2. Salema

3. Jawnij
4. Shtyk
5. Pawtos Oleksa
6. Gulko
7. Wassh Myron
8. Wysotskij
9. Zborowski
10. Chowrow
11. Barasa
12. Martynevich
13. Kochurka
14. Shkombora
15. (illegible)
16. Shkambara Konstantin
17. Pshzhemirski
18. Kucan
19. Mushka Taras
20. Shaderskyj
21. Chomowa, Secret Police Agent
22. Rychkowskij — Police Commander
23. Kobylenskij Kostia
24. Grinfeld (Jewish)
25. Blimfeld — Kommander Jewish Police.
26. Weinstein — Jewish Police
27. Fuchs — Police
28. Jampolex — Police

KOMMISSION

1. Dep. Supreme Soviet SSSR — Kompanets
2. P. S. Nasenko
3. Deputy City Soviet — Zuew I. P.
4. Captain — Gudemchuk J. A.
5. Head Med. Instit. — Wojtkewich M. I.
6. City Priest — Ivantiuw A. A.
7. Captain, Justice — Novikow A. M.
8. Major Justice — Kozachenko K. A.
9. Major M/C — Cherninskij P. J.
10. Represent. Extraordinary government Commission of the USSR — Kuzmin, S. T.

Osnovanye: Gato, Fond No, P-274, OP.1 D. 123 LL. 111-117.
Archive Director — L. I Lelekova
Archive Elder — G. W. Trotskaja
(STAMP)

(Translated by S. Brinstein)

ACT (Abridged)

Court-Medical investigation of the bodies of victims of German-Fascist crimes committed in the city of Tarnopol and region.

July 31, 1944.

Deputy of the main court-Med. expert, the First Ukr. Front, G. W. Major M/SL. Cherninskyj P. J., in the presence of Podpolk M/SL. Malaewa, Captain M/SL. Kogan, Capt. M/SL. Magomedova, Dir. Med. Instit., Dr. Wojt-Kewich, Major Justice—Kasachenko J. S., Capt. Justice—Novikowa A. M., investigated (from June 28-29, and from July 27-29, 1944), the excavated mass graves containing the victims of German fascism. The Commission established the following:

The German-Fascist occupation authorities systematically exterminated Soviet peaceful citizens in the city of Tarnopol and region during the year 1941, until April 1944. Among the murdered were Soviet Party members, the educated Polaks, Ukrainians, war prisoners, and partisans.

The Jewish populations was marked for special mass extermination. A Ghetto was created in the city of Tarnopol, in which the Jews were separated by barbed wire. They were forced to vegetate in anti-sanitary conditions, with very little food. The handing over of bread and other food products for the Ghetto inmates was forbidden. Regardless of age and health conditions, the Jews were forced to perform hard work: wood cutting, road building, and dirt cleanup.

All Jews were forced to wear a green color Star of David on the right arm. Under the excuse of resettlement to work, Ghetto residents were taken out in groups of 300–500, driven out on trucks and later shot. Such shootings the Germans called "Actions." There were five such "Actions" in Tarnopol. People who managed to evade the Ghetto were forced to hide in the forest, underground bunkers, attics, barns, etc. Part of the Jewish population were transported, in groups of 400–500 to the town of Belzec. Their fate is not known.

During the excavations of the Pits, the following was established:

To the west of Tarnopol, two km. past the village of Petrikow, along the roadway leading to the Village of Janowka, in the field at the right of the road, there are 17 Pits, and on the left, 3 Pits, with a downward top, grass covered, with sand underneath.

Pit No. 1, Size: 5 x 3 times 3 meters.

The bodies lie in disorderly manner, 1.5 meters deep. Sixty bodies were examined. The bones separated easily. All bodies were naked.

Numbers 1, 2, 3, 4, 5, and 6 describe in detail the condition of single victims. Shots in the back of the skull were visible.

Pit No. 3 is 5 x 3 x 2 meters.

Bodies lie in disorder, naked, strong decomposition stage. One hundred seventy bodies were excavated and examined. Among them: 4 children, 2 men and the rest women.

Numbers 1, 2, 3, 4 describe condition of single body skeletons.

Pit No. 4 is 5 x 3 x 2.5 meters.

Bodies in disorder, all naked. One hundred fifty-two body skeletons were examined. Among them: 18 men, 7 children, and the rest, women.

Numbers 1, 2, 3, 4 describe single bodies as above.

All the other skeletons show similar bullet holes in the back of the head, and the neck.

Pits No. 15-17, size: 5 x 3 x 2.5 meters.

Skeletons lie in disorder, naked. 120 were examined. Among them: 8 children, 23 men, and the rest, women.

Pits No. 18-19, size: 2 x 3 x 2.5 each.

All lie naked in disorder. One man found in slacks, jacket and shirt. Found in the pocket were: a ration card with the name Goldberg Kiwes, dated April 1943, and 20 Polish zlotyz. One hundred fifty-five skeletons were examined. Among them: 43 women, 19 children and the rest men. Five children ages 1 to 5, didn't show any bullet holes. All the others had bullet holes as described above.

Total in 17 Pits, size: 5 x 3 x 3 meters.

Total in 2 Pits, size: 20 x 3 x 3 meters.

Total in 1 Pit, size: 10 x 3 x 3 meters.

Were shot and buried over 15,000 people.

Westward from Tarnopol, 7 km. from the Dragunov Forest, right from the roadside leading to Brze D zany, six pits were discovered. Tops were sunken, covered with grass and with gray-red soil.

Pit No. 1, size: 5 x 3 x 2 meters.

Bodies lie in disorder, all dressed in jackets and slacks, and shirts. some have winter coats, boots, others with shoes and galoshes.

Twenty-eight bodies were examined. Among them: 18 men, 8 women and 2 children. In the pockets were found: combs, matches, tabac, pencils, etc. Two 2–3 year old children didn't show any bullet holes. The others had bullet holes as described above.

Pit No. 2, size: 5 x 3 x 2.5 meters.

Bodies lay in disorder, decomposed.

No. 1, 2, 3, 4 describe condition of bodies in detail.

The investigation of the other bodies and skeletons recalled similar damage from bullet wounds in the heads and other parts of the bodies as described above.

In 6 pits, sizes from 5 x 4 x 3 to 5 x 3 x 2.5 meters, between 2,500 and 3,000 people were found.

According to investigation materials and eyewitness accounts, some pits were camouflaged and not discovered.

Assist. of Main—Head Health Dept.
Court-Medic. Expert—Doc. Wojikewich
First Ukr. Front: Cherwinskij—Capt. M/SL. Kogan
Podpolkowik M/SL—Malaev—major Justice Kazacheuko
Captain M/SL.—Magomedov
Captain Justice—Novikow
Compiled: FO GATO Fond Nr. P. 274 op 1., 123, LL. 118-123.
Archive Director—L. I. Lelekova
Archive Elder—G. W. Trotskaya

(Translated by I. Gartner)

ACT (Abridged)

THE PLEBANOWKA MASSACRE

1944, July 2nd
Town of Trembowla, Tarnopol Region.

We, the undersigned below, The Commission of the Trembowla region: Lubarskoho Afanasievicha, Grebenszczykova Petra Grygorievicha, Dr. Deynickoho Olega Wladmyrowicha, Doc. Poleschuk Zygmunt Antomowych, Med. Koshushko Wladymyra, Comm. Shebelewa Ivana Nasyliewicha, Cap. Sec. Tarubara Mychailuc Ivanowicha, in the presence of Trembowla residents: Gondovicha Franca Ivanovicha, Wylki Petra Antonovicha, Naryneckoho Yosyfa Ivanovicha, Korezynskoho Y. Y., Kuncewa G. P., Gashchak C. Y., Kostelnika Yl., Wonsowych A. P., Strelecky Ivan, Trylycha M., Sydorov, I., Godlewski, T., Wylczynski M., Grycshyna, I., Zubyk Z., and other Trembowla residents took part in the investigation of the heinous crimes committed by the Nazis in Trembowla and surrounding areas.

The Commission, including the court-Med. experts, established the facts of brutal systematic extermination perpetrated by the Hitlerites, against the local residents: Jews, Poles, Ukrainians and war prisoners.

The above-mentioned Commission investigated the OPENED PITS, located 400 meters from the village Plebanowka, Trembowla region. Three large excavated pits revealed the dead bodies. On the order given by the Regional Commander of Tarnopol, Gestapo Major Miller, an "Action" took place in the town of Trembowla, April 7, 1943, in which over one thousand people were exterminated.

An eyewitness, Malinovski I. U., describes the "Action" in detail...The Court-Med. Commission established the following:

First Pit: 15 meters long, 3 meters wide, 4 meters deep. There were over 10 layers of bodies. The top layers were in the process of decomposition. The bottom layers were still intact. Some were with their clothes on. Women and children were found together.

Thirty-five percent of the victims were shot dead on the spot. Fifty percent of the people were injured, and fifteen percent were buried alive. A total of 1,100 bodies were in the first pit.

Second Pit: 10 meters long, 3 meters Wide, and 3 meters deep. Among the dead bodies in this pit were women with no visible injuries. They were buried alive. Some bodies were still intact, some others in a stage of decomposition.

The Second Pit contained 845 bodies.

Third Pit: 10 meters long, 2.5 meters wide, 3 meters deep. The condition of the bodies was similar to those described above.

The Third Pit contained 350 human bodies.

During the excavation of other pits, located in the "Koshary," Trembowla outskirt region of former war-prisoner camp, near "Red Army" street, mass shootings took place in 1941. Seven Pits (five in parallel order) were excavated. All were filled with human bodies. Some of the bodies were still intact. The bodies of the elderly persons, women, and children showed bullet wounds in the heads and other parts of the body.

The First Pit was 10 x 2.5 x 3 meters.

Four other Pits were of similar size as above, but only 1.5 x 2 meters deep.

In the Sixth Pit, 2 x 2 x 2, were found: Broken shovels, iron bars, and pieces of rope, with which the victims were probably tied.

The Seventh Pit was located near the street. It was 3 x 1.5 x 2 meters.

Nine additional graves were found nearby in the forest. There Red-Army prisoners were tortured to death and buried.

Among the dead bodies murdered in 1941 were recognized Christians: Seretny M. K., Chop S., and Cymbaluk Yosef G. Some were recognized by relatives, clothing and documents. The latter one (Cymbaluk) had his head split with a hard tool. In one pit a dead horse was found together with human bodies.

In the above mentioned Pits, over 800 bodies were found.

The investigation Commission established the following findings:

In the area of Plebanovka Village — 2,245

In "Koshary," town Trembowla — 800

Near Red Army Street — 8

Forest (war prison) Camp — 9

Region of German Police — 35

The mass extermination ("Actions") in the Plebanowka Village took place in April–July, 1943. In the "Koshary" region, the massacres took place in 1941.

The Commission made the following conclusions:

Responsibility for the criminal atrocities in Trembowla region — Government of Nazi Germany, and those directly involved:

German Lands-Commissar of the town of Trembowla-Weber. Regional Gestapo Commander of the city of Tarnopol — Major Miller. His Deputy-Captain Poikert. Commander of the German Police, town of Trembowla-Skylark. Commander of Ukrainian Police in the town of Trembowla-Goncharyk. Head of the Ukrainian Committee in Trembowla — Dr. Bazar, and the criminal — Lewkova.

Investigation Commission:

Chairman: Lubarsky

 1. Commission Member — Pylkik
 2. Commission Member — Grebenshchykov
 3. Commission Member — Dejnicki
 4. Commission Member — Poleshchuk
 5. Commission Member — Koshushko
 6. Commission Member — Schembelev
 7. Commission Member — Gorubara
 8. Commission Member — Gondowich
 9. Commission Member — Wylki
10. Commission Member — Narynetski
11. Commission Member — Korchynski
12. Commission Member — Kuncev
13. Commission Member — Gashchak
14. Commission Member — Wonsowich

Osnovanye: Gato, Fond Nr. P-274,
On. 2, A. 123 AA. 126-128
Archive Dir. — L. I. Lelekova
Elder Archivist — G. W. Trotskaya

(Translated by S. Brinstein)

ACT (Abridged)

October 28, 1944

The commission of Podvolochysk region, investigating the crimes committed by the Nazis, consisting of

Maluk, A. I. — Chairman

Commission Members: Karwacki, T. I., Ryabov, Alexsandrov, Waligura, Rudenko, Shterling, Merecki

Compiled on this day...

Location of perpetrated crimes by the Nazis.

In the village of Kamionki, Tarnopol, Reg., 19 km. West of the town of Podvolochysk, a huge pit was located, Size: 12 x 6 x 4 mt.

It contained 1,000 bodies, men, women, and children.

The second pit, size: 4 x 2.5 x 2.5. Twenty bodies were found.

Due to decomposition of the bodies, no identification was possible. Most

Архивная копия

А К Т

1944 года октября месяца 28 дня.

Комиссия содействия Подволочисского района Тарнопольской области, по установлению и расследованию злодеяний немецко-фашист-ских захватчиков и их сообщиков в СОСТАВЕ:

ПРЕДСЕДАТЕЛЬ КОМИССИИ: МАЛИК А.И.

Члены комиссии: КАРВАЦКИЙ ТРОХИМ ИВАНОВИЧ
РЯБОВ, АЛЕКСАНДРОВ, ВАЛИГУРА, РУДЕНКО,
ШЕТЕРДИНГ, МРЕДКИЙ.

Сего числа комиссия производила осмотр места злодеяний немецко-фа-шистских оккупантов. Осмотром встановленно, что в полтора ½ кило-метрах восточнее г. Подволочисск, на возвышенности обнаружено две могилы, первая из них имеет 6 м. длины 4, ширины 3 м., глубины, которые находятся 500 человек убитых, мужчин, женщин, стариков и детей жителей города Подволочисск, вторая могила имеет   3 м. длины 2 ширины 3 глубины, которые находятся 10 человек убитых.

Севернее г. Подволочисск в 100 метр, от города имеется оди-ночных 38 могил, в которых находятся 150 человек убитых мужчин и женщин жителей г. Подволочисск.

В селе КАМ"ЯНКИ Подволочисского района Тарнопольской области, в 10 километрах на запад от города Подволочисск, обнаруженная яма в размере 12 м. длины 6 м. ширины 4 м. глубины в которой находит-ся 1000 человек убитых мужчин, женщин, стариков и детей мирных жи-телей, другая могила 4 м. длинной 2,5 м. ширины 2,5 м. глубины в которой находится 20 человек мирного населения с.КАМ"ЯНКИ.

2.

Откопкой опознать трупы не представляется возможности, в силу их разложенности, одежды на трупах не имеется. установленно, что в большинстве расстрел производился с огнестрельного оружия в за-тылок головы обнаружено пробоины в затылках головы, установлено что трупы мужчин, женщин, детей и стариков лежат в беспорядковои виде.

Показателями свидетелей Задорожного, Шпигеля, Нагирного, На-лия, Павловича, Иней Анастасии Васильевой, проживающей в г. Под-волочисск и в с. Кам"янки Подволочисского района, устанавливается, что расстрелы производились Советских мирных жителей с 1941 г. по 1944 г. командой "СС", под командованием ВАГНЕРА и немецких сол-датоп. Районная комиссия ответственными за злодеяния нцд советски-ми гражданами считает вышеуказанных лиц, принимавших участья в расстреле мирных граждан.

ПРЕДСЕДАТЕЛЬ КОМИССИИ: МАЛИК

Члены комиссии: 1.   КАРВАЦКИЙ
2.   РЯБОВ
3.   АЛЕКСАНДРОВ
4.   ВАЛИГУРА
5.   РУДЕНКО
6.   ШЕТЕРДИНГ
7.   МРЕДКИЙ

Основание: ГАТО, фонд № Р-274, оп.I, д.I23, лл.I24,I25.

Директор архива   Л.И.Лелекова

Старший архивист   Г.В.Троцкая

of the people were naked. The majority were shot in the rear of the head. The bodies lie scattered.

According to eyewitness accounts made by local citizens: Zadorozny, Shpiegel, Nagomy, Palya, Pawlovich, Inej. A. W., the victims were shot during the years 1941–44, by "SS" commandos (detachments), under the leadership of Commander Wagner, and German soldiers.

The commission considers all those involved fully responsible for the crimes committed against peaceful Soviet citizens.

P. S.

According to survivors' testimonies, the KAMIONKI slave-labor camp was liquidated during the month of June or July 1943. The wooden barracks were locked up, with the inmates inside, and set afire. Those trying to escape were gunned down outside. Very few escaped.

Soviet war prisoners were housed also in the labor camps in the same area. They were exterminated before the Jewish slaves were brought in.

Archive Copies (Abridged)

1. Crimes Committed By German Nazis and Their Hirelings:

Thirty people shot dead. Date: 1.22.42, 6 people. 2.20.42, 18 killed. 7.25.42, 6 killed.

Place: Near village Kamionki, Tarnopol region, Shot by German SS and Gestapo, Eyewitness.

Buried alive: 7 people. Date: 7.7.1941 Place: village Kamionki. SS and Gestapo.

Fifteen people killed during bombardment. Date: 3.19.44.

2. Ten people shot dead. Date: 6.30.43. Place: Near village KACHANOVKA. German Sec. Police & LT. Wagner Sign: Lelekowa Trotskaya — Archivists

3. Shot dead — 1,020 people. Village KAMIONKI, Podwoloczysk region, Tarnopol obl. Date: 6.15.1943. German GESTAPO and their hirelings, and LT. Shwarts. War Crimes Commission Report. Date: 10.21.44.

4. Shot dead. 1 person. Village Myslova, Podwol. reg. German SS. Signed/

Lelekowa, Trotskaya — Archivists.

(Translated by S. Brinstein)

APPENDIX C:
MAY THEIR MEMORIES
BE BLESSED

ABE BRILLER

Do you remember the old, dilapidated, cramped house, in which my family lived? Do you remember our apartment, one out of the three in which three families lived? Do you remember how cramped it was, how difficult it was to turn around, to find a place where one could feel secure from bumping into the others present at the moment inside the small living room or the smaller kitchen? Maybe this was the main reason for meeting you most of the time outside the apartment rather than inside.

If you recollect, you were a frequent guest in our home. Even though much older, fully grown up when I was a teenager, we were best friends. There was something special about you. You were the incarnation of goodness. I still can see you before my eyes, a medium-sized man, somewhat plump, with two pink cheeks, eyes that shone eternally with friendliness and kindness, a face continuously covered with a smile, a willingness to be of help to those who occasionally might have tried to be not so friendly. You even practiced vegetarianism, refusing to eat the meat of once-living creatures. I remember how often you would sit down near me on the steps at our door and read Sholem Aleichem, Mendel Mocher-Sforim, or from the books of other writers to me. It was not the stories only that imprinted themselves in my memory. It was you, your way of reading, your active and imaginative rendition of the lines, your acting out every little nuance of what the lines were supposed to mean and say. You brought the stories to life and made them real. Not just once did I become so engrossed in the action of the tale that I shed hot tears of sorrow or joy. I suffered with the characters, laughed with them, and often saw them at night in my dreams.

You came from a destitute family. You lost your father when yet very young. I do not remember him; maybe I never knew him or saw him. Your mother was left with fifteen children. They died one by one, of different causes, but surely the main cause was malnutrition, the eternal grinding poverty. Your mother cried until she lost all ability to cry. Of all the children only you and a brother of yours in Lvov survived. I do not know how you managed it, but you not only survived, you also educated yourself—not in school but in the dark corners of your mother's poor dwelling. You learned by yourself. You learned to write letters for people, to fill out official papers; you learned to speak and write Polish, English, Ukrainian, Hebrew and Russian. Later you learned bookkeeping, and this became your main means of supporting yourself. By that time your mother had died. You were left alone, but you had your jobs, several part-time bookkeeping positions, that kept you busy and alive.

This was your life up to the outbreak of hostilities between Germany and Russia. You did not have to engage in politics to become the mortal enemy of the new conqueror of Europe, and you did not. It's the "pintele Yid," the fact that you were born Jewish, that became your undoing. You were unlucky—it was your lack of luck that followed your footsteps, as described by Sholem Aleichem. You were the proverbial "schlumazel"— but this time you had company—the entire Jewish nation.

It was on the first day of the triumphal entrance of the German army into Trembowla. You were by that time already married and the father of a sweet little girl. Maybe God himself envied you your new success. You were sitting at home when you heard the sudden noise of motors. Out of sheer human curiosity, you opened the door to see what all the commotion was about. A few Germans in shining uniforms and on shining new motorcycles came driving along the main road. One of them, an officer, noticed you and suddenly stopped.

"*Jude?*" he exclaimed, his hands grasping for the rifle that hung over his shoulder.

"*Ja,*" you answered, not realizing the gravity of the situation.

A sharp, short shot resounded. You fell to the ground, dead.

M. Briller

CLARA BRILLER

Dear Clara: I remember you and will never forget you. You were my sister, younger, but very close to me. We fought often and argued very foolishly, like all children and siblings. I remember you as a small child, wandering with me around the narrow streets of Trembowla, holding on to my hand and almost always following me. You were a skinny little thing, pretty and very friendly. Together we formed a picture of poverty, hidden poverty. Our mother cared that we looked respectable. She mended old clothes and turned them into looking like new. She kept us neat, and always clean. She also dreamed about a better future for us, about educating and bringing us up in a way that we would become good and worthy of esteemed people.

People teased us. They called us "Abele und Gritele" something like Hansel and Gretel. We were always seen together, walking and playing together. You held on to me and followed me. Maybe I was not a great hero; surely, I could not have protected you had we been faced with real danger. I was bigger than you, but physically weak. Somehow God watched over us.

Then we grew up. I remember you as a very gifted little girl. At the age of twelve you were already tutoring smaller children and helping them with their homework. The few pennies that you earned you handed over to our parents. I did the same. Poor children, under conditions such as we lived in, tended to be sympathetic to their parents' problems. At a very young age they worried and tried to help their elders if they could; especially with the passage of years, and as we grew older, our household increased and with this, so did our difficulties.

Then came Gymnasium. At a great sacrifice to our parents, you and I were enrolled in the local high school, called the Gymnasium. You proved to be an exemplary student. You won a government scholarship and passed the eight years of schooling with flying colors. You were especially talented in writing. Your compositions were often read to whole classes as examples of how such compositions should be written. You were in general adept in languages, but you did well in all subjects. I must say that I hardly ever saw you studying. Knowledge came easily to you. You liked to read and you had your friends, many friends. You were friendly and outgoing. You were popular and easily won the respect of all around you.

The war was the beginning of our new troubles. By then you were engaged to your future husband, a lawyer. Poland was again dismembered, torn apart between its closest neighbors, Germany and Russia. You landed a good job. Luckily, our family was poor and as such could easily find employment under the Russians. Life had changed under the new rulers, but the changes did not greatly affect our family.

The worst was yet to come.

On June 22, 1941, the Germans unexpectedly attacked the Soviet Union. The war proved to last almost four years, bringing destruction and desolation to the land and its inhabitants. The Nazi rule reached new heights of cruelty, treachery and pure bestiality in the treatment of the population. Trembowla was overrun on July 5, 1941, by the Nazis, less than two weeks after the commencement of hostilities, and the population almost immediately began to feel the effect of the Nazi rule. Murder, unabashed, cruel, and in most cases completely senseless and unnecessary became the order of the day. The avowed policy of the German Nazis was terror, as a way to turn the whole population of these regions into modern slaves, working for the glory of Germany. It was the old saying: "Deutschland über Alles."

The Jews suffered the most. Driven into new compounds, denied the most fundamental means for survival, beaten, shot at will, hanged and subjected to the most refined methods of extortion and confiscation, the people soon realized that the "New Order" had nothing to offer but misery and deprivation.

You, my sister, found yourself in the midst of this new "valley of tears." You struggled, you fought to survive. I was not there to witness this, but I can imagine that it was a terrible life. Driven from meager living facilities, thrown into successively more cramped one-room apartments, having, on top of everything, to share it with more and more people, your life could not have been anything but sheer misery. With your husband away in the far regions of Russia, with no outlook for any means of supporting yourself, with daily shootings and killings going on in all parts of Trembowla, with the constant threat of being caught by the Germans or their helpers, there remained but little hope for your deliverance. Then Mother died; Father and a younger brother were shot on the steps of their miserable lodgings.

Then you made your decision. You decided to go into hiding. You joined a group of more than a hundred people and hid in a basement of one of the houses. There were rumors of an upcoming new "Action" — the German word for mass execution. Conditions in your hiding place were unbearable; hunger; lack of air; unsanitary conditions; and not even the possibility of venting one's frustrations in screaming, begging for help, or just raising one's voice. There were also a few children in your midst. You had to use all your ingenuity to keep them quiet; it would be your immediate end if the Germans and their Ukrainian Nationalist helpers found you out in your hiding place. You could only hope for a miracle.

The miracle never happened. As I learned after the war, Rudolf, a friend of yours, a dear, personal friend, brought over a few SS men, and, pointing out the entrance to the basement, told them about your presence in the hiding place.

The rest is history. You were marched in an orderly column, and in the spirit of German efficiency and thoroughness, led to a village behind Trembowla, to Plebanowka. You and all those you were with were shot, one by one. All were buried on the hill in a common grave.

M. Briller

JOSEPH CHAIKIN OF STRUSOW

I only became acquainted with my friend and companion Joseph Chaikin (he perished in the Second "Action") in 1943 when I was joined by a friend from Tarnopol, Samuel Weisman, of blessed memory (he fell on the Soviet front in the Second World War), and together we traveled to the world conference of the Zionist organization Hapoel Hamizrachi. It took place that year in Cracow, Poland's royal capital. Joseph Chaikin was also a member of this group of Tarnopolians who traveled to the conference. From that point on we established a relationship of true and sincere friendship despite the fact that we met only rarely because he spent all his time in Western Galicia.

He was a teacher in Bielsko-Biala for several years and had very close ties to Rabbi Dr.Hirschfeld, the Rabbi of Bielsko Biala and one of the most active and important rabbis in the ranks of Hapoel Hamizrachi before the Second World War.

Joseph Chaikin was born in 1912, and, according to the information I received from his brother, after finishing elementary school in Strusow, he studied for several years with Rabbi Alexander Lipa Eichenstein, but for the most part, he completed his education on his own. He taught for a period of time in Strusow in the local Hebrew high school and then moved to Western Galicia, where he spent several years. He was active in the Bnai Akiva movement and afterwards went on to teach in Bielsko Biala.

I got to know him, of course, after he turned twenty because he was exactly my age. Of the many good qualities by which he distinguished himself, particularly kindness, humility, and a willingness to help the next person, I shall lay special emphasis on the aspiration which dominated all his thoughts, and this was the yearning for Zion. He tried in every way to acquire an immigration certificate for Eretz Yisrael. He was waiting for the summons that his elder brother Yechiel, of blessed memory, who had arrived in Eretz Yisrael in 1935, was about to send him from Rabbi Kook's Yeshiva. Joseph told me this during the period of Soviet administration when he got to my house after wandering about on out-of-the-way roads in real mortal danger as the Germans advanced into Poland after the outbreak of the war. He had been in Bielsko when the war broke out and was able to get back to his native town, Strusow. Yechiel verified this for me when we met after I arrived in Israel and told him how Joseph had died. Clearly, because of the outbreak of the war he was unable to reach his sought-after goal — the land he longed for.

His poetic soul, his longing and yearning for Eretz Yisrael, which expressed itself in our conversations whenever we met, have remained embedded in my memory to this day. Before writing these lines I contacted his brother, Holocaust survivor Samuel Zainwill of Rehovot in order to get some details about his childhood and youth. He handed me a copy of a letter that Joseph had written to a friend. The girl had kept the original, but Joseph's brother made a copy of it. The letter had been written in the month of January, 1935. I shall excerpt from it the sentences which express his longing for the land of Israel: "There is no way for me to put into words the tremors that shake my body and soul when I hear the word *Aliyah*. The people weltering in blood on its native land will anchor its restored national life in the black clouds of its soil. Glory to those who are creating something out of nothing with all their youthful fervor, who are redeeming every piece of land even at the cost of their own blood."

Finally I must mention his act of self-sacrifice which I witnessed in our house after the "Action" in Strusow, which took place on the Sabbath, the sixteen of Elul, 5702 (August, 1942) in which his mother and sister perished. That was the Sabbath whose weekly Torah reading, "Ki Tavo," includes the Reproof Section in Deuteronomy. He moved to our house when the Jews of Strusow were expelled from their town and ordered to move to the Jewish district of Trembowla. He did so after the First "Action." We dug a hidden, well-camouflaged bunker, which was not detected even after the city was declared *Judenrein*. He worked hard, together with us, to dig the tunnel and take the excavated earth far away from the area of our house. The "Action" came suddenly and caught us all off guard and in the house. And, in fact, my brother and I were among the fifty survivors who took shelter in that bunker. I don't know why he lingered outside the bunker. At any rate, as I was told afterwards, many strangers had squeezed in, and there was no more room. So he said, "Never mind, I'll hide here somewhere in front of the entrance," and that apparently is how he was discovered. It may well be that when they found him there they didn't bother to look any further. They assumed that the place where he was found was the hiding place and that the others must have already been taken out and he alone managed to continue hiding until he, too, was discovered. Therefore, there was no need to search that area any longer. Thus by remaining outside our hiding place, he saved everyone else.

With these words which I have dedicated to his memory, I am fulfilling a sacred duty to a friend and companion who sacrificed himself for others. May his memory be blessed and may God avenge him and all the martyrs of Plebanowka where he perished together with another fifteen hundred victims of the Second "Action."

I. Goldfliess

REB BARUCH DLUGACZ

His thin delicate figure and yellow beard with its copper-colored hue stand alive before me. Also his bespectacled face with glasses for a very near-sighted person in a yellow frame, the same color as his beard, leaps about in front of me. He took them off frequently in order to look at the small print of Rashi's script (Rashi, A.D. 1040–1105, one of the greatest commentators on and interpreters of the Bible) and that of other commentaries in the numerous pocket editions of the Talmud which he owned. He himself was a native of Zalazac. I believe that he was the son of a shochet in town (retired slaughterer). Here in our town he was the son-in-law of Mordechai

Mester. His father-in-law was not one of the town's scholars. But the son-in-law, Baruch Dlugacz, devoted his life to the Talmud and its commentaries, even when he engaged in wheat trading, from which I very much doubt whether he eked out a living. I remember studying in the temple several times and approaching him with a question about the German or the Tosephot (religious laws), and, instead of answering me, he became entangled in unsolvable problems. Finally he would say: "Why, this is so simple I don't understand how I got so involved."

I think that he was the most learned man in our town. He was always arguing with the rabbi and not only about complex Talmudic matters, but also about a great variety of issues. At one time he wanted to be appointed to the post of rabbinical judge, and the rabbi naturally objected. He was a great book lover and had a broad knowledge of German language and literature. I would not be exaggerating by saying that his library and especially his wife's was one of the biggest in the entire district. It was valued in the thousands of dollars. I recall that he had the big eleven-volume set of Graetz, the unabridged first edition in German, which was already then a collector's item. He had some very old books from the early days of printing. He never sold a book without buying another more expensive one in its place. He traded books and expanded his library, making it truly glorious. I know that during the German occupation he dug many tunnels beneath his house in which to hide his library. It may still be buried in some underground tunnel beneath the ruins of his house without anyone's knowing about the treasure lying there.

His older son, Elazar, was a student of mine in Bnai Akiva and also his younger son Itchele belonged to Bnai Akiva. They appear in one of the pictures of the movement. His oldest child was named Seril. She was one of those who approached me with a request to establish and organize a Bnai Akiva Youth Movement in order to save the youth from the clutches of the left-wing organizations, not a few members of which ended up in the Communist camp, for which the Polish authorities sentenced people to long prison terms.

To the best of my knowledge Reb Baruch leaned to the Jewish organization Agudah, but he realized that in Trembowla an Aguda would not take root. His entire family perished in the Holocaust. May their memory be blessed.

I. Goldfliess

REB YITZCHAK (ISAAC) FRIEDMAN

Reb Yitzchak Friedman was a person who aroused enthusiasm because of his simplicity and kindness. He, I believe, was one of the few individuals in Trembowla who came to town to study Torah before the First World War and went to learn in the Stanislawow Yeshiva. He also sent his only son Leybele to study in the same institution during the period of Polish rule. I know of at least one other person who studied there before the First World War and that was my mother's cousin, Saul Weiser, of blessed memory, whom I have already mentioned.

But I do not wish to stress Reb Yitzchak Friedman's learning in this sketch, but his passionate love of Zion. All his thoughts were centered upon the Land of Israel, and he deeply yearned to go and live there despite the fact that his family was not small. Aside from his son he had three or four daughters. I don't recall the exact number.

He earned his living by selling leather for the production and repair of shoes. Stores with ready-made shoes produced in factories made an appearance only in the 1930's. In the 20's everyone and especially the farmers bought pieces of leather and soles and gave them to a shoemaker who prepared custom-made shoes or boots. At first he made a handsome living, but when the ready-made-shoe stores opened, his income shrank. Only villagers then bought material with which to sew boots.

I shall never forget this: when he heard that I was going to an agricultural training farm after my studies with the rabbi of Proworzna, despite the objection of my father, of blessed memory, he ran to my house and slipped ten gold pieces into my pocket. In the nineteen thirties this was quite a sum of money. He wanted me to have some financial reserves. Of course I returned the money somewhat later. He helped organize and expand the Bnai Akiva movement. Because of his tireless Zionist efforts, he was promised a certificate but the promise was not realized, and he perished like many others at the hands of evil men.

In my heart I have only feelings of love and affection towards him and his family, towards his daughter Feige who was a friend of my sister, may she be set apart for long life, towards his son Leybl, his daughters Mimi and Alte — all members of Bnai Akiva, and they appear in pictures of the Movement. The rest of the names I cannot remember. To all of them I dedicate these words: May their memory be blessed forever.

I. Goldfliess

DAVID-SALOMON GANS

David-Salomon Gans was a butcher by profession. In comparison with the others in this trade, he was the poorest one. I have always wondered how he was able to exist, how he managed to support a family of seven, three daughters, two sons, his spouse, and himself.

Two of his daughters and two of his sons emigrated to the United States before World War II. His wife died (if my memory is correct) in the early 1930's. David-Salomon remained with his daughter Ewa (Chawa) in Trembowla in his small clay house. Thanks to the periodic help from his children in the U.S., he managed to "make a living."

In the late 1930's David-Salomon was in his sixties or a little older. In those years he had no butcher shop anymore and was living in retirement. His physical condition was remarkable for his age. I never remember his being sick.

The Jewish community in Trembowla was not a classless one. There were well-to-do people, a middle class, and the poor. The former two were preoccupied mostly with their own problems, and their own business, caring little about their poor Jewish "brothers" in the town. The community leadership showed little concern about the fate of the underprivileged. The poor were on their own, with no place to turn for help.

Once a year some material help for the needy arrived from the Trembowla society in the U.S.A. The financial help was mailed to the Rabbi, the head of the community.

Periodically, some assistance also came from the Joint Distribution Committee in the United States.

But in the meantime, many Jewish families continued to struggle for a piece of bread. How simple and easy it would have been to open up a communal kitchen for the poor in Trembowla, where the needy could get a warm meal daily. About this, the Jewish community leadership did not seem to care at all. It wasn't their business to alleviate the need of the hungry Jewish "brothers."

Did I say that there was nobody in Trembowla who was concerned about the fate of the poor? My apology for this mistake. There was an elderly gentleman: his name was David-Salomon Gans.

I am sure that I'm not the only survivor who remembers David-Salomon, walking in the streets of Trembowla with a loaded sack on his back. He went from house to house, door to door, to collect bread from the affluent for the poor. His job was a double one—pick-up and delivery. "When some refuse to give," he would say, "I come back again and again. I don't go away; I don't leave empty-handed." He knew that the poor and hungry were waiting for him.

Moshe, the "Water-carrier," known in Trembowla as *'Der Wasserträger,'* was an old, half-paralyzed man, barely able to walk. The few groshen (pennies) earned from his hard job weren't enough to feed his family. It was David-Salomon Gans who saw to it that Moshe and his family did not starve. In Trembowla, there were many, many other poor and hungry (Jews and Gentiles) waiting for David-Salomon. He knew them well. He never complained about the heavy load on his back. He considered it his duty as a human being.

Being a poorly educated Jew of the old generation, he had more understanding and compassion for the needy than the entire Trembowla Jewish community establishment — including the Rabbi. All this happened in the 1930's.

On Saturday, July 5, 1941, the German Nazi army marched into Trembowla. David-Salomon was relieved of his job walking the town's streets carrying the sack on his back to collect bread for the poor. Gradually the rich and the middle class were brought down to the level of the poor.

In 1943, during one of the two mass round-ups ("Actions") of Trembowla Jews, David-Salomon was included in the group. Still being robust, he was able to keep up with the rest. Marching together with the other Jews from the old part of the town where the Jewish Ghetto was located, passing the bridge dividing the two parts of the city, they made a right turn toward the main street. Did they know that this was to be the last walk on the familiar road?

Standing on the sidewalk were Gentile spectators, looking toward the marching "parade." Bewildered, without shoes, in their underwear only, the rounded-up Jews were herded to their final destination. From the onlooking crowd, a middle-aged Gentile lady recognized the butcher, David-Salomon. She knew that he was a religious man. The deadly silence was pierced by the lady's voice: "Shlomko" she cried out, "now you'll take a ride straight to heaven." Some of the spectators smiled.

To the spectators it was no secret as to where the Jews were going. All of them knew that this was their last walk through the Trembowla streets. There was little chance for the Jewish victims to escape from the mass graves waiting for them on the Plebanowka mountain. Special Nazi extermination squads, assisted by the local Ukrainian police, took good care to see that none of the marching Jews escaped the "parade."

Just a few weeks before the above described "Action" took place, a small group (ten) of religious Jews sneaked in the dark of the night into the old Synagogue. There they prayed, reading a few chapters of "Thyllim" — Psalms, hoping earnestly that God the Almighty would save them from annihilation. They still hoped that a miracle would rescue them in time, and make the Nazis disappear, or change their policy.

The great majority of the Jewish community in Poland (and not only in Poland), did not comprehend at that time the deadly Fascist menace, especially to the Jewish people. They were blinded by many things. They didn't understand the world they were living in. Many still believed in miracles.

In Trembowla, and in Plebanowka, no miracle happened; the loud tra-ta-ta noise of the Nazi machine guns was heard clearly by Gentiles in the neighboring fields.

The victims' beliefs and prayers were undoubtedly sincere. Most of them were deeply religious. All the waiting and prayers were in vain. There was no miracle to stop and destroy the Nazi war machine. To accomplish this task, hundreds of Allied divisions were needed. The price of victory over Fascism was a costly one. Millions of people had to sacrifice their lives.

For David-Salomon Gans and all the other Jews in Trembowla, the liberation came too late. He, like the others, never had a chance to see a picture of his grandchildren in the U.S. His lovely great-grandchildren know him from pictures their grandfather preserved and brought from Europe.

David-Salomon: You are alive in our memory. Your good deeds for the Trembowla poor will be remembered forever. Trembowla survivors cherish your sacred memory. The recently erected monument in Plebanowka, a Memorial Dedicated to the Jewish (and some non-Jews) Nazi victims of Trembowla, Mikulince, Strusow, etc., is a reminder of Nazi barbarism against innocent people. It will never be forgotten. It shall never be forgiven.

S. Brinstein

JACOB-DAVID (DUNYE) GOLDFLIESS

My brother Jacob-David was called Dunye Goldfliess by family and friends. He was born in March 1913. He received the same education in the house that I received, but we never studied together. That is, we both studied with Reb Pinchas Arak and Ashkenazi, but separately. He also did not attend the Polish elementary school. In his childhood years he wasn't drawn to schoolwork. But as he grew into adolescence, his desire to study increased. He had better than average talents, and he particularly excelled in math and the sciences. He managed to learn Polish in one year, although he had not studied the language at all in childhood. He covered all the material until the last year of high school and even beyond that. The principal of the government high school, a man named Mirtinski, liked him, and he accepted him into the school—after taking entrance examinations, of course—even though he was over age. He began his studies in the next-to-the-last year of high school. He studied in the same class with our sister Shoshanna.

After our sister came on Aliyah (emigration) to Palestine, he began to study in the commercial academy in Lwow. He studied in the academy for two years but did not manage to complete it because the Second World War broke out. He earned a living during his stay at the academy by giving private lessons to his colleagues at the academy, and he taught mathematics to high school students. Under the Soviets he was a head bookkeeper in the tax department, in Russian "Pinadyel." During the Polish regime he was an active member of the "Zionist Youth." He was traditional and never missed putting on Tfillin to pray. . . . He, too, studied with Reb Yehuda Dlugacz. My brother had a fine ability to understand difficult Talmudic issues. Even during the Soviet rule we studied a page of Talmud daily. We finished tractate "Ketubot" (marriage contracts), as I remember, and others. He took a sober view of all aspects of life.

His strongest ambition was Aliyah to the land of Israel. He looked for various ways to leave Poland, and Europe for that matter, because he foresaw the outbreak of war. He stressed this in conversations with me many years before the war broke out. Our financial situation did not allow us to help him immigrate to Palestine as a student after we assisted our sister in immigrating there. He told us during our stay in the forest that he turned to our uncles for assistance in this matter. These were Mother's brothers who had emigrated to the United States before the First World War. They assisted Mother from time to time after she was widowed. He asked that they send him at least a loan to pay for travel expenses, but they didn't respond. I am mentioning this point in order that we be aware of the many people who remained in the Diaspora simply because they didn't have funds for travel expenses, even if they had the opportunity to come on Aliyah.

When the Soviets left Trembowla, nine days after the outbreak of the German–Russian war and many of the citizens of our town joined them, so did my brother. But that same day towards evening he returned home because he had simply forgotten to take a few rubles with him for the journey, and so he remained in the German Occupation Zone.

We were together throughout most of the Holocaust. Under the Germans he spent several months in a camp, Halowocek, near Tarnopol. The members of the Judenrat by some miracle, were able to get him out of there. Judah Leisner, of blessed memory, will be remembered kindly, for he was the person most active in the efforts to gain my brother's release from the camp.

He was with me all the time in the forest, and once when the Germans went hunting, according to one version, or were looking for a Soviet plane, according to another version, they shot right and left, in all directions. My brother was struck by a stray bullet. That is how local residents who heard those shots in the forest explained what had happened to us after the liberation. It happened the Ninth of Kislev (January) 5704, three months before the Soviets returned to capture Trembowla in March 1944. I didn't even have a shovel with which to dig a grave for him. That night a heavy snow fell and afterwards there was frost. I left the forest and went to stay in the home of a farmer who had supplied us with food for a long time.

Since then I hear, deep in my heart, the great pain over our loss because he was cut down in his prime brutally, such a short time before the liberation. His powers of judgment and thought guide me to this day. I always marveled at his steadfast refusal to join the Judenrat under the Nazis, despite having been urged to do so from the start of the German occupation.

When I returned from the "Burki Wielki" camp and toyed with the idea of finding a little work with the Judenrat he said: "Only on condition that you leave our house." Not only in this matter but in every matter I was amazed at his brilliant talent and indomitable will which never wearied or let an obstacle stand in its way. He overcame difficulties with an almost superhuman power.

I. Goldfliess

THE TEACHER ABRAHAM LEDERMAN

I don't know where and when he was born. I knew him at the last stage of his life when he moved near us, at the entrance to the same corridor. He was then more than sixty. I knew that he came from the Ukraine and, like many young people from Russia, he arrived in Galicia before the First World War and wandered through several places as a Hebrew teacher. This role was very important in the literature of the Haskala (Enlightenment). We find in Hebrew Enlightenment literature many descriptions of this special type of person.

I don't know all the stops he made in his wanderings. I remember only from his stories that during the First World War he was in Czortkow. His elder daughter, who has been living in Israel for many years in Kibbutz Mizra, came here with a group of friends from Czortkow. I also know that he spent a period of time in Lancut, a town in Western Galicia, and from there, I believe, he arrived in Trembowla and lived for many years in our town. Even during the period when there was no school, he did not move away because his wife became paralyzed, and he was past the age of mobility, as he put it to me on more than one occasion.

I lived right near Lederman; we were neighbors. We used to meet almost every day after I gave up my teaching position in Czortkow and returned home at the outbreak of the Second World War. I heard many illuminating comments from him about life and war. I think they are worth recording and their underlying philosophy is worth remembering. He was the true representative of "the Hebrew teacher" as he is depicted in our literature. In him a knowledge of our sources blended with a broad education in Western European culture and formed a smooth combination. His marvelous memory always found analogies from the past to events unfolding before our eyes.

I remember that when the Russians retreated, a large part of the Jewish population was bewildered and did not know what to do, whether to join the retreating Russians or stay in Trembowla. He said repeatedly that his fate was already sealed. Clearly, he could not leave his paralyzed wife and his daughter who was also not completely well (his daughter was a friend of my sister and studied together with her in high school), and whatever happened he would have no pangs of remorse for not running away. "But of one thing I am certain. The current chaos and retreat are much more pleasant to live with than what awaits us under German Nazi rule."

I also remember his wise comment upon the outbreak of the German–Polish War in 1939. The barbaric onslaught of the Germans on Poland angered all the town's residents, and they shouted that they would never forgive them for this wrong. He would chuckle and say: "That noise of yours reminds me of an incident that happened in your town several years ago. One of the villagers had moved to town a short while before and then suddenly died. The community's committee demanded a lot of money from his relatives for a place in the cemetery (this was one of the committee's main sources of income). The relatives had always refrained from contributing to public causes, and they now also stubbornly refused to pay the sum demanded of them. The deceased was kept in a pre-burial state for several days which made many citizens angry with the community's committee and the burial society. Many announced that those responsible for the delay would face the wrath of heaven for their misdeed. Then a *shochet* (a ritual slaughterer) got up and shouted: "What do they think that only heaven will punish them? And what about the deceased? Will he let them get away with this?"

The comparison was obvious. Whoever says that the world will not let the Germans get away with it is not facing reality. "Who is the world? England has not yet begun to dig a well, and from where will she draw water? The world is simply not ready for a war against Germany which has not ceased to prepare for war since the peace treaty was signed after the First World War. They also confiscated many weapons in Czechoslovakia which submitted to the pressure of the western countries without firing a single shot."

Likewise, I cannot forget what he said to me several months after the outbreak of the German–Russian War: "Israel, listen to me, get a gold pen and stationary and write down for eternal memory that Germany has already lost the war and that she will be vanquished despite the fact that they have captured by brute force almost all of European Russia. I am not certain whether I shall live to see their downfall, but if you do, remember these words and also these which I shall now add. You see these haughty, victorious Germans, how forceful they are. After their first defeat even a youngster without weapons will be able to dominate them." And this prophecy was also fulfilled. In general, he remembered the First World War, and every detail which he drew from it for comparison to the Second World War was completely appropriate.

I shall end my sketch of this dear man with an interesting and enlightening anecdote that I heard from him about an experience in the First World War in Czortkow: After the Austrians retreated and the Russians conquered the city, a Cossack on horseback suddenly appeared, and he had a whip in his hand. The streets were deserted; only the uncle of Knesset

(Israeli parliament) member Gidon Hausner, Hillel Hausner, who came to live in Israel after World War I dared to go out into the street. The Cossack riding by struck him with his whip. Hillel Hausner then boldly asked him: "Well, you hit me, what can I do: But why did you hit me?" The Cossack answered him immediately and laconically: "I hit you because I have a whip in my hand." "Yes," added Mr. Lederman, "whoever has a whip in his hand strikes without thinking. That is the way things are with the Germans. They have no need to justify their provocations. If they win, they won't need explanations, and if they lose, explanations won't help them."

I could add stories from his treasure chest, "but the bed is too short for a man to stretch himself." (Isaiah). I just wanted to portray one of the ideal representatives of the type of Hebrew teacher in the Diaspora who played a major role in building the land of Israel. Many of them did not live to arrive here themselves. He perished together with his family in the First "Action," as he forebode. May their memory be blessed.

I. Goldfliess

RABBI ELIEZER LEITER

During the years I lived in Trembowla until the liquidation of our town's Jews, I can remember only one rabbi who served continuously from Austrian rule before the First World War until the liquidation of the community by the German Nazis, may their names be blotted out. The rabbi stayed with us until Trembowla was declared free of Jews: *Judenrein.*

It was several days after the last "Action" on Thursday, June 3, 1943, the eve of Rosh Chodesh Sivan, 5703. The rabbi, Reb Eliezer Leiter, was discovered in his hiding place and was taken from there to the barracks, where he was shot.

The news reached me after we were liberated by the Soviets on Wednesday the twenty-seventh of Adar 5794 — March 22, 1944. I don't know the exact date of his death.

I heard a long story about the appointment of Reb Eliezer to the post of rabbi in our town. The events took place before my time so I cannot provide details from my own memory. Perhaps one of our townsmen in the United States remembers more than I do. He was appointed rabbi even before I was born.

I remember the rabbi after we returned from the vicinity of Vienna where we spent the First World War as refugees. I believe that the rabbi, too, returned at the same time as we did, although it may have been a little before we returned. When I went to the synagogue I always passed his house. When I reached the age of Bar Mitzvah boy, and I was eligible to participate in a Minyan (prayer quorum), I once went with my Uncle Leib

to attend the Sabbath afternoon prayers and to sit at the rabbi's "third
Sabbath meal" which was called *shali shides* in Yiddish. The rabbi held it
in his house for a limited group of people. My uncle was one of this group.
I became a regular participant and I never missed a "third Sabbath meal"
unless I was away from home as a student or teacher. When I came home
on vacation, I would visit the rabbi's "third Sabbath meal." Although I was
a regular participant on the Sabbath, I never studied with the rabbi. I did
hear him share his insights into the Torah with us during the third Sabbath
meals, but he didn't always have time to "say Torah," as it was called,
between the end of the singing and the conclusion of the Sabbath.

Our rabbi came from a long line of rabbis. His father was the rabbi
in Zawalow, a small town near Podhayice Peremyszlan. All of his brothers
were also rabbis. His brother, Reb Neta, was the rabbi in his parents' town
and afterwards in Zalazec. After the First World War he was appointed to
the post of rabbinical judge in the main religious court in our region, which
was in Lwow. Reb Neta's sons are distinguished rabbis in large American
cities such as Pittsburgh. One of his brothers, too, became a noted American
rabbi. To this day members of the rabbi's family named Leiter are serving
as rabbis. In Israel a book was published by Mosad Harav Kook in 5727
(1967) whose author was a relative of Rabbi Leiter and also a practicing
rabbi, first in Dunayev and later in the United States. The book is entitled
In the Margins of My Notebook. It is a collection of comments and commentaries
on the weekly Torah reading. Even the opponents of the rabbi, who weren't
many in town, admitted that the rabbi had great talent and had studied
a great deal in his youth, but later on became more preoccupied with
communal affairs than he was with his studies.

During the Polish administration he was a member of the city council.
He was an excellent speaker. While his sermons on the Long Sabbath (before
Passover) and the Sabbath of Repentance (after Rosh Hashonah) were not
characterized by learned analyses (and perhaps justifiably, his audience had
no need for such analyses), they were sprightly, they contained Talmudic
legends, and they were full of ideas suited to the contemporary spirit. His
sermons were very tastefully presented. In every Zionist gathering his speech
was the center of attention, and it even surpassed those of Zionist activists
including doctors and lawyers. The rabbi Reb Eliezer Leiter spoke at every
Polish national holiday as a representative of the Jewish community, but
his Polish speeches were weak; he didn't have a good command of the
language. But he did have a good command of German, as did every product
of the Austrian system before the First World War.

There wasn't a single survivor of the rabbi's family. His eldest son
Welwel (Zev) perished in the Janowska camp in Lwow. His eldest daughter
Regina (Hucya) married Shimon Eichenbaum, a graduate of Warsaw
University and the Institute for Judaic studies. He was a friend of Hillel
Seidman, may he be set apart for long life. He was a high school teacher

in Tarnopol, his native city. Regina, I believe, perished there together with her husband. The second daughter of the rabbi, Malkah (Mali as she was known in town and in the Bnai Akiva movement of which she was a member), had a clear, wonderful voice, and she brightened every festive occasion with it. She perished in the Second "Action" in our town. The younger son of the rabbi, Dudye (Darrol), who had been a pupil at the Polish municipal high school (gymnasium) was a member of the Judenrat police during the Third "Action." According to one account, he was one of the first shot and thrown into the pit. The rabbi's wife perished in the First "Action" which ended on trains to Belzec. This was the "Action" in which my mother, too, perished.

I shall end with this anecdote, which I remember in connection with the rabbi. I was about to go to study at the Yeshiva in Stanislawow. Before departing for that Torah center my father, of blessed memory, asked the rabbi to provide me with a letter of recommendation. I remember some of the contents of the letter. The rabbi pointed out that although my name was "Goldfliess" (Goldflow), in reality I was unable to let gold drip from my purse, and he recommended that I be given a big reduction in the cost of tuition. The rabbi's special Hebrew interpretation of my family name has remained embedded in my memory to this day.

I. Goldfliess

GERSHON (HASYO) NAIGEWIRZ

Young and exuberant, energetic and indeed, sometimes stubborn, possessed of a rare organizing capability — so will his image be forever fixed in my memory. He was born in 1916 and received an education which was quite common in our town in those days. After four years of elementary school, he passed a test and was accepted to the Polish high school (my brother and my sister learned together in the same class with him). His parents' home was near the synagogues in town. Even while attending the Polish high school, he did not absent himself from the synagogue. In his free time he always frequented the synagogue, and also studied in the afternoons with one of the teachers. He devoted most of his free time to religious studies and Judaism. He was obviously a good neighbor of the synagogues and he prayed every morning and evening with a *minyan* in one of the synagogues.

Thus, when Bnai Akiva was being organized we tried to draw him into our activities. At first, he reacted with indifference and even a little suspicion. But after several visits he agreed to help us, and he was only a boy of sixteen at the time. This is how he joined us and became a committed activist.

By nature he couldn't bear to make only half an effort. When he joined the movement, he did so with all his youthful vigor. He worked tirelessly.

Even after finishing high school and remaining in town for a year or two without continuing his studies at some institution of higher education, he devoted himself at all times to the movement. He invested all his youthful energies in it. Thanks to his unflagging work, a model branch of the movement was established in Trembowla. And he dedicated himself not merely to the one movement, Bnai Akiva. All Zionist causes fell within the scope of the Bnai Akiva movement — the Jewish National Fund, Keren Kayesod, and anything connected with Zionist and cultural activity. He also organized an agricultural training camp in the form of a kibbutz for Bnai Akiva pioneers who came from the surrounding area and needed a place to stay and work, organized agricultural training and many other communal undertakings.

On his young shoulders lay the burden of keeping the local organization functioning. He was the leader of almost all of the groups and, in addition, attended to the administration side of the movement. And he followed closely the progress made by all of the young people affiliated with the movement. He organized all the parties. Even after he left town to study at the university in Lwow he would come home during vacations and devote most of his time to the local branch of Bnai Akiva.

Whenever I think of the effervescent activity, the conversations, the dancing, and the other events in the Bnai Akiva chapter, I associate them with his personality. Thanks to him alone the chapter developed so rapidly that even after he went away to study, he could rest assured that it would continue to flourish and produce a magnificent national religious youth.

According to what I know through the grapevine, he perished in the forest after he managed to survive all the "Actions" in our town. I was unable to find out details of what happened to him when I made inquiries after the liberation.

May it be God's will that his memory be blessed among the builders of the Zionist movements in our town. His memory will forever remain a part of us.

I. Goldfliess

DAVID MILGROM

My friend and companion David Milgrom was born eight days before Rosh Hashana, in 1912. He went to public elementary school in town and after taking the examinations he entered grade four of the high school. He received religious instruction from Reb Shalom (Leykes) Landau. I never studied with him in my childhood or in my youth. We were just linked by bonds of friendship because we were about the same age, both of us were religiously observant, and we prayed together in the Husyatin Kloiz (Synagogue) in town. He was one of my closest friends and remained so even after going away to Warsaw to study at the university and at the Advanced Institute for Jewish Studies. During vacations, when he returned home from Warsaw and I came back from Zerobinca, near Zbaraz, from the Altstadter Home, where I taught for several years, I would study German with him and help him prepare texts in the Hebrew book Gemara, which he had to know for his studies at the Institute. We used to take walks and spend time together until late at night since we lived near each other, on the same street. We would discuss a variety of subjects.

When I founded a branch of the Bnai Akiva Zionist organization in our town, he assisted me and he also led discussion groups frequently at our meeting place, during vacations when he was at home rather than in Warsaw. After completing his studies I suggested that he would be a suitable candidate for a teaching vacancy in the new Jewish high school that had just been opened in Czortkow, where I had been working as a teacher. He was given the position and he began to work there. We sometimes met in our leisure hours. During the Soviet rule, until 1941 when the school was turned into a Yiddish language school, he continued teaching there. I did not want to return to the school, where I had taught Hebrew and Zionism. I didn't wish to stay on in the profession by renouncing my values. I fully remembered the contents of a book by Zenzifer; which came out in Eretz Yisrael before the war. I had read it in Poland. The author described the Soviet persecution of people active in spreading Hebrew culture and I was afraid to remain in Czortkow. I preferred returning home and remaining anonymous and not known publicly as a Zionist. But during the German occupation in 1941 he, too, did not return to Czortkow and stayed at home.

I remember, as if it were today, his coming to consult with me, as the Soviets retreated, about whether to escape with the Soviets or remain in Trembowla. He feared that he would not be able to leave Russia. I told him then that I was certain the Russians would open the gates now that it was time, but I didn't like the Soviets and whatever was to be the fate of all the Jews would be mine as well. Of course this opinion was incorrect, and I paid for it, although I remained alive. At any rate he stayed in Trembowla and did not flee with the Soviets. I was one of the first to be sent to the labor camp at Burki Wielki near Tarnopol, by the Judenrat, and I was legally released.

As I mentioned in the chapter on the Holocaust, my friend and companion David arrived at the camp several months after I was released. I believe he was sent to relieve an earlier group of prisoners. Some time after he went to the camp I heard that he had been killed in an accident while working in the camp in 1942. Let these remarks be a monument in memory of my friend and companion who devoted himself wholly to the Torah and Judaism and died a Martyr's death in the Burki Wielki camp. May his memory be blessed.

I. Goldfliess

HASYO NEUBAUER

Trembowla, a beautiful town, is surrounded by forests and fruitful fields.

Only the Jews of Trembowla are no longer, for gangs of Germans and Ukrainians murdered them brutally. Only a small remnant survived.

My beloved unforgettable brother, Hasyo Neubauer, perished at the hands of the henchmen in Treblinka. He was brought there from Czestochowa.

He was a son of Trembowla. He spent his childhood and youth there. An unforgettable personality. An ardent Zionist, organizer, and leader of "The Zionist Youth" devoted entirely to the Zionist movement, he dreamed of Zion.

He didn't live to see a free Israel with his own eyes, which he so yearned to do. He didn't live to see the brave wonderful soldiers of the Israeli army. He didn't live to see the gay, healthy children of Israel, the kibbutzim, the citrus groves, and the beauty of our land.

He fell in the prime of his life. And I have felt ashamed, more than once, that I, not he, am in Israel. And all that remains for me to do is cry bitterly that I shall never again see his beautiful face, his smiling clever eyes, his hearty smile, his faith in the future, and his joy of life.

Never, till my dying day, will I forget him.

Ada Neubauer-Blautel

DR. ISRAEL STERN

Dr. Israel Stern was born in the village of Humnisk near Trembowla into a family of Jewish farmers and agricultural laborers, but from childhood his parents planned for him and his younger brother, Willy, a high school education (unlike their two older brothers Getsl and Meir who took care of their farms and engaged in farm management even after getting married).

And indeed when he was born in 1894 one really had to plan such an education because Trembowla still did not have a high school. He was sent to Tarnopol for his high school studies, which, needless to say, was very costly. After completing high school he pursued medical studies in Vienna. The First World War caught up with him there before he earned his degree. He was drafted into the Austrian medical corps and served as an officer until the collapse of the Hapsburg monarchy in 1918. He married his cousin, the only daughter of our Uncle Moshe Gerye.

After the war he settled in Trembowla, and engaged in his medical practice throughout the period of Polish rule. In the 1930's he set up a laboratory to repair teeth near his office and together with a dental technician who rented facilities from him, he threw himself wholeheartedly into this branch of therapy.

He suffered several family tragedies. His first children, who were born the end of the First World War, died in a typhus epidemic that was raging in the city in 1918–19, after the end of the war. Only his two children who were born in the second half of the twenties survived.

He devoted his whole life to public affairs. He was a member of the communal committee and for a period of time was the head of the community. He was very active in Zionist life. He headed the Jewish National Fund and the Keren Hayesod. The Zionist leadership even promised him a certificate (for Palestine) as a tribute to his active Zionist endeavors, but in the meantime the Second World War broke out, and he remained stranded along with many others who were about to immigrate from Poland to Palestine in the last years of independent Poland when anti-Semitism was increasing and Jews were being driven out of their branches of the economy, one after the other.

During Soviet Rule he continued working in his profession. At the start of the German occupation he, as a public figure and member of the Communal Council under the Polish regime, was appointed to the Judenrat and served on it. In the First "Action" on the twenty-fifth of Marheshvan 5703 (November 5, 1942), he was dragged to the "Sammelplatz" (the assembly point) in the center of town (which, by the way, was not far from his house), and when he stood up without permission, the German guards surrounding the area didn't let him utter a word; they shot and killed him on the spot (as I was told the next day). His family, his wife, children, and also his old mother were sent to Belzec extermination camp.

In the memory of our townspeople he will be recalled as one of the most active workers for Zion. May his memory be blessed together with all the residents of our community.

I. Goldfliess

CHAIM HERBST

I met Chaim Herbst in the Zionist Organization, where he was an active member. He was an idealist, and worked with devotion to inspire the Jewish youth with love of their heritage and the Hebrew language. At that time the idea of a Jewish state was still a dream. How happy he would have been to see it!

Chaim had a beautiful Hebrew library and he mastered the Hebrew language. David Turkel, of blessed memory, was his best friend, and they worked together towards a common goal. They organized an elementary Hebrew school, and Chaim was a very successful teacher.

We were married in 1936, and in 1938 our daughter was born. In 1941 the German–Russian war broke out, and Chaim was one of the first victims of the Holocaust. I shall never forget Chaim, my dear friend and husband.

It was a magnificent spring. Blue skies, the bright sun warming the earth. The first green shoots breaking through the ground and the world coming alive with color. There was a loud knock at our window. The war is OVER! There'll be no more running and hiding. We are FREE! Now my husband will come home.

We rushed outside. Music in the streets. Crowds, khaki uniforms everywhere; soldiers handing out chocolates to children. I search through the crowds; surely my husband will be among them. But the faces of the soldiers belong to strangers. The memory I clung to for three desperate years — in the Ghettos, hiding in caves, in the attic — will remain only a memory. There's just my daughter and I. Two people alone; thrust into a big empty world. How do you begin again when death is all around? And spring! — that teases with false promises!

Sabina Herbst